IN HER OWN VOICE

GENDER AND GENRE IN LITERATURE
VOLUME 9
GARLAND REFERENCE LIBRARY OF THE HUMANITIES
VOLUME 2043

GENDER AND GENRE IN LITERATURE

MOTHERS IN THE
ENGLISH NOVEL
From Stereotype to Archetype
by Marjorie McCormick

FEMALE HEROISM
IN THE PASTORAL
by Gail David

GENDER IN THE THEATER OF WAR
Shakespeare's Troilus and Cressida
by Barbara E. Bowen

SOUTH AFRICAN FEMINISMS
Writing, Theory, and Criticism,
1990–1994
edited by M.J. Daymond

THREE RADICAL WOMEN WRITERS
Class and Gender in Meridel
Le Sueur, Tillie Olsen,
and Josephine Herbst
by Nora Ruth Roberts

AIDS NARRATIVES
Gender and Sexuality,
Fiction and Science
by Steven F. Kruger

HOMEMAKING
Women Writers and the
Politics and Poetics of Home
edited by Catherine Wiley
and Fiona R. Barnes

IN HER OWN VOICE
Nineteenth-Century
American Women Essayists
edited by Sherry Lee Linkon

In Her Own Voice
Nineteenth-Century American Women Essayists

Edited by
Sherry Lee Linkon

Garland Publishing, Inc.
New York and London
1997

Library of Congress Cataloging-in-Publication Data

In her own voice: nineteenth-century American women essayists / edited by
Sherry Lee Linkon.
     p.   cm. — (Garland reference library of the humanities ; vol. 2043).
(Gender and genre in literature ; v. 9)
    Includes index.
    ISBN 0-8153-2652-1 (alk. paper)
    1. American essays—Women authors—History and criticism. 2. Women
and literature—United States—History—19th century. 3. Women and journalism—United States—History—19th century. 4. American essays—19th
century—History and criticism.   I. Linkon, Sherry Lee, 1959– . II. Series.
III. Series: Gender and genre in literature ; v. 9.
PS427.I5   1997
814'.3099287—dc21   97-16446
                                                          CIP

Printed on acid-free, 250-year-life paper
Manufactured in the United States of America

This book is dedicated to Burton Raffel, who
started me down this path.

Contents

Preface

In Her Own Voice examines the literary history of women's nonfiction writing through studies of individual writers, their works, and their careers. The essay and other forms of nonfiction prose have received little attention from feminist critics, but nineteenth-century American women's essays add an important element to critical understanding of women's literary history. In their essays, women writers often claim an overtly public voice despite the restrictions their culture may have presented to keep them silent. They make their personal lives objects of public display, and they offer both direct and covert political commentary. By studying such writing, the contributors to this volume offer thoughtful analyses of how ideas about public and private, political and personal, feminine and masculine voices affected and were reflected in nineteenth-century American literary history. The essays in this collection consider the development of women's public voices, relationships between women essayists and their editors and readers, and the fuzzy line that divides—or seems to divide—fiction from nonfiction. The book includes studies of some of the best-known American women essayists, including Margaret Fuller, Lydia Maria Child, and Fanny Fern, and articles on women writers whose work has received very little attention, such as Gail Hamilton, Anna Julia Cooper, Ann Sophia Stephens, and Zitkala-Sa.

Acknowledgments

I am grateful to the Graduate School of Youngstown State University for providing me with a one-quarter leave to work on this collection and, even more important, funding for two research assistants. Those assistants, Michelle Donley and Karen Burnett Ford, invested incredible energy, care, and meticulous labor in this book. They caught my errors, remembered to ask important questions, and provided enthusiasm and encouragement through a sometimes frustrating process. The contributors to this volume taught me much about the subject, and their positive attitudes and prompt work were essential in seeing this project through. I received encouragement from many friends, but I want to note especially the support and advice of my colleagues Jim Schramer and Stephanie Tingley. I am fortunate to have a family that supports my work even when they don't quite understand it; I appreciate their interest and encouragement. Special thanks, of course, go to Frank Bongen, for his endless patience, his willing ear, and his good heart.

Introduction

Sherry Lee Linkon

In his preface to the 1852 edition of *The Female Prose Writers of America*, John Seely Hart noted that "a ponderous volume of nearly five hundred pages is hardly sufficient to enrol [sic] the names, and give a few brief extracts from each of our female writers, who have already adorned the annals of literature by their prose writings" (vii). In fact, the volume ran 432 pages and offered readers brief biographies and excerpts of writing by forty-eight women, as well as portraits of eight of the writers, including Maria McIntosh and Margaret Fuller. By the time Hart produced the fifth edition in 1870, the volume had expanded to 536 pages with sixty-one authors. While only a few names are familiar to readers today, the five editions of Hart's anthology suggest that women prose writers were important enough to mid-nineteenth-century readers to lead them to buy out four printings in less than twenty years.

Based on the literary histories written in the past two decades, we might assume that most of those profiled in Hart's collection were fiction writers. But most of the women Hart included wrote essays as well as fiction, and many appeared in the volume solely on the basis of their nonfiction writing. A few were recognized exclusively for writing about religion, politics, or history, not topics that fit our twentieth-century images of nineteenth-century women writers. Hart's collection provides ample evidence of a large body of women's writing that has escaped critical attention not, like the private writings some historians have so fruitfully studied, because they were unpublished but because they do not fit comfortably into our definitions of "women's literature." In some cases, we have simply focused our attention on one part of a writer's work and ignored essays and magazine articles that seemed to exist "only" as part of her breadwinning efforts. We have ignored whole bodies of work by other women because their pieces look more like journalism than essays or because their topics—housekeeping, gardening, even travel and so-called "women's issues"—seem to offer interesting historical information but nothing worth considering in literary terms. As Nina Baym has suggested, contemporary narratives of women's literary history, with their emphases on women's use of fiction and on "recovering . . . private, putatively unpublished forms," have led critics "to perceive women writers as largely sealed off from public discourse" (108–9). With this as our guiding understanding of women's literary work, no wonder we have not recognized women's essays, travel writing, histories, and other nonfiction on everything from homemaking, art, and music to economics and politics as literature worthy of critical study and even pleasurable reading.

In reading nonfiction, we often assume that the narrator's voice is synonymous with the author's voice. While we should be skeptical about this assumption, as several essays in this collection suggest, we can fairly say that in their nonfiction writings, especially in essays, women claim an overtly public voice despite the pressure from the culture to remain silent. In nonfiction, women seem to present themselves, not their characters or their narrators, as public figures. They make their personal lives objects of public display, and they offer both direct and covert political commentary. By studying such writing, we can understand more completely how ideas about public and private, political and personal, feminine and masculine voices affected and were reflected in nineteenth-century American literary history.

This volume of critical essays contributes significantly to the project of describing and analyzing women's own voices, their other words. While a few presses have reprinted some nineteenth-century women's essays in the past five years, including, for example, a collection of Gail Hamilton's work (Rutgers UP, 1991) and some pieces in the recent anthology *American Women Writers: Diverse Voices in Prose* (St. Martin's, 1992), very little critical work has yet been done on these texts. Nina Baym has published several groundbreaking essays and a book on nineteenth-century women historians and essayists,[1] but few critics have taken up her challenge to "recover a different sort of writing woman from the madwoman in the attic and acquire materials to begin constructing a different narrative of American women's literary history" (*Feminism* 109).

The problem stems not only from our limited histories of women's writing, but also from our ideas about prose genres. Indeed, for twentieth-century critics accustomed to assigning generic labels to various kinds of prose, one of the biggest surprises in Hart's book is his lack of distinction among genres or topics. In most of his critical introductions to the excerpts in the book, he does not indicate whether the work is fiction or nonfiction. Hart may have assumed that his readers would so easily recognize the difference that no critical markers were needed, but given that many writers used fictional strategies in nonfiction and included extensive social commentaries in their fiction, this seems unlikely. Rather, the difference seems not to have mattered to Hart or, presumably, to his readers. This assumption is supported when we look at the places where Hart does comment on genre. He presents generic boundaries as quite permeable, so that while a political argument might be different from a novel, the line between the two is easily crossed. Some pieces that are written in narrative form, that look to twentieth-century eyes to be short stories, he describes as critical examinations of contemporary issues. Even today, of course, we would agree that fiction often reads like public debate about politics, religion, or the family, but we nonetheless identify fiction as fiction and therefore different in some significant ways from the essay. Indeed, a significant body of recent critical work has appeared with the specific aim of defining how the essay differs from other genres. Yet Hart describes Catharine Sedgwick's *A New England Tale* as a religious tract that was developed into a novel (17) without any sense that the two might not be quite naturally joined. Similarly, he makes almost no distinction between different topics. He discusses Lydia Maria Child's political writing alongside her housekeeping guides with no comment on the variety of her writing nor any hint that one type of writing might be different from another (116–118). According to Hart's introductions, we should not see advice about how to bake bread as any different from commentary about slavery, descriptions of a journey to Italy, or a history of the rise of Congregationalism. Thus, Hart's anthology suggests that we should worry less about assigning generic labels to prose and that we should take more seriously the work that our habitual labeling has led us to ignore.

How, then, do we define the prose works that the contributors to this collection have studied? This project began as an attempt to examine nineteenth-century women's use of "the essay," but both Hart's work and the work of the critics included in this book suggest that we must keep our definition of that form open and flexible. If, as Hart's anthology suggests, nineteenth-century readers did not worry about whether the work they were reading was intended as fact or fiction, and if they did not see a value in separating various topics and types of prose, then we should make our study as inclusive as possible. Baym's argument that we should "recover a different sort of writing woman from the madwoman in the attic" (109) points to the importance of reading beyond familiar generic categories so we can recognize literature that we have previously set aside. The critical discussions included in this volume begin to identify the more varied images of the writing woman that we can bring into clearer focus by reading a wider range of women's writing.

But even with such an awareness of the value of reading women's nonfiction without a limiting generic framework, recent critical writing about the essay can help us understand more clearly the guiding concerns and the importance of the criticism in this volume. After years of being what Graham Good terms "the 'invisible' genre in literature" (ix), the essay has recently begun to receive fresh attention from critics and practitioners. Since 1989, at least four major critical works have appeared, and both anthologies and literary journals devoted exclusively to "creative nonfiction" have become regular features on the contemporary literary landscape. After a century of serving primarily as a text for first-year English courses, the essay seems to be coming into its own again. Contemporary essays and recent criticism suggest two main themes that are central to the articles in this collection: the essay's form and its cultural work. By connecting these themes in essay criticism with concerns for women's gender roles and awareness of their literary and social histories, the articles in this collection help build a bridge that will link and enrich both fields of study.

Perhaps the most commonly repeated point made in critical writing about the essay is that the form resists definition. G. Douglas Atkins, in attempting to describe the contemporary version of the genre, refers to it as "baggy," "unwieldy," and "slippery" (19), and he points out that "the essay form itself encourages some of the blurring of distinctions that often accompanies discussion of the genre." Indeed, while he argues that we should set the essay apart from "articles, columns, reviews, pieces, themes (in composition courses), and what have you" (5), he later admits that the essay is "impossible to confine, to define precisely, and so to distinguish unequivocally from other forms, its next-door neighbors" (8). Similarly, Good suggests that we should view the essay as "a sort of fiction," similar to the novel, as defined by Ian Watt: a text that "purports to be an authentic account of the actual experience of individuals" (qtd. in Good 9), but a fiction that is "rightly classed in most libraries as *non*fiction" (12). Thus, even in their attempts to define the genre, contemporary critics recognize its slippery nature. Such attempts at definition remind us that we should not limit our understanding of the essay form too narrowly.

Rather than succumb to the temptation of leaving the genre entirely undefined, however, Atkins, Good, and other contemporary critics cite two key texts as valuable starting points: Montaigne's *Essais*, the 1580 text generally seen as offering the first examples of the genre, and Georg Lukács's "On the Nature and Form of the Essay." Good, whose study of eight major essayists offers the most thorough, careful effort toward definition of the genre of any of these recent works, draws primarily on Montaigne to identify the following points as essential elements of the essay: it is critical but based on personal experience and learning rather than on disciplinary scholarship; it presents its claims as an effort toward the description of truth, what Good terms "a claim to count as knowledge" (3); it is "held together by the concept of the self" because it foregrounds the author's perspective as valuable knowledge rather than a supposedly objective or universal truth (8); and it "presupposes" the combination of "an independent observer, a specific object, and a sympathetic reader" (4), thus emphasizing the essay's assumption of a personal relationship between writer and reader and its often narrow topical scope. Good also effectively incorporates Lukács's definition into his effort to describe the genre, noting especially Lukács's emphasis on the essay as an art form, "intellectual poems" (qtd. in Good 16) that attempt to offer both "a kind of truth" and "imaginative response" (17). Atkins similarly suggests links between truth and art in the essay. "These truths require story," he writes; they "take root in, blossom, and bear fruit as story, argument and demonstration evidently lacking the arable and fertile soil necessary for the cultivation of the heart's truths" (76). In an essay, then, we find the author reflecting on his or her vision of some object, event, or experience, attempting to cast personal knowledge, "the heart's truths," in artistic form. Clearly, such a definition is vague, leaving open a wide range of options and encompassing a variety of texts and topics. Yet it can nonetheless help us recall that, in studying essays, we must consider how the author combines the personal and the public, using private experience as a source of authority. The openness of the essay form may also work especially well for women, as Ruth-Ellen Boetcher Joeres and Elizabeth Mittman suggest, because it may operate as a kind of *écriture feminine*, an unstructured form that highlights nonlinear thinking and creative expression (14).

In offering personal reflection as a kind of truth, the essay constructs the author as a subject as well as a creator. An essay is as much about its author as it is about its supposed topic; as Good suggests: "the self finds a pattern in the world and the world finds a pattern in the self" (22). O.B. Hardison, Jr., in his essay defining the form, takes this even further, suggesting that the essay functions as "an exercise in self-fashioning" (25). This emphasis on the personal, Joeres and Mittman point out in their introduction to *The Politics of the Essay*, "would seem to be consonant with the subjective trimmings long considered acceptable for women writers" (13), yet for nineteenth-century women writers, as Mary Kelley's work shows, revealing the private self in a public forum is useful but also threatening to both the writer and her readers. Joeres and Mittman remind us that the "experience, wisdom, and contemplation" associated with the essay did not fall "within the province of [women's] expected behavior," which they argue explains why women have only appropriated the form in the past century (13). Many authors discussed here wrote essays before that period, however, and their efforts to claim the authority of the personal, not surprisingly, led them to use the form in unusual ways.

The cultural work of the essay, in part because of the form's close association with the personal, can be difficult to define. Because it mediates between private and public, personal and political, the essay cannot be brushed aside as "merely" incidental, topical, or reflective. While the notion of "truth" has become quite complicated in the context of poststructuralist criticism, the essay's claim to offer a kind of truth—not merely personal reflection but personal reflection as truth—makes it a valuable and, in the context of nineteenth-century ideas about gender, potentially dangerous tool for the woman writer. As Joeres and Mittman suggest, "it takes a certain degree of radical thinking to appropriate a literary form unintended for you and to make it conform to your own wishes" (14). In choosing the essay rather than fiction as her genre, the writer made a forceful claim for female authority. As Katherine V. Snyder points out in her discussion of Florence Nightingale's novel-turned-essay "Cassandra," nineteenth-century readers "took the immediate presence of the author and his consciousness as a preeminent and uniting generic feature" (24), an assumption that concerned Nightingale. She had to choose, Snyder argues, between aligning herself closely with a fictional heroine or revealing her own experience "without the mediation of the novel's characters." Given the closer proximity of author and subject in the essay, Snyder understandably sees Nightingale's decision to make her text an essay as a "bid for authority or even a sign that she had attained it" (25). If essay writing is a sign that a woman writer has attained authority, then it suggests that nineteenth-century women writers may have accomplished even more than previous literary histories, with their focus on women's fiction, have identified. For women essay writers to succeed as they did, for their work to be recognized with the publication of a collection like Hart's, and for that collection to have sold out four press runs, they must have been viewed as more respectable, authoritative public figures than we have previously understood them to be. The essay may well have served as a tool not only for women's participation in public discourse but also for the legitimation of women's knowledge and experience as a kind of authority.

All these elements of the essay play significant roles in the criticism in this volume. This book attempts to trace the process of legitimizing women's discursive authority and to begin to map the previously unexplored terrain of nineteenth-century American women's nonfiction. The critics here examine issues of authority and self-representation in the essay, of the authors' relationships with their readers and editors, and of how essay writing served women's efforts to construct themselves as public figures in a period that defined women as private persons. The essay's ability to slip between fact and fiction, personal observation and generalization, served women well because they could offer their opinions in forms that would be acceptable to their contemporaries and that allowed them the freedom to criticize, as Beatrice Jacobson and Margaret Lukens argue here. Because of the strong connection it implies between private and public worlds, because of its definition of authority as based on personal experience, and because it suggests that the author is trying to define herself as much as to address the reader, the essay allowed women writers to participate in public discourse while remaining private individuals. At the same time, however, as Laura Laffrado, Dorothy Baker, and other critics in this volume suggest, the apparently open representation of the self as authority also posed challenges for women writers.

This collection follows two main paths in its exploration of women's use of the essay. First, it considers how scholars can use the theoretical and historical frameworks developed by feminist critics of nineteenth-century fiction to analyze other kinds of texts. Many essays in this collection ask the same kinds of questions of women's nonfiction that critics have long asked of women's fiction: Is there a distinctly female or feminine voice in this text? How have readers and editors responded to women's writing? How did women present themselves as public figures in their writing, and what problems did their public stances create? Several pieces in this book also consider the relationship between fiction and nonfiction as literary forms and as elements of an individual writer's career, raising questions about what we ought to include in a study of women's "literature" and how we ought to use generic approaches to literary criticism.

Second, this collection will introduce readers to writers and texts with which they may not have been familiar. It includes pieces that examine the best-known American women essayists, including Margaret Fuller and Fanny Fern; forgotten essays by women who are remembered mostly for their fiction, such as Lydia Maria Child; and women writers whose work has received very little attention, such as Ann Sophia Stephens and Zitkala-Sa. The collection thus begins to describe the literary history of women's nonfiction writing through studies of individual writers, their works, and their careers. It is intended not as a comprehensive study of the field but as an opening gesture, an invitation to readers to consider how the study of nineteenth-century women's essays may revise our understanding of American women's literary history.

The collection begins with a study that provides a history of one portion of nineteenth-century women's essay publishing, their work for the *Atlantic Monthly*, the most prestigious magazine of the nineteenth-century. While the *Atlantic Monthly* published fiction and poetry by many of the most important figures in American literary history, including many of the best-known women writers of the day, its pages were dominated by informative essays on a wide range of topics, mostly by men. Although relatively few women published essays in the *Atlantic Monthly*, the number increased over the years, as did the variety of subjects on which women wrote. Shirley Marchalonis complements her overview of *Atlantic* women's essays with a case study of Harriet Waters Preston, whose work appeared in the magazine regularly during the last three decades of the nineteenth century. As Preston's case demonstrates, *Atlantic* women essayists moved from writing an occasional piece based on narrow expertise to assuming authority on many subjects, a development Marchalonis argues was occasioned by increasing educational opportunities for women over the course of the century.

Marchalonis also raises another central issue in our discussion of women's essay writing—the question of gendered style. While Marchalonis argues that women writing in the *Atlantic Monthly* did not display a "feminine" writing style, Judith Mattson Bean suggests that Margaret Fuller had employed a strongly gender-based voice in *Woman in the Nineteenth Century*, published earlier in the century. According to Bean, Fuller uses both a power-based rhetoric associated with masculine discourse and a rapport-based rhetoric associated with feminine discourse. Fuller used informal strategies at the levels of words, sentences, paragraphs, and segments of her text, and these dialogic techniques produced a multivoiced but smooth-flowing and spontaneous conversation that is impressive in its diversity and enlivened by engaging narratives. Bean argues that this informal, conversational style operates as an alternative rhetoric with an aesthetic of its own, suggesting the possibility of a feminine "tradition" of essay writing.

Lydia Maria Child also contributed to this emerging tradition. As Stephanie A. Tingley shows, Child's newspaper writing often took the form of informal, personal essays or "opinion pieces" that offered perceptive, often witty commentary about social justice issues, gender politics, domestic life, and women's issues. Many of these pieces were collected in two volumes of "Letters from New York" in the 1840s, and Tingley argues that the pieces in these volumes represent some of Child's most innovative and experimental writing. By deliberately blurring genre boundaries, mixing lyrical, poetically impressionistic passages with argumentative prose passages, Child both entertains and informs her readers. These pieces exemplify some of the nonlinear, nonhierarchical writing strategies that appear in much of the work identified as "personal" or "private" women's writing. Her work thus suggests that critics should be cautious about the distinctions we draw between public and private voices.

Like Child, Anna Julia Cooper combined personal experience with political and intellectual discourse to construct an authoritative public presence for women's voices, but Cooper's work, unlike Child's, had to negotiate tensions surrounding differences of race and class as well as gender. Writing near the end of the century, Cooper constructed a new form to represent a new kind of identity, the African-American intellectual woman, as Elizabeth Alexander argues in "'We Must Be about Our Father's Business': Anna Julia Cooper and the In-Corporation of the Nineteenth-Century African-American Woman Intellectual." In *A Voice from the South* (1892), Cooper draws on representations of the body, the physical presence of the author, to assert her presence in public discourse. She also draws on philosophy and literature to represent herself as intellectually credible. This combination of the authoritative third-person intellectual voice with anecdotes from her own experience, often presented in a first-person voice, allows Cooper to construct a form through which she could convey both individual authority and collective responsibility. Her writing, Alexander argues, creates a public space for an African-American intellectual woman's movement.

Issues of public and private voice and persona take center stage in Laura Laffrado's examination of how Sara Payson Willis created the public persona of "Fanny Fern," a fictionalized representation of the self, authorized to speak publicly. This public persona allowed Willis to address topics of cultural significance, to revise expectations about appropriate female speech and behavior, and to write anonymously and androgynously. Laffrado argues that the newspaper essay genre was particularly well-suited for Willis's project because its fluidity allowed commentary on social issues and made it possible for Willis to play out various scenarios of self-representation. Laffrado focuses on the essays Willis wrote concerning readers' conjectures on her gender, appearance, dress, and values. She argues that Willis, writing as Fanny Fern, used the newspaper essay to reflect and transform concepts of self and gender, feminine discourse, and public voice.

Yet women's public personae were not always entirely of their own making, Dorothy Baker suggests in "Excising the Text, Exorcising the Author: Margaret Fuller's *Summer on the Lakes, in 1843*." Baker traces the reasons for and effects of Arthur Buckminster Fuller's editing of his sister's travel narrative, focusing on how his deletions of embedded tales changed both the message of the text and Margaret Fuller's public image. She argues that Arthur approached the task of editing as a way of recuperating Margaret's reputation as a "true" woman, but that in attempting to present her as a more conservative commentator, he changed the form of her essay significantly. He seems to have attempted to force her work to be strictly a travel narrative rather than a combination of social commentary, storytelling, and description. This radical revision reveals Arthur's patriarchal assumptions about the authority of a woman's voice and transforms Margaret's conversational prose into a more direct and spare style closer to a classical masculine voice.

While Baker argues that Fuller's brother created a "masculine voice" for her, Beatrice Jacobson explores how Ann Sophia Stephens created one for herself in her public persona, Jonathan Slick. Stephens's adoption of a male persona represents not only a transitional point in her own literary development but also a crucial stage in the evolution of women's humor in the early nineteenth century. Adopting the perspective of a comic male Yankee figure, Stephens studies New York in the 1830s through a series of letters, *High Life in New York*. Like her character, Stephens was a recent arrival to New York, and she expresses her ambivalence toward urban life through Slick's eyes. Using the voice of the naive Yankee, Stephens critiques, satirizes, and parodies a variety of class and gender codes, including those associated with parlor manners. Stephens's literary cross-dressing also allows her to evade the contemporary prejudice against humorous women. Located between the early male Yankee figures, products of male writers, and the later female Yankee figures created by Frances Witcher and Marietta Holley, Stephens uses Jonathan Slick to experiment with humor while avoiding the stigma usually assigned female wit. While doing so, Stephens accomplished more than a complaint against artifice and excessive sentimentality; she transformed the down-east Yankee into a wisely foolish, ambiguously gendered personality.

Stephens was not alone in borrowing and revising genres usually associated with male writers during this period. The classic "American jeremiad" is a good example. Women writers used the form in much of their public writing on the "Woman Question," and in doing so, they added gender considerations to a genre that emphasizes cultural consensus. Gail Hamilton adopted both the authorial stance of prophecy and the standard rhetorical pattern of the jeremiad, but she altered it to fit her antisuffrage ideology by addressing men and women separately. By examining two of Hamilton's extended essays on women's rights, I argue that her gendering of the jeremiad and her own apparent discomfort with the authoritative form reflect the complexities of both the women's rights debate and women's participation in public political discourse.

Zitkala-Sa also used a common nonfiction form to engage in political discourse. As Margaret Lukens discusses, Zitkala-Sa's autobiographical essays offered a unique and important contribution to public awareness of Native American issues. When Zitkala-Sa's essays were published in the *Atlantic Monthly* in 1900, they were among the first Native American writings to appear in such a form "without the aid of an editor, an interpreter, or an ethnographer," according to Dexter Fisher. In this essay, Lukens argues that this freedom allowed Zitkala-Sa to voice harsh criticisms of the dominant culture's methods of educating Native American youth, the culturally genocidal intentions behind the inculcation of white culture in Native American students, and the government bureaucracy's mismanagement of the welfare of Native Americans as wards of the nation. Despite Zitkala-Sa's choice of the dominant cultural media of publishing and the written word, her inspiration had its source in the traditional oral culture of the Sioux. Her writing exemplifies the condition of a Native American writer in transition between two cultures.

Together, these essays sketch a rough history of nineteenth-century American women's use of various nonfiction genres. As these scholars and their subjects illustrate, women essayists created a public space for their social commentary in a much more direct way than literary history has previously recognized. In constructing a feminine version of the authoritative self of the essay, women writers negotiated not only with editors and publishers but also with their culture's ideas about public discourse and women's roles. Their success can be measured in works such as Hart's anthologies as well as in the rich sources their essays provide for contemporary literary scholarship.

NOTES

1. Baym has almost singlehandedly laid the foundation for work on American women's nonfiction in her two books, *Feminism and American Literary History* and *American Women Writers and the Work of History.*

REFERENCES

Atkins, G. Douglas. *Estranging the Familiar: Toward a Revitalized Critical Writing*. Athens, GA: U of Georgia P, 1992.

Baym, Nina. *Feminism and American Literary History: Essays*. New Brunswick, NJ: Rutgers UP, 1992.

———. *American Women Writers and the Work of History, 1790–1860*. New Brunswick, NJ: Rutgers UP, 1995.

Good, Graham. *The Observing Self: Rediscovering the Essay*. New York: Routledge, 1988.

Hardison, O.B., Jr. "Binding Proteus: An Essay on the Essay." *Essays on the Essay: Redefining the Genre*, ed. Alexander J. Butrym. Athens, GA: University of Georgia Press, 1989. 11–28.

Hart, John Seely. *Female Prose Writers of America*. Philadelphia: Butler, 1851.

———. *Female Prose Writers of America*. 5th ed. Philadelphia: Butler, 1870.

Joeres, Ruth-Ellen Boetcher and Elizabeth Mittman. *The Politics of the Essay: Feminist Perspectives*. Bloomington: U of Indiana P, 1993.

Snyder, Katherine V. "From Novel to Essay: Gender and Revision in Florence Nightingale's 'Cassandra.'" Joeres and Mittman 23–40.

In Her Own Voice

Women Writers and the Assumption of Authority:

The *Atlantic Monthly*, 1857–1898

Shirley Marchalonis

From its first issue in November 1857 to the end of the century, the *Atlantic Monthly* was America's outstanding magazine. Pre-publication advertising, both paid and word-of-mouth, had been skillful and the names connected with the magazine renowned, so from the beginning, it was the voice of the literary and intellectual establishment in the country at a time when that establishment was widely known and honored, even when its New England voice irritated some. Although there were other good magazines, notably *Putnam's*, *Harper's*, *Scribner's*, and later *The Century*, none attained quite the literary and intellectual prestige of the *Atlantic*. Founders and editors were dedicated to the best and took great pride in the quality of their magazine. The austere format (unlike other magazines, it had no pictures or decorations) and the refusal to print authors' names indicate the founders' emphasis on the content and quality of the offerings.[1] Under its nineteenth-century editors, the magazine assumed so great an authority that appearing in its pages gave luster and status—what Thomas Wentworth Higginson called "the *éclat* attendant on writing for the *Atlantic Monthly*"—to its contributors (*Cheerful Yesterdays* 172). And though there were difficulties with circulation and scandal through the period, the *Atlantic* never lost its prestige or reputation for quality.

In his *The Atlantic Monthly and Its Makers*, M. A. DeWolf Howe, chronicler of literary and social Boston, sums up the founders' dream in a statement that described the magazine through the century: "The *Atlantic Monthly* was started with the definite purpose of concentrating the efforts of the best writers upon literature and politics, under the light of the highest morals" (27).[2] "Highest morals" included, in pre-Civil War days, an abolitionist stance, the only strongly defined political position the *Atlantic* ever took. The back cover of the first issue stated that the magazine would "rank itself . . . with that body of men which is in favor of Freedom, National Progress, and Honor, whether public or private." And,

> while native writers will receive the most solid encouragement, and
> will be mainly relied on to fill the pages of the *Atlantic*, they [the editors] will not hesitate to draw from the foreign forces at their com-

mand, as occasion may require, relying rather on the competency of an author to treat a particular subject, than on any other claim whatever.

In his study of American magazines, Edward Chielens notes the *Atlantic*'s awareness of mission: "This sense of obligation to establish authoritative literary and intellectual standards and to promote high literate culture continued to influence the magazine's identity and its editorial policies in an increasingly democratic and pluralistic society" (50–51). Whatever changes in format occurred, that desire for the best in the magazine did not change throughout the century—though editorial judgments of what constituted the "best" might.

The *Atlantic* has been the subject of personal reminiscences from those who remembered their connection with the magazine as a happy experience and a source of pride; its importance in the nineteenth-century letters has given scholars evidence of American thought, intellectual climate, and the work of major authors.[3] With a few exceptions, such as Harriet Beecher Stowe and Sarah Orne Jewett, the women who published in the *Atlantic* have had little critical attention. Overall there are fewer women contributors; the significant difference is not in fiction, where the numbers of men and women writers almost balance, but in nonfiction. Even though the number of women contributors is comparatively small, there is no indication of a bias against women, nor did the magazine ever take a stance toward the "Woman Question." In 1859 it published Thomas Wentworth Higginson's "Ought Women To Learn the Alphabet?" with its bold and revolutionary thesis that women were just as intelligent and capable as men—or would be if they were permitted the same kind of education, a thesis that he supported with innumerable examples from history.[4] While Higginson notes that James Russell Lowell thought the essay too "radical," it was published without changes and signifies the magazine's willingness to discuss any topic as long as it was important and the essay well-written.

Higginson also noted one editor's attitude toward women writers:

> I have also known [James T. Fields] to increase the amount paid, on finding that the author needed the money, especially if this were the case of a woman. His sympathy with struggling women was always very great; and I think he was the only one in the early *Atlantic* circle, except Whittier and myself,—with Emerson also, latterly, who favored women suffrage. (*Cheerful Yesterdays* 185; Howe 43)

With no indication of a prejudice against women authors and with men and women writers of fiction almost equal numerically, the fact that only a very small number of women published nonfiction essays in the magazine becomes a point worth examining. Nonfiction essays constituted most of the *Atlantic*'s content and, in a sense, provided its reason for existence. The few women whose informative essays met the magazine's high standards and were published in its prestigious pages did something that, given the time, the attitudes about women, and the lack of educational opportunities, was unusual. We have paid little attention to women who wrote nonfiction (with the exception of Margaret Fuller) and, in doing so, assumed the authoritative masculine voice. Those who wrote essays for the *Atlantic*, their achievements, and their preparation need to be placed and examined within the context of the magazine's history and procedures.

The founders and controllers of the magazine, literary men with similar interests and backgrounds, made up a network whose members understood one another and spoke a common cultural language. Their shared values and their innocent conviction that all wisdom came from Boston made them see the magazine as far more than a commercial venture; it was a voice of culture, intellect, and authority. James Russell Lowell, like Emerson, Longfellow, and the other founders, belonged to the group by birthright; James T. Fields, a farm boy from New Hampshire, made his place not only by his position as junior partner in the most prestigious publishing firm in the country, but through intelligence, personality, and his deep love of literature and admiration for its creators. Arthur Gilman's essay "Atlantic Dinners and Diners" is virtually a record of male conviviality, with good conversation, good food, and flowing wine. "Most of the decisions regarding the early courses of the *Atlantic* were taken at dinner-tables," says Howe, and the reminiscences are full of vignettes of these revered figures walking the streets of Cambridge in a state that must be called mellow (19).

The festive dinners to plan the magazine or to celebrate various things connected with it were exclusively male. Part of this exclusion may be explained simply by the mores of the time and part, perhaps, by the presence at an early planning dinner of Harriet Beecher Stowe, who as a teetotaler refused to have wine served; the gentlemen were forced to sneak wine into their water glasses, and her presence resulted in an awkward evening (Howe 21–24; Higginson, *Cheerful Yesterdays*, 176–180).[5]

No contemporary account, however, minimizes Stowe's importance; her recommendation of the proposed magazine to the first publisher, Phillips Sampson, along with her promise to be a regular contributor, gave the *Atlantic* its start. Another woman important to the establishment and early days of the magazine was Annie Adams Fields, who, when James T. Fields took over as editor, became a major player. Fields clearly adored his young second wife, finding her not merely an object of affection but an intellectual partner. When Ticknor and Fields bought the house on Charles Street, Annie Adams Fields became the city's (and therefore, in Bostonian eyes, the world's) foremost literary hostess, a position resulting from her husband's job but enhanced by her own personality, intelligence, and old Boston family background. More important, during Fields's editorial reign, the years when the magazine was consolidating itself, Annie Adams Fields influenced both policy and the choice of content to the point of being an informal assistant editor.[6]

Though the network excluded women from festivities and from the planning and policy that went on during such occasions, it did not exclude them from the pages of the magazine. In fact, from the beginning, well-known women fiction writers were courted as eagerly as were men.[7] Stowe's name would sell issues; established writers like Rose Terry (Cooke), Caroline Chesebro', and Lydia Maria Child were assets; and the youthful Harriet Prescott (Spofford) was a major discovery. Examination of the contents over the period shows that in fiction, men's and women's contributions are about equal in number and show no significant differences in content.[8]

While the controllers of the magazine displayed no bias against women writers, scholars have been less interested in or friendly to the women who were connected with the magazine. Most mention a name or two in passing, and the one study that devotes time and space to women contributors does so in a negative way. James C. Austin's *Fields of the Atlantic Monthly* (1953) is a major source of information about the magazine and its second editor. At first glance, this work seems so thorough a study that no more needs to be said; it is especially strong in its analysis of the editorial relationship of Lowell and Fields. To read it today, however, in light of our changed attitudes toward and greater interest in women writers, is to see its imbalance. Austin treats male contributors in standard critical fashion but has very little time or space for women.[9] When he does mention them, he is at best patronizing, at worst contemptuous, and the result of his work is to reduce women writers to producers of filler. The few women he does discuss are writers of fiction and poetry.

The history of the magazine is usually and logically presented as the history of its five nineteenth-century editors. Throughout the century, the format and philosophy of the magazine remained consistent, but each editor had preferences that affected what was selected for inclusion. To examine the magazine this way is to present a kind of panorama that displays changing interests, the movement from literary Romanticism to Realism, and an array of names that surface, stay for awhile, then disappear.[10]

James Russell Lowell (1857–61), with his advisors, established the format, goals, and the balance of fiction, poetry, and nonfiction for the magazine, and his issues are dominated by the great names of the literary establishment in fiction, poetry, and nonfiction.[11] Though Lowell was not a practical editor and offended some writers by his unauthorized tinkering with their work, his policy decisions seem to have been so wise that successive editors felt no need for major changes.

Four years after its founding, Ticknor and Fields bought the magazine and James T. Fields, junior partner of the firm, became editor (1861–71). The change was friendly; Lowell served as a consultant for years. With the same format, Fields shortened the essays and put more emphasis on the topical so that his magazine seems livelier. The Civil War was a major topic, although Howe notes that war themes and issues appeared chiefly in "the political article, editorial in its character" and were never deliberately sought (45). Later there were reminiscences and war-based fiction from men who fought or women who nursed or taught contrabands; political essays discussed reconstruction, impeachment, and President Johnson. He introduced Gail Hamilton, a witty, fearless critic of society, a regular contributor until her quarrel with Fields in 1869. He liked Harriet Prescott's romanticism, but, although the encouragement of Realism is always attributed to Howells, it was Fields who accepted Rebecca Harding's "Life in the Iron Mills." Too, he personalized the magazine, making it, with its Authors' Room and the famous Book in which authors could write their bits of humor or wisdom and with his own genial presence, both a literary and social center (Ticknor). More concrete changes were managerial: Fields paid when works were accepted, which endeared him to his writers, and in volume X (1862) he revealed the authors' names in the semiannual index; in volume XXVI (1870), names appeared in the text.

Fields had made two significant editorial changes: he ended anonymity, and in 1866 he hired the young midwesterner William Dean Howells as assistant editor. When Fields retired in 1871, Howells became editor (1871–81). He widened the scope of the magazine beyond New England, keeping the older writers while encouraging the new. There were fewer pieces overall and more literary comment, and of course, he invited Realism, discovering Sarah Orne Jewett, Mary N. Murfree (who wrote as Charles Egbert Craddock), Helen Hunt (Jackson), and Mark Twain. In volume XXXIX, he initiated the Contributor's Club, pages in which authors could anonymously comment on anything they chose.[12]

When Howells left Boston for New York in 1881, he was succeeded by Thomas Bailey Aldrich (1881–90).[13] Aldrich published less fiction in his volumes, and the new women writers he introduced were all writers of nonfiction. His most significant change was his emphasis on the review essay, which not only told about books but commented on fiction and literature with the assumption that these mattered. The reviewers he relied on were highly intellectual in their approach, believed in literature as a feature of civilization, and continued the discussion of Realism and Romanticism in the creation and identification of literary art.

Aldrich left in 1890 and was succeeded by Horace Scudder (1890–98), described by Howe as "the last of the *Atlantic* editors who belonged, even as a younger contemporary, to the group of writers which dominated the magazine through its early years" (93). Scudder kept most of the same contributors, although the new women writers he introduced were writers of fiction, like Alice

Brown and Kate Douglas Wiggin. He continued the review essays, written by the same group of critics.

The *Atlantic*'s basic policies did not change, though editorial preferences did create different emphases. Sampling from randomly chosen years, each representing an editor, gives a picture of the magazine's contents at different times and the comparative proportions of fiction and nonfiction as well as of men and women writers. Numbers do not tell a whole story, but they do allow a rough comparison.

	Lowell III–IV	Fields XV–XVI	Howells XXXVII–XXXVIII	Aldrich LIX–LX	Scudder LXV–XVI
	(1859)	(1865)	(1876)	(1887)	(1890)
Titles	69	90	76	107	131
Fiction	21	19	18	19	24
By Men	10	10	12	11	9
By Women	11	9	6	9	15
Nonfiction	48	71	57	88	107
By Men	46	59	46	64	86
By Women	2	12	11	24	21

For several reasons, this count must be an approximate rather than an exact one[14]; it does, however, show some significant points. Those who study American literature today tend to think of the *Atlantic* as the home of the great names of the time and as a repository for the best nineteenth-century fiction. In reality, fiction made up a small proportion of the total content: about one-third to one-fifth overall. Important as the fiction was to the magazine and to scholars today, comparative numbers indicate that it was never the main focus. While the *Atlantic* clearly cherished good fiction and poetry, its major focus was to inform: to produce the best writing and thinking on subjects of importance. From Emerson and Higginson to Theodore Roosevelt and Woodrow Wilson, the editors chose essays that treated a variety of subjects with a shared basis of concern for the nation's intellectual and moral health. In this area of informative and scholarly writing, women are noticeably in the minority. Yet there were women who contributed ideas, who were knowledgeable enough by the *Atlantic*'s high standards to inform the public, and who in some cases became regular contributors to the magazine. While the proportion does not change much over the years, numbers do: two women writers of the erudite *Atlantic* essay in Lowell's sample volume to twenty-four in Aldrich's.

The essay form established by Lowell was learned, but in a sense informal: leisurely erudition. In a note to Higginson, Lowell described an essay as "just to my liking,—scholarly, picturesque, and, above all, earnest."[15] He might have added that it should be in no hurry to get to its point. An essay by D. W. Cheever called "The Gymnasium" on present-day sports serves as an example; it opens with the beginning of sport in ancient Greece, moves through times and cultures, pauses whenever the author has a comment to make or wishes to reflect, and finally gets to the present and its topic in fourteen closely packed pages. These meditative essays are as far away from today's thirty-second sound bite as one can imagine; later editors might shorten the number of pages, but through the nineteenth century, the *Atlantic* essays assumed an audience of thoughtful readers with the time and desire to think about what they read. They assumed as well a language of allusion reflecting a shared background of reading, study, and thorough knowledge of the Bible, mythology, Latin and Greek classics, literature, and history. Perhaps the most striking feature of the essays, regardless of differences in content and style, is their voice of effortless, nonstrident, but completely secure authority—the voice of knowledge and wisdom in an age that still liked and expected to be taught as well as entertained. The magazine's first volume announced that while "native writers" were preferred, it would rely on "the competency of an author to treat a particular subject" above any other factor. This stated policy of going to the "experts" for its nonfiction allowed the *Atlantic* to tap the knowledge and intellectual rigor of the well-educated.

However wide the range of topics, the essays were alike in their desire to inform rather than to argue a cause. Though they became shorter and livelier under Fields and his successors, they never lost their easy erudition nor the authority that they all had in common. They project a calm, easy, unself-conscious confidence that the writers know what they are saying, know how to say it, and never doubt that what they say is valid because it is based on their expertise. From Emerson on, the essays quietly assert the right of the author to inform the world—a right based on ability, intelligence, and education.

The small number of women contributors in this area might suggest that the editors could accept women as creators of fiction but not as learned beings, but again there is no indication of such a bias. There are several possible explanations for the fact that so few women ventured into the area of informed nonfiction. Susan Coultrap-McQuin has shown in *Doing Literary Business* the difficulty women might have with editorial and business relationships and the reconciliation of womanly standards with this normally masculine activity. Diffidence might come from the fact that while women writing fiction could fall back on the myth of the creative muse for which they were merely instruments, those who wrote nonfiction were displaying their own knowledge and thought. Furthermore, women's education as it was in the early years of the magazine made the knowledge and wide reading needed for the kind of expertise that the magazine demanded far less available than these tools would later become. While there were some good seminaries, such as Mount Holyoke, Hartford, and Troy, it is significant that when Vassar opened in 1865 the attacks against it focused on Matthew Vassar's stated intention of offering women the same curriculum given their brothers at Yale or Harvard—including not just history and science, but those hallmarks of male superiority, Latin and Greek, the classical background for that shared language of allusion from which so many women were barred. Opportunity was indeed restricted by gender, as it was by economic class and by the social definitions of propriety that might make a woman hesitate to achieve or claim the implicit authority of the expert.

Even in the early volumes, however, a few women demonstrated their expertise. Well-known social critics like Harriet Martineau and Lydia Maria Child were welcome, and Gail Hamilton was a regular contributor under Fields. More characteristic, however, were women knowledgeable on specific topics: Maria Mitchell wrote of another woman astronomer, Harriet Hosmer on sculpture, Elizabeth Peabody on kindergartens, Fanny Kemble on Shakespeare, and Caroline Kirkland on the West. Their knowledge tended to be narrow and deep, and once they had written about their subjects, they did not appear again. Essays on traditional "women's topics" were few and early, and they have some odd twists: Stowe's "House and Home Papers" have a male narrator, and Melusina Fay Peirce's "Co-operative Housekeeping" series presented a radical formula for communal work and escape from women's sphere.

Women nonfiction writers flourished during the editorial reign of Thomas Bailey Aldrich, who shifted emphasis away from fiction to the informative essay and to reviews. Himself a craftsman and conscious artist, Aldrich clearly liked the well-shaped, well-written essay or sketch, and his tables of contents show that he preferred shorter essays and more of them. More than any preceding editor, he accepted nonfiction written by women, although it is impossible to know whether this was deliberate choice, the larger number of available slots, or simply the fact that more educational opportunities for women existed. Probably all these factors were responsible. The numbers given for the sample volumes, twenty-four out of sixty-four essays by women, remain representative through Aldrich's tenure.

By the 1880s, there was a group of women whose nonfiction appeared regularly in the magazine. They were not like the fiction-writing "regulars" of James T. Fields, who could encourage talents to publish only in the many prestigious outlets he controlled, nor were they a kind of women's literary community from Boston and its suburbs, all of whom knew one another. Instead, they contributed to other magazines, had other publishers, and came from all locations, so that they are individual careerists rather than a literary group.

Although essay topics could come from almost anywhere, there are several categories that appear consistently enough to be considered staples of the magazine. Biography had been a feature from the beginning; for the most part, these were the lives of the great who gave examples for others to follow. Women wrote these pieces as well as men and might even be subjects of them, especially if they were figures of historical significance. Though few women wrote directly on politics and economics, Fields had called on two Englishwomen, Frances Power Cobbe and Sophia Collet, for analyses of their country's politics. Social criticism, ranging from comments on behavior to serious studies of labor problems, poverty, and social ills, was an open area. Harriet Martineau contributed several essays, and Lydia Maria Child wrote on slavery and religion. Later Helen Hunt Jackson's subjects included the treatment and lives of American Indians and the West. Rebecca Harding Davis wrote essays as well as fiction. Lillie Buffum Chace Wyman did a series called "Studies in Factory Life," and her autobiographical "From Generation to Generation" told of growing up in a Quaker family committed to abolition. Octave Thanet's "The Indoor Pauper: A Study," about poorhouses, offers analysis based on fact and observation with discussion of political implications. Journalist Kate Gannet Wells wrote about women in various situations and places: "Women in Organizations," "The Transitional American Woman," and "Caste in American Society." Women observed, analyzed, and wrote.

After Elizabeth Cary Agassiz, few women wrote about science, but the world of nature inspired many essays. Edith M. Thomas, today a lost name but then a respected poet, wrote sensitive nature essays; her "A Spring Opening" describes the coming of spring with a naturalist's eye and a poet's pen. Olive Thorne Miller's essays, beginning in volume LII, translate bird behavior into human terms, redeemed from cuteness by her refusal to anthropomorphize and her precise observation. These, like nature essays by John Burroughs, a lifelong contributor, John Muir, and Bradford Torrey, combined the belief that the natural world gives both pleasure and guidance through its beauty with an emphasis on exact scientific reporting.

Humor was never an aim of the magazine, but its serious approach to life was occasionally breached by wit. Oliver Wendell Holmes, of course, is an example, and Howells began publishing fiction and essays by Mark Twain in volume XXXIV. Gail Hamilton's work was witty, often ironic, social criticism; in volume LVII, Aldrich introduced essayist Agnes Repplier, whose gentler humor examined individual follies and behaviors rather than social ills. She was a regular writer for the magazine for many years. Humor functioned as a tool to point up an issue rather than for its own sake, as in Mary Boardman Sheldon's "A Literary Model," which tells the perils encountered by an overzealous author in search of Realism.

Early writing about literature had been chiefly literary history and biography, with current fiction briefly noted, but that approach changed over the years into the long and serious review essay. As the amount of space given them indicates, the later *Atlantic*, beginning under Howells and maturing with

Aldrich, took its review essays very seriously, finding them a way to talk about both literature and the society that generated it. A major preoccupation was, of course, the competing ideas of Romanticism and Realism, and many review essays sought to define the relationship of the two to each other and to standards of literary art.

A staple of the magazine from its earliest days was the essay of place. These essays were not travel guides or descriptions of pretty places, but close analyses of a city or region, its history, geography, politics, people, and culture. One writer sums up the goal in the beginning of an essay titled "A Florentine Family in the Fifteenth Century," based on letters and other documentation, noting that

> Details of personal traits and domestic life have an inexpressible charm for all readers of average human sympathies. We turn with more relief than we are willing to confess from the brilliant generalizations of the historian to the pages of the humble chronicler or diarist. (Bianciardi 672)

Later Agnes Repplier would add, in an essay called "Children, Past and Present,"

> As a result of this modern tendency to desert the broad beaten roads of history for the bridle-path of biography and memoir, we find a great many side lights thrown upon matters that the historian was wont to treat as altogether beneath his consideration. It is by their help that we study the minute changes of social life that little by little alter the whole aspect of a people, and it is by their help that we look straight into the ordinary every-day workings of the past, and measure the space between its existence and our own. (508)

These statements are assertions, not veiled apologies, and from the number of essays with exactly this focus, they could almost be stating magazine policy. No issue was without at least one essay of this kind, and even though we often generalize about women being more interested in people than in issues, the writer's gender has little to do with the finished product. Again, while these essays may include subjective impressions, they are primarily observations of customs, behavior, and attitudes solidly grounded in history. Under Lowell, J. W. Palmer wrote about British India, stressing terrain, history, and politics to help readers understand the country, and Julia Ward Howe's trip to Cuba provided analysis of an exotic neighbor, as later Helen Hunt Jackson's "Bergen Days" examined geography, climate, legends, and work in Scandinavia and saw people and their character as a product of these forces. But Jackson, in her essays on Colorado and the American Indians, wrote about another place of interest, almost as exotic in eastern eyes: the American West.[16] Readers and editors clearly liked this kind of informative writing, perhaps logically in a still-growing country seeking its own definition and welcoming knowledge about the rest of the world against which to measure and identify itself. And perhaps the editorial and public appetite for realistic details of other lives and cultures parallels the growing appreciation of Realism in fiction. The men and women who wrote place analyses were obviously, like the local color Realists, close observers, but they had to be informed, well-educated, travelled, and capable of drawing intelligent and objective conclusions and generalizations from what they saw. These essays combine solid but easy learning with the ability to write well.

The women who wrote essays for the *Atlantic* were intelligent, perceptive, and well-educated; among them are a few whose work shows the kind of study and methodology that is characteristic of scholarly writing. Although most of these scholarly women wrote toward the end of the century, Lowell published an essay on the Faust legends by Theresa Albertina Robinson, a well-known European scholar who had married an American minister; much of her work was in German and analyzed the United States for European readers. According to one source, Goethe had described her as having "the heart of a woman but the brain of a man."[17]

By Aldrich's time, there were more women who had won reputations in their various scholarly fields and whose essays appeared regularly in the *Atlantic*. A sampling of their work must include Isabel Hapgood, who published a series of essays on Russia between 1888 and 1894. She translated from French, German, Italian, and Spanish, but her primary expertise was in Russian and Slavic dialects. Besides her sixteen-volume translation of Turgeniev, which became the standard text, she translated works by Leo Tolstoy, Fyodor Dostoyevsky, Anton Chekhov, Victor Hugo, and others, and she wrote critical works on Russian literature and a scholarly examination of the forms of the Russian Orthodox Church.[18] In 1916 and 1917, she was a correspondent for the *New York Times*, reporting on the Russian Revolution. Her *Atlantic* pieces focus on the life and culture that she had observed on her several long stays in Russia.

Elizabeth Robins (Pennell) wrote chiefly for the *Nation, Century,* and *Harper's,* but beginning with her "Mischief in the Middle Ages," she published fourteen knowledgeable studies of comparative mythology and folklore in the *Atlantic* between 1881 and 1888. These cover a wide range and are clearly the result of serious study. In 1884 she published a life of Mary Wollstonecraft, but after her marriage to illustrator Joseph Pennell in the same year, her work became more popular than scholarly; they moved to England and traveled throughout Europe—"he with his sketchbook, I with my notebook"—writing and illustrating their travels, many of which were by bicycle

(Pennell 109). After his death, she wrote his biography and several reminiscences of places and people she had known, and she worked as a journalist for several London newspapers.

Aldrich's emphasis on the review essay led to the consolidation of a group of reviewers who argued the value of Realism vs. "literary art" and used fiction as a way to comment on life and society. Ferris Greenslet credits Aldrich with developing

> the critical department of the magazine to a high degree of competence by marshaling what has seldom been seen in this country, a thoroughly compact and capable coterie of critical reviewers. This group, which was composed of Richard Grant White, G. E. Woodberry, George Parsons Lothrop, Horace Scudder, and Miss Harriet Waters Preston, contributed a surprisingly large proportion of the material [which is] still remarkable for penetration of insight and felicity of expression. (85)

These writers kept their connection with the magazine for years.

Of all the women who wrote nonfiction essays for the *Atlantic*, Harriet Waters Preston (1836–1911) is numerically the outstanding *Atlantic* woman nonfiction writer of the period covered in this paper; between 1873 and 1904 she contributed forty-one essays, sixty-seven signed review articles, as well as pieces for the Contributor's Club, and seventeen essays with her niece, Louise Dodge, as collaborator. Her career certainly asserts that women could present themselves as experts and authorities and that, by this time, instead of a narrow expertise, could use their intelligence on a wide range of subjects.

In *Perish the Thought*, a study of intellectual women before the Civil War, Susan Conrad pictures their isolation, their vulnerability to stereotypes and labels, the privacy of their education, and the lack of opportunity to use their minds. Although Preston was late in starting a career and did indeed meet problems, her life contrasts sharply with those Conrad describes in an earlier generation. Concepts of womanly behavior were changing and variable through the latter half of the century, influenced by the agitation for women's rights, the opening of women's colleges, and the founding and growth of the club woman movement, so a woman asserting her right to ideas may have been less conspicuous. Preston's letters display confidence in her ability, intelligence, and judgments, and that confidence informs her essays as well.

Born in 1836 in Danvers, Massachusetts, the youngest daughter of a wealthy shoe manufacturer who encouraged his three bright daughters to study, the young Harriet Preston had a gift for languages. After attendance at local schools and study with tutors, she went to boarding school in Brunswick, Maine, where the faculty was enhanced by moonlighting professors from Bowdoin College. She describes her studies there in 1853, when she was seventeen:

And now I must tell you how scientifically my day is divided, and what a regular, busy life I lead. I rise at four (!!!), study German from half past four to half past five, read from half past five to half past six, then have breakfast. From seven to nine I prepare my French and algebra lessons, from nine to ten practice, from ten to eleven recite French, from eleven to half past twelve I study whatever is not ready and the same from one to two. From two to three [I study French]; from three to four thirty our occupations vary on the different days. From half past four to six we walk; from half past six to eight, study, and from eight to nine, enjoy ourselves. . . . I thought from what Pa said that you were all a little afraid that I had too many studies. But I do not think I have. (15 Oct. 1853)

Other letters show that she was not taking Latin formally because she already knew it so well, and a year later she mentioned that she was getting along well in her study of Greek (10 July 1854). During the time that she was away at school, there are long weekly letters between Harriet and her father, with added notes from her mother and sisters. The Preston family letters are warm, affectionate, thoughtful, and full of the details of everyday life; they reveal a family whose love and respect for one another is very strong, and perhaps this secure background explains Preston's confidence in herself and her abilities.

Her literary career began in the late 1860s; before then, she had been reading and studying at home. There is a gap in biographical information for these years, with only a hint now and then in a few family letters. In 1855 her older married sister, Louisa, wrote her concern: "But Mary and Hatty need action, not rest. Hatty in particular is dying for want of an object in life" (20 Mar. 1855). Mary married in 1859, Louisa died in 1860 and their mother in 1868, leaving Harriet the daughter at home. She and her father had a close relationship, and they lived and traveled together until his death in 1878. She was a friend of Essex County neighbor Gail Hamilton and later of Sarah Orne Jewett.[19] She spent time in New Hampshire, Boston, and Washington, D.C. Whether marriage was a possibility at any time during this period is not clear.

By 1873, the time of her first *Atlantic* essay, which was a study of the French poet Frederic Mistral whose *Mirèio* she had just translated, Preston had written a story for children, the first of her four novels, and many pieces for the *Independent*; she was established in her major work, translation and criticism of French literature.[20] Other analyses of French literature followed, and as she became a regular contributor to the *Atlantic*, she began reviewing books and widening her range of subjects. In 1879, after her father's death, she left for extensive European travel, which resulted in her own kind of learned place essays for the magazine. For her, Rome evoked history and inspired a series of essays on Cicero, using the scholar's tools: analyzing all available sources, comparing versions, and weighing evidence to get at truth ("Cicero in the Senate," "A Changing Order," and "Assam Igitur"). Her "Oxford in Winter" begins and ends with scenery, topography, and architecture, but these frame the lives and work of poets who were students there. She displays impressive literary scholarship in "The Arthuriad" as she compares Tennyson's version of the legends with Malory and other redactions; she knew the medieval romance literature in English, French, and German thoroughly and, somewhat surprisingly, is aware of the relationship between this early literature and oral transmission in the formation of the metrical, then cycle, romances. She concludes with the intelligent judgment that while Tennyson reflects current moral values, Malory is the better writer.

Unlike our image of mid-century women writers, who are often glibly accused of writing only for money, Preston was not dependent on her earnings. Ellen Ballou says, "Of her articles that had been in the editor's drawer for nine months, Harriet Waters Preston demanded in frustration, '. . . please print them or pay for them or something, before the leaves are much greener'" (208). Later Ballou calls her "impoverished," apparently on the basis of this letter (268).[21] There is plenty of evidence that she became annoyed when payment for her work was not immediate, but the Preston family was wealthy, and she had an inherited income that allowed her to read, study, travel widely, and write when she chose. Isabel Hapgood and Elizabeth Robins, too, were independently wealthy; in fact, the lives of these three women more closely parallel those of the gentleman-scholar than the striving author.

Competent and secure as Preston seems to be in her work, she still met frustrations. Like her friend Gail Hamilton, she was not inclined to suffer fools gladly or in silence. An unsigned fragment from Hamilton suggests trouble with the *Independent*:

Washington, D.C. May 9, 1872

My dear—It is seldom in a lifetime one puts his head in a lion's mouth so deftly as you have put yours in mine. I have always hitherto as you know been in an inferior and subordinate position. You have lorded it over my hats and silks and I have waited for the tables to be turned and now you have been and gone and done it, you silliest of all silly women. You are just like a man. Strong in streaks, utterly weak, impracticable, inharmonious as a whole. What evil spirit possessed you to quarrel with the Independent? Where will you find such an audience as there? I suppose you don't care to write for the mere expression. If you do you need never go off the Hill [the Preston home]. But if you want to communicate as well as express your thoughts, a great paper like the Independent, reaching through the country, is as good a medium as either you or I can command by our own unaided resources. Then who is to be judge of length, he who has been making up Independents for a dozen years or you who don't know anything but to squat on the Hill.[22]

Preston responded snappishly to the editor of the *Literary World*, who asked her to review books for him without pay because she would increase his circulation: "I have no doubt that it is very right that your fortune should be made before mine, but I do not quite so clearly see why I should help you make it." The letter goes on:

> If I understand what you mean by "books of value"—no one whom I know is rich enough to read such books conscientiously and review them properly for the price of the volumes. On the other hand—to review books of little or no intrinsic value, even at the highest market price, is extremely expensive for the reviewer. I "did" the novels for the *Atlantic* for two years, and then threw over the engagement because I found ten dollars a page no sort of compensation for the misery of reading the books. (5 Jan. 1881)

In fact, she "threw over" the engagement partly because of disagreements with William Dean Howells, whose judgments of poetry she later described as "purblind, provincial, *borné*" (27 Oct. 1878) and who finally offended her beyond bearing. In his study of the *Atlantic Monthly*, Ellery Sedgwick notes that in 1902 she wrote "a strong condemnation of Howells, based partly on an old but virulent personal feud . . . Howells, she said, was provincial, half-taught, intolerant, dictatorial and dogmatic—not the great reformer he pretended, but an obstructionist who needed deflation."[23] Evidence from her letters, however, suggests that her dislike of Howells was professional, not personal; as she explained to a correspondent at the time, she was reviewing Henry James's *The American*, *The Europeans*, and *Daisy Miller* and was pleased with the result, which "really came somewhere near my ideal of critical discrimination." Since she admired James, most of the review was favorable, but there were some negative comments with her praise, and Howells hastily wrote that they must be removed:

> "Oh no," he said. "You must take this all back. *I know Henry James so well* I could not appear to attack him. You must take out all you said of *Daisy Miller* and all but your praise of *The Europeans*. *On the whole I think I'll cut the article down myself.*" (Preston's emphasis)

Worse was to follow, as the same letter indicates:

I had already corrected the proof of my *Last Songs of Chivalry, entire,* just as I wrote it . . . so you may judge of my emotions when it appeared in the January Atlantic, with the *four most interesting pages taken out without a word.* All the earliest fragments of English verse were gone— a dozen or more collected with great care out of the Harleian mss.— together with the discussion on their forms of versification so clearly derived from the Romance poetry and on the wide difference between these and the first really indigenous English poetry—Chaucer, Skelton, etc. And so on through the article, everything that was rare, curious, and difficult of access—everything which might not have been found in any one of forty collections—everything as it appeared which the editor did not know about himself, was thrown away, without a word to me,— mutilating the article fatally. When I beheld the ruin, I cared no more for Henry James. (22 Dec. 1878)

That James knew nothing of this disagreement is suggested by a note in the Preston Papers from him to Edward Niles: "I am seldom so much disappointed about anything, as that Miss Preston has not written that notice. Can't you get her to do it yet? Telling her that Mr. Howells said he would be very glad to have it? . . . I really think Hatty Preston might do it. It wouldn't take her two hours to write the thing." He adds after his signature, "I'd about ask her my-self—now that I know she likes the book so much;—but I do not like ever to ask such a personal favor as that" (18 Nov. 1876). We can only wonder whether Howells would so freely have tampered with the work of a male writer, but clearly the paternalism he displayed toward women writers did not work with this one. Soon after this he left the *Atlantic,* to be succeeded by Thomas Bailey Aldrich, with whom Preston maintained a long and friendly working relation-ship.

Preston's writing and letters reveal her awareness of the limits society placed on women or that women placed on themselves. In a later Contributor's Club piece called "Women and Politics," she deplored the fact that American women did not inform themselves and that they accepted the general belief in their own inability to understand politics. To prove her point, she instanced Queen Victoria, who as a "moderately endowed woman" was still able "to grapple vigorously with what are usually considered, in a very special sense, the affairs of men" and displayed a "rare political intelligence" that was learned. She points out that "the average Englishwoman of good birth and education" un-derstands politics and has a "thorough acquaintance both with public events and issues and the character and record of public men." In America, she iden-tified Gail Hamilton as "the only . . . woman I ever knew who had exactly the sort of political savoir-faire which is possessed by hundreds of strictly domes-tic Englishwomen" (589–90). Preston herself, in a long correspondence with southern poet Paul Hamilton Hayne, seriously tried to understand the southern mind, attitude, and pre- and post-war politics. Obviously she was interested and informed, but her insights and understandings of current politics do not appear in the *Atlantic*; for it, she restricted herself to the politics of ancient Rome.

Her awareness of women's status does not intrude into her formal *Atlantic* essays, but does display itself in her fiction. She wrote thesis novels, more rational than eventful, but because she was good at creating characters, reviewers forgave her her thin plots, which are little more than lines on which to hang ideas. For example, *Love in the XIXth Century* (1873) is a courtship novel, but a most unusual one, describing the "wary siege-approach" of two young people who meet in a rural New Hampshire boarding house. Both intelligent, their conversation is civilized argument; they disagree courteously over the Franco-Prussian War, Matthew Arnold's idea of culture, money and society in the city of Trimountain (Boston), death and afterlife, and other topics. This searching of each other's minds continues in letters when the summer ends, and eventually, though they may hold their different opinions, their understandings lead to marriage and the establishment of an ideal home based on respect as well as love.

In the novel, a discussion of Anthony Trollope's fiction leads to ideas about women characters created by male authors with which today's feminist scholars would agree. Clara comments:

> men . . . have been in the way, instinctively, of regarding women, like other subordinate creatures, as something less than individuals. And so they have not thought it worth their while to study them from life as they have their men, but instead they have given us their several ideals of feminine grace and goodness, or the reverse. Their men have been men, and their women have been types, abstractions. . . .

As for women novelists depicting men,

> we know you better than you think; better than we quite dare say; better, I verily believe, than you know us. . . . women have always been more dependent for their happiness . . . on the characters of the men with whom they were associated, their fathers, sons, husbands, and so on, than men on their female relatives. . . . this dependence has made them very acute. All dependents are acute. How well your servants know you! (22–27)

While there is no indication that Preston was ever active in feminist causes, she was consistently aware of women's issues.

Preston is unusual, but in a sense, she represents a group of women, small but growing as the century ended, who moved into male territory to speak with intellectual authority and expertise in the country's most prestigious magazine. Her writing impresses the reader with its breadth and depth of knowledge, its quality, and certainly its confidence. By the latter years of the nineteenth century, intelligent, well-educated women could have unapologetic literary careers as journalists, satirists, social critics, or scholars. The work of such women as Preston, Hapgood, and Robins shows that they could and did assume the authoritative voice of the expert on subjects that were not "womanly," and they did so over their own names. They are a long way from sweet singers or untutored nightingales, and they do not appear to have needed the protection of these labels.

Significantly, the women who wrote informative nonfiction for the prestigious *Atlantic* do not display an identifiable "woman's voice." The nonfiction is genderless—the neutral voice of the scholar or detached observer, with conclusions drawn from knowledge and logical thinking. The lack of a woman's voice raises questions: Is it proof that women could think and write *as well as* men? Or that in order to be published in a prestigious outlet, they had to achieve the androgynous voice of the scholar? Is this a sinking of personality or the logical result of the kind of writing? There is a slight but significant difference in saying that a woman could assume the scholar's voice and saying that she could assume the scholar's identity. In the preface to her translation of Sainte-Bueve's *Portraits of Celebrated Women*, Preston hopes that the work

> may serve to remind some of the more gifted among the "anxious and aimless" sisterhood, of the possibility of sober and useful literary careers, which they may enter easily by abjuring vanity, and paying the enobling fee of patient thought and conscientious study. (10)

Preston, in fact, betrayed suspicion of "woman's voice" in her letters; she praised a novel that had no "taint of womanhood" (29 Sept. 1878), and about one of her own novels she commented, "Women are so taunted with perpetual self-revelation in what they write that I began with the firm resolution to make no one person my own mouth-piece" (3 Mar. 1878). For this late-century intellectual, an identifiable woman's voice was clearly undesirable. Her denial of a woman's voice is at the same time denial of a standard in which masculine is better than feminine and an insistence that if the standard for good writing is the gender-neutral, scholarly, authoritative voice, she—and other women—can achieve it. She seems to bear out Higginson's earlier assertion that if women are given the same intellectual tools as men, they can produce the same result.

Perhaps the numbers of women mentioned here are too small to lead to a general conclusion, and because some women had expertise and adopted the authoritative voice, we should not ignore what we know to be the legal and social status of all women and the attitudes that kept many voices muted. Clearly those attitudes, though diminished in force and often contradictory, still existed. But just as clearly, by the end of the century, there had been changes: more women were better educated, and even for those who did not attend, the establishment and success of the women's colleges made a strong positive statement about women's abilities. Some, at least, were not afraid to assert the kind of authority more characteristic of men and found good outlets for their work. And within this period and the magazine, there is a progression from an occasional woman writing in depth on a single subject to women like Preston who combined a wide range of knowledge and therefore a variety of subjects with the methods and voice of scholarship and who chose their own topics within wider limits and displayed the confidence of authority. The question of whether gender mattered would seem to call for a negative answer, but a negative that still has qualifications. Women who wrote out of wide knowledge and with authority could be published in the most prestigious magazine in the country; the problem lay in acquiring the education that qualified them to do so and the courage to enter a traditionally masculine arena. Here gender was indeed a limitation.

The *Atlantic*'s fame was probably always greater than its readership, since it was never a circulation leader, but its influence was strong. It remained the voice of the great patriarchs, Emerson, Longfellow, Whittier, Holmes, and others whose fame lingered into the twentieth century, long after they were available to contribute. It prolonged the great day of New England even after that day was past. For its authors, it represented a forum that elevated their stature, and no one doubted its quality. Whatever we may think of individual pieces now, publication in the *Atlantic* bestowed not just credibility but luster; for women, such a forum made a statement of intellectual competence and equality. In 1858 Thomas Wentworth Higginson had promised and prophesied that women, given education and opportunity, would prove to be as intelligent and capable as men. He might have been pleased to see his words fulfilled in the magazine for which he wrote the piece.

NOTES

A shorter version of this paper was presented at the Modern Language Association in December, 1992.

1. Authors' names were used in the advertising for the magazine, and letters indicate that guessing who wrote what made a kind of pleasant literary game.

2. M. A. DeWolfe Howe, *The Atlantic Monthly and Its Makers* (Boston: Atlantic Monthly Press, 1919) 27. The driving force in the creation of the magazine was Francis Underwood, whose role has been overshadowed by the names of his great contemporaries (Emerson, Whittier, Lowell, Holmes, Motley, Whipple, and others); see Bliss Perry, "The Editor Who Was Never an Editor," *Atlantic Monthly* 100; John Townsend Trowbridge, "The Author of Quabbin," *Atlantic Monthly* 75; 111.

3. For personal reminiscences, see Volume 100 (1907), celebrating the fiftieth anniversary, which contains pieces by Arthur Gilman, John Townsend Trowbridge, William Dean Howells, Charles Eliot Norton, Thomas Wentworth Higginson, and others; see also an anonymous piece, "Forty Years of the *Atlantic Monthly*," *AM* 80 (1897): 571–76. Howe's *The Atlantic Monthly and Its Makers* is probably the most complete record of the personalities involved. Autobiographies like Howells's *Literary Friends and Acquaintances* and Higginson's *Cheerful Yesterdays* make clear the importance of the magazine in their lives.

For scholarly works, see W. S. Tryon's *Parnassus Corner*, a biography of James T. Fields (Boston: Houghton Mifflin, 1963); Robert E. Mitchell's unpublished Harvard dissertation, "American Life as Reflected in the Atlantic Monthly, 1857–1881" (1951), a vast examination of content; Helen McMahon's *Criticism of Fiction: A Study of Trends in the Atlantic Monthly, 1857–1898* (New York: Bookman Associates, 1952), a study of the work of reviewers and their part in shifting literary emphasis from Romanticism to Realism; Ellen Ballou's *The Building of the House: Houghton Mifflin's Formative Years* (Boston: Houghton Mifflin, 1970), a history of Houghton Mifflin that is particularly interesting because its viewpoint is so very different from the literary; James C. Austin's *Fields of the Atlantic Monthly* (San Marino: Huntington, 1953), which will be discussed further in the text; Ellery Sedgwick's *The Atlantic Monthly, 1857–1909: Yankee Humanism at High Tide and Ebb* (Boston: U of Massachusetts P, 1994), the most recent and best study of the magazine. While Sedgwick does not emphasize women, he does not ignore them but treats them as individuals and contributors.

4. See also Higginson's comments in *Cheerful Yesterdays*, 184, and his preface to *Women and the Alphabet* (Boston: Houghton Mifflin, 1880).

5. This exclusion continued for years; "the ladies" did not share the friendly dinners. They were invited to the Holmes breakfast in 1877, an occasion large, formal, and rewarding rather than policy-making. Festivities after that were more inclusive; Stowe's seventieth birthday celebration was a garden party held at the home of Governor and Mrs. Claflin in Newtonville.

6. For a study of her influence, see Rita Gollin, "Subordinated Power: Mrs. and Mr. James T. Fields," *Patrons and Protégées*, ed. Shirley Marchalonis (Rutgers UP, 1988) 141–60.

7. In "The Editor Who Was Never an Editor" (*AM* 100), Bliss Perry quotes from letters by Francis Underwood to well-known authors requesting work for the magazine.

8. *Atlantic Tales* (Boston: Fields, Osgood, 1867), a collection of the magazine's best fiction, shows the proportion. There are fourteen stories, eight by men and six by women. The men are Edward Everett Hale (two titles), FitzJames O'Brien, Robert T. S. Lowell, George Arnold, Charles Nordhoff, J. D. Whepley, and Bayard Taylor; the women are Rebecca B. Harding Davis, Gail Hamilton (whose short story "The Pursuit of Knowledge under Difficulties" proved that fiction was not her forte), Caroline Chesbro', Lucretia P. Hale, Rose Terry Cooke, and Elizabeth Haven Appleton. Of the stories, the two best known are Harding's "Life in the Iron Mills" and Hale's "The Man without a Country"; comparison of the two stories points up the futility of making judgments about gender marking: Harding's grim realism contrasts with Hale's patriotic romanticism.

9. In *Fields of the Atlantic Monthly*, Austin has a chapter each for Julia Ward Howe and Harriet Beecher Stowe, but his focus is chiefly on their disagreements with Fields, caused, he suggests, by their unreasonableness; other women are gathered into a chapter called "Ladies, Militants and Dilettantes." He praises Harriet Prescott, not for her writing but as a "docile girl" who obeyed her editors (312); he describes Celia Thaxter as "one of the small fry who abounded in prettinesses and commonplaces" (319) and Gail Hamilton as a writer of "light essays on domestic matters" and "semi-serious meanderings on general subjects" (316). His superficial treatment of "The Battle of the Books," which should be read next to those of William Tryon and Susan Coultrap-McQuin, absolves Fields of all blame and dismisses Hamilton as a silly, ungrateful hysteric. He reserves his

greatest contempt for Stowe, calling her "the least dignified" of the contributors, a "rabble-rouser," and a "fanatic" (266). He names her as a founder in passing but minimizes her importance; when he admits her popularity or that *Oldtown Folks*, for example, is a good novel, he does so grudgingly. This hostility is surprising in a scholar, and there are curious gaps in his reasoning: he says that Stowe was paid well, but her "financial ineptitude" made her spend too much and therefore demand more money. Shortly after that, he says (approvingly) that Calvin Stowe resigned his position to do his own writing, but Austin does not connect that and come up with what Stowe scholars have shown: that Harriet was the sole support of her large family. Attitudes like Austin's have not encouraged study of these women.

10. For example, Harriet Prescott Spofford was a sensational discovery for Lowell and a steady contributor for Fields; after volume XXVII (1871), she vanishes from the pages except for an occasional poem, although she still published regularly in other magazines. Presumably Howells did not like her romanticism, although notably the *Atlantic* did not always pay as well as other magazines.

11. For example, in bound volumes I and II (14 issues, November 1857 through December 1858), there are sixty-nine poems, and of these, thirty-one were written by Emerson, Lowell, Longfellow, and Whittier; eight were by women. The second year is more representative of what would be the norm: thirty-nine poems, four by the greats and eighteen by women. While the poems range from Emerson's "Days" and "Brahma" and Whittier's "Telling the Bees" to short celebrations of whatever the season was, they are fairly free of sentimentality. Lowell seems to like especially the long narrative poem.

12. See Philip B. Eppard and George Montiero, *A Guide to the Atlantic Monthly's Contributors Club* (Boston: G. K. Hall, 1983). I am indebted to these authors for their identification of Harriet Waters Preston's "Women and Politics."

13. Aldrich had been editor of *Every Saturday*, another of the firm's magazines. Business changes affected editorial choices; in 1861 Ticknor and Fields bought the *Atlantic* and, when Ticknor died three years later, Fields was senior partner of what became Fields, Osgood. When James R. Osgood took over, he gave the firm his own name, but Osgood, for all his charm, was no businessman and by 1871 was forced to sell (See Carl Weber, *The Rise and Fall of James Ripley Osgood.*Waterville, ME: Colby College Press, 1959). The firm became Hurd and Houghton, then stabilized as Houghton Mifflin. Whether Howells felt it was time for a career change or whether, as several accounts suggest, he did not like the rigid, highly moral, and thoroughly businesslike Henry Oscar Houghton, he left the magazine for *Harper's*.

14. In a few cases, it is impossible to determine gender, since the writers remain hidden behind initials even in the two thorough indices which give full names and pseudonyms wherever possible; some women, too, chose to write under masculine names. Among the totals are features, probably written by staff members or editors, unsigned and unidentified. Still another difficulty comes from genre; Lowell and Fields, especially, liked frame tales and sketches, and it is sometimes hard to know where fiction ends and fact begins. Holmes's "Professor," for example, uses the fictional frame of the breakfast table to comment on people and society.

15. Lowell, letter to Thomas Wentworth Higginson, 1858; qtd. by Edward Everett Hale, *James Russell Lowell and His Friends* (1899; New York: Chelsea House, 1980) 166.

16. J. W. Palmer has seventeen titles in volumes I to XXIX; Julia Ward Howe's six-part series on Cuba appears in volumes III and IV and is the only prose she wrote for the magazine. Helen Hunt Jackson (also listed in the index as Helen Hunt) has thirty-six pieces, as well as many poems, between volumes XXVI and LVII.

17. The passage comes from her entry in the *National Cyclopedia of American Biography*, one of the few sources of information about these scholarly women. Theresa Albertina Louise von Jacob (1797–1869) married Edward Robinson and lived in

Andover, Massachusetts, until his death, when she returned to Germany. She was fluent in several languages and was an active scholar all her life.

18. Isabel Hapgood (1850–1928), *Service Book of the Holy Orthodox Catholic Church* (1907); other titles, besides her many translations and her magazine articles, were *The Epic Songs of Russia* (New York: Scribner's, 1885); *Russian Rambles* (Boston: Houghton Mifflin, 1897), which included her *Atlantic* essays; *A Survey of Russian Literature* (New York: Chautauqua, 1902).

19. Preston may have been connected by marriage with Gail Hamilton, since her sister married into the extensive Dodge family. There are frequent mentions of her in volume II of *Gail Hamilton's Life in Letters,* ed. Mary Augusta Dodge (Boston: Lee and Shepard, 1901), particularly through the late 1870s.

20. Unless otherwise noted, all Preston's books were published by Roberts Brothers, Boston. Translations: Frederic Mistral, *Mirèio* (1873); C. C. Sainte-Beuve, *Memoirs of Madame Desbordes-Valmore* (1873) and *Portraits of Celebrated Women* (1868); Paul de Musset, *Biography of Alfred de Musset* (1877); *The Georgics of Virgil* (1881); *The Life and Letters of Madame Swetchine* (1870); *Studies in the Correspondence of Petrarch* (1893).

Fiction: *Theda and the Mountain* (Boston: Walker and Wise, 1861); *A Summer with the Little Grays* (Boston: Walker, Wise & Co., 1860); *Aspendale* (1870); *Love in the XIXth Century* (1873); *Is that All?* (No Name Series, 1876); *A Year in Eden* (1887).

Nonfiction: *Troubadours and Trouveres, Old and New* (1876); *The Guardians* (1881) and *The Private Life of the Romans* (1893) with Louise Dodge.

Edited *The Complete Works of Elizabeth Barrett Browning* (Boston: Houghton Mifflin, 1900); with Martha Lebaron Goddard, *Sea and Shore: A Collection of Poems* (1874).

21. Ballou does not give a source for the quoted passage.

22. This fragment is in the Preston Papers in the Massachusetts Historical Society. Although the signature is missing, handwriting, content, and style indicate Gail Hamilton as the author.

23. Sedgwick, *Atlantic Monthly*, 297. The letter he quotes is to Bliss Perry, 7 Nov. 1902; the original is in the Houghton Library, Harvard.

REFERENCES

Austin, James C. *Fields of the Atlantic Monthly*. San Marino: Huntington, 1953.

Ballou, Ellen. *The Building of the House: Houghton Mifflin's Formative Years*. Boston: Houghton, 1970.

Bianciardi, Elizabeth Dickinson Rice. "A Florentine Family in the Fifteenth Century." *Atlantic Monthly* 48 (1881): 672–81.

Chace, Lillie Buffum Wyman. "From Generation to Generation." *Atlantic Monthly* 64 (1889): 64–72.

———. "Studies of Factory Life." *Atlantic Monthly* 62 (1888): 16–29; 63 (1889): 69–79.

Cheever, D. W. "The Gymnasium." *Atlantic Monthly* 3 (1859): 529–543.

Chielens, Edward. *American Literary Magazines: The Eighteenth and Nineteenth Centuries*. New York: Greenwood, 1986.

Cobbe, Frances Power. "The Fenian 'Idea.'" *Atlantic Monthly* 17 (1866): 572–577.

Collet, Sophia. "England and Emancipation." *Atlantic Monthly* 8 (1861): 742–756.

Conrad, Susan Phinney. *Perish the Thought: Intellectual Women in Romantic America, 1830–1860*. New York: Oxford UP, 1976.

Coultrap-McQuin, Susan. *Doing Literary Business*. Chapel Hill: U of North Carolina P, 1990.

Davis, Rebecca Harding. "Life in the Iron Mills." *Atlantic Monthly* 7 (1861): 430–451.

Eppard, Philip and George Montiero. *A Guide to the Atlantic Monthly's Contributors Club*. Boston: Hall, 1983.

Fields, James T., ed. *Atlantic Tales*. Boston: Fields, Osgood, 1867.

Gilman, Arthur. "Atlantic Dinners and Diners." *Atlantic Monthly* 100 (1907): 646–657.

Gollin, Rita. "Subordinated Power: Mrs. and Mr. James T. Fields." *Patrons and Protégées: Gender, Friendship and Writing in Nineteenth-Century America.* Ed. Shirley Marchalonis. New Brunswick, NJ: Rutgers UP, 1988. 141–160.

Greenslet, Ferris. *Under the Bridge.* Boston: Houghton, 1963.

———. *The Life of Thomas Bailey Aldrich.* Boston: Houghton, 1909.

Hale, Edward Everett. *James Russell Lowell and His Friends.* Boston: Houghton, 1899. New York: Chelsea, 1980.

Hamilton, Gail [Mary Abigail Dodge]. Letter to Harriet Waters Preston. Fragment. n.d. Preston-Dodge Papers. Massachusetts Historical Society, Boston, MA.

Hapgood, Isabel. *The Epic Songs of Russia.* New York: Scribner's, 1885.

———. *Russian Rambles.* Boston: Houghton, 1897.

———. *A Survey of Russian Literature.* New York: Chautauqua, 1902.

Higginson, Thomas Wentworth. *Cheerful Yesterdays.* Boston: Houghton, 1898.

———. "Ought Women To Learn the Alphabet?" *Atlantic Monthly* 3 (1859): 137–50.

Hosmer, Harriet. "The Process of Sculpture." *Atlantic Monthly* 14 (1864): 734–737.

Howe, Julia Ward. "A Trip to Cuba." *Atlantic Monthly* 3 (1859): 601–608, 686–692; 4 (1859): 184–193, 323–327, 455–460, 602–614.

Howe, M. A. DeWolfe. *The Atlantic Monthly and Its Makers.* Boston: Atlantic Monthly P, 1919.

Jackson, Helen Hunt. "Bergen Days." *Atlantic Monthly* 47 (1881): 770–784.

James, Henry. Letter to Mr. Niles. 18 Nov. 1876. Preston-Dodge Papers. Massachusetts Historical Society, Boston, MA.

Kemble, Fanny. "Some Notes on Shakespeare." *Atlantic Monthly* 6 (1860): 288–294.

Kirkland, Caroline. "Illinois in the Spring-time." *Atlantic Monthly* 2 (1858): 475–488.

McMahon, Helen. *Criticism of Fiction: A Study of Trends in the Atlantic Monthly, 1857–1898.* New York: Bookman, 1952.

Mitchell, Robert E. "American Life as Reflected in the *Atlantic Monthly*, 1857–1881." Diss. Harvard U, 1951.

Peabody, Elizabeth. "Kindergarten—What Is It?" *Atlantic Monthly* 10 (1862): 586–593.

Peirce, Melusina Fay. "Co-operative Housekeeping." *Atlantic Monthly* 22 (1868): 513–524, 682–697; 23 (1869): 29–39, 161–171, 286–299.

Pennell, Elizabeth Robins. "Mischief in the Middle Ages." *Atlantic Monthly* 48 (1881): 1–8.

Preston, Harriet Waters. "The Arthuriad." *Atlantic Monthly* 38 (1876): 129–142.

———. "Assam Igitur." *Atlantic Monthly* 64 (1889): 1–8.

———. "Background of Roman History." *Atlantic Monthly* 64 (1889): 150–64.

———. "A Changing Order." *Atlantic Monthly* 62 (1888): 51–68.

———. "Cicero in the Senate." *Atlantic Monthly* 61 (1888): 641–61.

———. Letter to E. Abbott. 5 Jan. 1881. Bowdoin College Library, Brunswick, ME.

———. Letter to Paul Hamilton Hayne. 3 March 1878. Duke U Library, Durham, NC.

———. Letter to Paul Hamilton Hayne. 29 Sept. 1878. Duke U Library, Durham, NC.

———. Letter to Paul Hamilton Hayne. 27 Oct. 1878. Duke U Library, Durham, NC.

———. Letter to Paul Hamilton Hayne. 22 Dec. 1878. Duke U Library, Durham, NC.

———. Letter to Preston family. 15 Oct. 1853. Preston Papers. Massachusetts Historical Society, Boston, MA.

———. Letter to Preston family. 10 July 1854. Preston Papers. Massachusetts Historical Society, Boston, MA.

———. "Mistral's Calendau." *Atlantic Monthly* 33 (1874): 406–16.

———. "Oxford in Winter." *Atlantic Monthly* 52 (1883): 49–59.

———. "Women and Politics." *Atlantic Monthly* 87 (1901): 589–90.

Putnam, Louisa Preston. Letter to Samuel J. Preston. 30 Mar. 1855. Preston-Dodge Papers. Massachusetts Historical Society, Boston, MA.

Repplier, Agnes. "Children, Past and Present." *Atlantic Monthly* 57 (1887): 508–517.

Robinson, Therese A. "The German Popular Legend of Dr. Faustus." *Atlantic Monthly* 2 (1858): 551–566.

Sedgwick, Ellery. *The Atlantic Monthly, 1857–1909: Yankee Humanism at High Tide and Ebb.* Boston: U of Massachusetts P, 1994.

Sheldon, Mary Boardman. "A Literary Model." *Atlantic Monthly* 78 (1896): 256–262.

Stowe, Harriet Beecher. "House and Home Papers." *Atlantic Monthly* 13 (1864): 40–47, 201–209, 353–363, 458–465, 621–629, 754–761; 14 (1864): 93–98, 230–240, 434–443, 565–579, 689–702.

Thanet, Octave [Alice French]. "The Indoor Pauper: A Study." *Atlantic Monthly* 47 (1881): 749–764; 48 (1881): 241–252.

Thomas, Edith M. "A Spring Opening." *Atlantic Monthly* 47 (1881): 764–769.

Ticknor, Caroline. *Glimpses of Authors.* 1922. n.p.: Books for Libraries, 1972.

Tryon, W. S. *Parnassus Corner.* Boston: Houghton, 1963.

Weber, Carl. *The Rise and Fall of James Ripley Osgood.* Waterville, ME: Colby College P, 1959.

Welles, Kate Gannett. "Women in Organizations." *Atlantic Monthly* 46 (1880): 360–367.

———. "The Transitional American Woman." *Atlantic Monthly* 46 (1880): 817–823.

———. "Caste in American Society." *Atlantic Monthly* 48 (1881): 823–831.

Conversation as Rhetoric in Margaret Fuller's *Woman in the Nineteenth Century*[1]

Judith Mattson Bean

Walter Ong describes women's writing in the early nineteenth century as less formal than writing influenced by classical rhetoric, a discourse tradition associated with manliness in the nineteenth century. From Cicero forward, classical rhetoric was assumed to demand toughness and power to persuade listeners—as opposed to "effeminacy," which would vitiate the speaker's effectiveness. Ong writes that in the nineteenth century, "most literary style throughout the west was formed by academic rhetoric, in one way or another," with the exception of women, who "normally expressed themselves in a different, far less oratorical voice, which had a great deal to do with the rise of the novel" (111–12). He argues that the style of early women writers was "more like a conversation than a platform performance" (159–60). The exclusion of women from formal rhetorical training, which Ong sees as the source for differences in women's styles, was only one factor contributing to perceived differences in style. Although Ong defined women's writing as a deviation from a male norm, an informal, conversational style is more clearly understood as an alternative rhetoric with an aesthetic of its own.[2] Developing in a variety of settings, according to Christine Oravec, the informal style was "a rhetoric of mass communication in a politically pluralistic society, as distinguished from a specialized rhetoric addressed to a ruling elite" (405). Sources for the principles of this rhetoric include contemporary critiques of rhetorical performances and advice books for conversation, which was a genre of discourse in its own right in antebellum America and nineteenth-century Europe.

Analysis of individual women writers' public discourse—essays and speeches—has only just begun. Early analyses of American women's public speaking employ classical rhetorical approaches, as exemplified by Lillian O'Connor in *Pioneer Women Orators*. More recently, Karlyn Kohrs Campbell describes women's speeches as having a characteristic style that is personal in tone, relies on personal experience, invites audience participation and attempts to create identification with the experiences of the audience. This rhetorical style aims to persuade listeners that they can be agents of change (13). Nineteenth-century women essayists have not generally received as much scholarly attention as public speakers, but Margaret Fuller's extended, complex essay *Woman in the Nineteenth Century* has been the object of rhetorical analysis and considerable stylistic commentary. Marie Urbanski's analysis links Fuller's text to the structure of a sermon, but she finds that Fuller does not employ strict syllogistic logic, but rather free association and "an unfolding from the subconscious" characteristic of Transcendentalist writing (135). She cites contemporary responses to this text (such as those of Thoreau and Poe), which equated Fuller's writing and speaking voice (143). Several recent scholars describe Fuller's text in terms of dialogue: Julie Ellison writes that *Woman* is based on an "implied contract that binds all members of the group to an ethic of sincerity" (237), and Elaine Showalter notes that "Rather than forcing her readers' consent, Fuller wanted them to engage in a dialogue with her, to be respected rather than manipulated" (318). Annette Kolodny finds an intersection between nineteenth-century rhetoric and conversation, providing a rhetorical analysis that relates Fuller's *Woman* to Whately's *Elements of Rhetoric* (1832) and indicating that Fuller drew on that source for "suggestive style." Such a rhetoric would be suitable for investigation and "rational conversation." Kolodny also points out that Fuller disregarded Whately's suggestions for persuasion by addresses to passion and emotion, and that Fuller preferred to base her address on areas of mutual agreement rather than direct confrontation of differences with her audience. Despite growing consensus on the conversational nature of *Woman* and its relationship to Fuller's "Conversations," none have pursued analysis of Fuller's text according to the elements of conversation identified by linguistic scholarship or the implications for rhetorical history.

Since the 1970s, linguists have been developing descriptions of the systematic nature of conversation and contributing to a new field: conversation analysis. Some linguists have explored the implicit cultural norms of conversation, including gender restrictions and taboos.[3] Others have described various subgenres of conversation, such as polite small talk, serious discussion, didactic talk, and competitive forms of talk. Among the elements of conversation that have been analyzed are the protocols of turntaking, repair of disruptions, topic control and shifting, and functions of repetition. Deborah Tannen, drawing on earlier scholarship and creating new insights, has contributed significantly not only to scholarly but also to popular understanding of conversational practice relative to gender and ethnic cultural assumptions. Applications of conversation analysis to literary criticism have usually been confined to discussions of dramatic and fictional representations of dialogue. However, conversation analysis should also provide insight into stylistic choices of essayists who directly address their readers in a conversational manner.

Fuller often relies on strategies of conversation in *Woman*. She employs informal strategies at the lexical, sentence, paragraph, and segmental levels. At the sentence level, Fuller uses comments inserted by parentheses or dashes, giving the impression of a comment spoken aside in a different tone. She also uses question-and-answer pairs and sentences that begin with the indefinite "it." Besides informal features at the sentence level, three other elements give Fuller's text an interactive, conversational style: self-disclosure, dialogic techniques, and topical cohesion. Her style creates involvement or engrossment, establishes bonds of trust, initiates interaction with the reader, and emphasizes immediacy, fluidity, and interaction among multiple voices. Her style serves the purposes of her feminist work, as Mary E. Wood has pointed out, because Fuller "follows a model of conversation in which one woman, the narrator, opens the space for the subjectivity of another woman" (12). Despite the persuasive aim and public nature of *Woman*, its style challenges the classical ethos of unitary self, blurs boundaries of genre, and disregards structural and persuasive strategies central to traditional rhetorical practice.

Fuller's choice of an informal style was influenced not only by Whately's rhetorical principles but also by cultural trends, gender expectations, and individual talents. Her speaking skill gave her a reputation as the most brilliant American conversationalist of her age. She turned that talent into a vocation by inaugurating educational Conversations for women in Boston. Her writing was often compared to her speaking, both favorably and unfavorably. The duality of her style, integrating formal rhetoric with conversation, provoked criticism for both its informality and its formality, depending on the perspective of the critic.

Cultural factors that stimulated development of informal styles generally included literary and rhetorical trends as well as Jacksonian democracy. Political forces of democratization pressured all speakers and writers to use a more informal, conversational style as compared to the neo-classical grand style that aimed to overpower the audience with linguistic elegance. Literary Romanticism and Transcendentalism encouraged the shift toward informality by advocating a more conversational literary style, not attempting to reproduce everyday conversation, but evoking the "art of conversation" (Buell 79). A writing style would be considered conversational if it seemed informal, spontaneous, and dialogic; an informal style might or might not be personal, that is, featuring self-revelation, individual tastes and experiences, and a confidential manner. Matters of style are more than evidence of mastery in the production of literary art. As Kenneth Cmiel points out in his delineation of the nineteenth-century democratization of rhetoric, "Linguistic styles are not simply personal idiosyncrasies, . . . [but] cultural practices encouraged, perpetuated, and challenged through time . . . one indication of the way we have organized our lives" (16). Fuller should be seen as one who challenged not only rhetorical styles, but also the principles behind the organization of life.

In the nineteenth century, conversation styles became a way of differentiating between genders and among nationalities. According to travel writers, lecturers, and writers of advice books, women's conversational style differed from men's, and American conversation differed from British. Beatrice Knolly, in *The Gentle Art of Good Talking* (1899), wrote that:

> The society of brilliant men may temper and strengthen the steel blade of eloquence with the logic and discretion so wanting in women, but it is the society of brilliant women that gives the point and polish to that steel blade as they sharpen it with their repartee and brighten it with their tact. (qtd. in St. George 325)

Differences in British and American conversation styles were a source of commentary by many writers, including Emerson in *English Traits*. In England, the great talkers, such as Browning, Carlyle, and Macaulay, recorded in Victorian memoirs, tended to be men. Bostonian Oliver Wendell Holmes achieved great commercial success with his "table talk" books, beginning with *The Autocrat at the Breakfast Table* (1857). Conversation served as the basis not only for literary discourse, but also for lecturing and speech-making. An active proponent of conversational public speaking was Henry Ward Beecher, one of the most popular speakers of the nineteenth century. In addition, Fuller's contemporaries employed discussion as literary critical discourse in conversation clubs and literary circles.

Both topic and style in Fuller's *Woman* were outgrowths of her Boston Conversations (1839–1844), which were primarily for women. In a time when lecturing was not seen as an appropriate female genre, it was acceptable for women to speak to other women (while remaining seated) if the discourse was called a "conversation." Fuller's method of presentation simulated Socratic dialogues: she posed questions to which her audience members were expected to respond. She was the primary speaker and leader of discussion, providing an introduction to a topic, then inviting responses, definitions, and criticisms. She hoped to stimulate women to think for themselves and to express their thoughts on basic philosophical and cultural matters in an age that provided women with largely superficial educations (Chevigny 211–12). Unfortunately, the only Conversation series for which an account was published (by Caroline Dall in 1895) was the series opened to men, noted as an exception in that the men generally turned the Fuller-led discussions into their own debates.

Fuller's interactional style in *Woman* may also have resulted from personal factors, as Jeffrey Steele has argued. Noting that Fuller's nonlinear style has been "a source of embarrassment for most critics," Steele posits that her "intertextual and pluralogic style" resulted from Fuller's intellectual and emotional development and that this style represents "a new way of viewing and

writing the self's development—one that supplants . . . self-reliance with
. . . other-reliance" (289). Whether Fuller's intertextual style was new or characteristic of women in general, as some have argued, depends on one's point of
view; nevertheless, Fuller seems to have developed it more extensively than
her contemporaries.

Nineteenth-century culture sharply distinguished between men's and
women's oral and written discourse styles. Double standards for speaking and
writing according to gender meant, for women, a stricter standard that discouraged slang and encouraged genteel speech. Women were praised for writing
spontaneous, "artless" prose and poetry, while men were lauded for their control of language. The double standard is illustrated by a writer of advice books
on conversation, Andrew Peabody, who presented two lectures on conversation, one to men and one to women, markedly different in their admonitions
and the degree of insistence on the moral implications of women's speaking.

Modern scholarship indicates that women's preferences for establishing
friendly contact with their audience contributed to the development of conversational prose (Donovan 214). Nineteenth-century women's style has also been
characterized as having a "vibrant surge of personality" (Walker 152). Although
Fuller's style in *Woman* is not entirely a question of gender, some elements of
her style have been associated with a woman's style, exhibiting qualities of
vibrancy, immediacy, and personal rapport through self-disclosure. However,
Fuller's style cannot be characterized broadly as conversational in all her works.
In her later *New York Tribune* columns, she is less conversational, yet she often
maintains an informal voice and occasionally engages in dialogue with others.
Her works do not rely entirely on an informal style but display a variety of
styles.[4]

Fuller was not singular in adopting a conversational style; a similar style
has been attributed to her contemporary Caroline Kirkland, an essayist and
sketch writer whose work Fuller admired. Lori Merish writes that Kirkland's
style is characteristic of much antebellum women's writing and "mobilizes
both the emotional immediacy of 'feminine' private language and Romanticism's
valuation of immediacy and discursive fluidity" (493). Merish also importantly
notes the flexibility of voice provided by a conversational style. Kirkland, more
than Fuller, directly acknowledged gender expectations for an associative style,
as in her collection of essays and sketches *Western Clearings*. For example,
Kirkland writes that, "a slender thread serves sometimes to string female reveries, and it is doubtless best they should not aim too much at 'consecution of
discourse,' lest they be accused of lecturing. I shall tell my little story, 'pro-
miscuous like,' claiming my feminine privilege" (98). Kirkland's ambivalence—
her claim that an associative style is both a privilege and a defense from social
censure—indicates the problematic nature of stylistic choices for women of
her era.

An extended essay, Fuller's *Woman* (1845) was the first American work to examine the political, economic, and philosophical aspects of feminism. Her work was a significant impetus to the women's rights movement in America. In this text, Fuller unsettles her readers' expectations by defying received stylistic boundaries of genre—blurring autobiography, fiction, and nonfiction to express, as she does in *Summer on the Lakes*, "disparate aspects of her consciousness" (Stowe 242) and to establish a dialogue with her readers. The features of the text that make it a dialogue can be described in terms of conversation analysis.

Fuller's use of the first-person singular pronoun "I" challenged her culture's belief in a unitary self, reshaped authoritarian hortatory discourse into dialogue, and recast the impersonal written voice as a personal autobiographical voice. The use of the autobiographical "I" is an interactive strategy that creates involvement. The pronoun "I" implies the presence of a listener, "you," and helps create a conversation between writer and reader, inviting the reader to participate in sense-making. Fuller uses first-person pronouns to speak to the reader and disclose her feelings. For example, she writes: "But whatever were the facts of daily life, *I cannot complain* of the age and nation which represents its thought by such a symbol *as I see before me at this moment*" (emphasis added, 32). Fuller's self-disclosure creates personal intimacy, rapport, and involvement, which are characteristics of conversation. An important index of style, self-disclosure is one method used by discourse analysts to distinguish formal from informal discourse (Chafe 46–48). The informal writer uses the autobiographical "I"—not the representative, impersonal "I"—to incorporate personal experience and self-disclosure into the discourse. The term "actual I" has been used to describe the woman writer or poet who uses the pronoun to speak autobiographically as a woman with a certain history and background and who "felt a need to give the voice a self" (Walker 68–69). Thus, Fuller's use of "I" creates a more personal voice and individualized self.

Self-disclosure is also closely connected to the writer's portrayal of subjectivity, selfhood, and relation of the speaker to the listener. In *Woman*, Fuller speaks confidentially to her readers and shows her responsiveness to past readers. She discloses decisions she made in composing this text in response to readers of its earlier form, "The Great Lawsuit," saying, for example: "In the earlier tract, I was told, I did not make my meaning sufficiently clear. In this I have consequently tried to illustrate it various ways" (112). Displaying her cooperation with her readers, Fuller rejects a rhetoric of control over her readers.

Fuller also unsettles expectations for nonfiction prose by using narrative as a poet might to display dramas of selfhood and to challenge the customary ethos of a unitary, nonfictional self. Fuller's variety of self-presentations was a disruptive technique in an age that demanded an orator or writer be governed by a morality of style—a consistency in presentation of character and discourse. An "uneven style" might be called "vice-ridden." By contrast, nineteenth-century refined gentlemen exhibited that hunger for wholeness of self, which was reflected in linguistic proscriptions against dialect, slang, and informality. These were more than matters of expressive choice; they were questions of maintaining a unified self in the face of growing fragmentation of self into discrete social roles (Cmiel 92–93). Fuller's letters and journals reveal her desire that others understand her expression of multiple aspects of herself and her resentment against expectations for consistent presentation of a singular self. Contemporaries noted her ability to adapt to her interlocutors, and this ability reflects her flexibility of self-presentations and styles of discourse. As Vimala Herman has pointed out, a "dispersal of roles . . . ensures that subjectivity is not a static or unitary affair but a series of displacements in which the dramas of selfhood are displayed" (217). Fuller not only expressed various facets of herself, but she also relied at times on dramatic modes of presentation.

Narratives of personal experience with conversational self-disclosure present Fuller's dramas of selfhood. Fuller uses first person to relate narratives and to comment on them, simultaneously expressing separate selves as narrator and listener to her own story. This combination of narrative and commentary blends autobiography with fiction.[5] She presents her own experience as if it belonged to Miranda, an imaginary girl who was taught to be independent. Through Miranda, Fuller dramatizes a youthful, dynamic self and distances her current self from the constructed persona. Through the veil of a fictional self, she becomes both first and third person, "I" and "she." Fuller begins by writing: "I was talking on this subject with Miranda, a woman, who, if any in the world could, might speak without heat and bitterness of the position of her sex" (21). Miranda remarks that "we must admit that I have been fortunate. . . . This self-dependence, which was honored in me, is deprecated as a fault in most women" (22). At the end of the narration, the first speaker engages Miranda in a dialogue to interpret the experience (22–23). Thus, Fuller is, in effect, talking to her past self—an act which recognizes growth and represents how one of her selves (an optimistic one) feels about the issue of women's position. Whereas a more formal approach might have impersonalized Miranda's views into exposition without a specific speaker, Fuller creates another person who relates her experience—simulating a conversation in which experience is often presented as evidence.

Employing the autobiographical "I," Fuller also presents narratives of consciousness. Presenting examples from experience, she describes their effect on her thinking. Her account implies the presence of listeners who could challenge her conclusions, a stance indicated by her use of evidential constructions, which are phrases that express a speaker's strength of conviction in terms of available evidence. Fuller employs evidential constructions to demonstrate her progression from observation to belief that something must be done to improve the legal status of married women. She presents a series of examples which lead to her conclusion:

> Such instances count up by scores within *my own memory. I have seen* the husband who had stained himself by a long course of low vice . . . *I have known* this man to install himself in the chamber of a woman who loathed him . . . *I have known* these men steal their children . . . *I do believe* that this mode of kidnapping . . . will be by the next age viewed as it is by Heaven now. (emphasis added, 16–17)

The evidential verb phrases indicate her progress from personal observation to understanding and finally to belief in the principle illustrated. In these ways, Fuller uses the autobiographical "I" to present personal experience and engage in dialogue with her readers.

Not only does she set up her discourse as a conversation with her readers, she also uses dialogic elements *within* this text. Beyond her use of the autobiographical "I," Fuller creates a conversational text in other ways by employing fictional dialogue, equating writing with speaking, and incorporating the voices of other individuals or groups in her discourse. These devices contribute to the creation of an inner context, a sense that in reading one is overhearing the voices of others. Fuller creates what Henry Louis Gates, Jr. has called a "speakerly text, one that is oriented toward imitating one of the numerous forms of oral narration" (181). She combines persuasion with exposition when she presents informal, colloquial-sounding debates within the text. One such debate appears as a confrontation between a women's-rights advocate and a merchant. The dialogue begins with the merchant protesting:

> [Y]ou have done all you could to break up the national union, . . . but now you must be trying to break up family union, to take my wife away from the cradle and the kitchen-hearth to vote at polls, and preach from a pulpit? . . . She is happy enough as she is. She has more leisure than I have,—every means of improvement, every indulgence. (14)

An opposing speaker counters, "Have you asked her whether she was satisfied with these *indulgences*?" and the trader replies, "No, but I know she is" (14). After the dialogue ends, Fuller adds interpretations in her analytical voice, writing: "Thus vaguely are these questions proposed and discussed at present" (15). Here—as a third person—she distances herself from conventional positions expressed in the dialogue.

Colloquial expressions and proverbs common to conversation also recreate the voices of cultural groups. Colloquialisms are introduced both as support for Fuller's arguments and as examples of stereotypical thinking by which women were defined. She calls attention to the status of proverbs as "proof" when she says, "Knock and it shall be opened; seek and ye shall find. It is demonstrated; it is a maxim" (7). However, she often challenges conventional wisdom that defines expectations for women and men, as when she writes, "there exists in the minds of men a tone of feeling toward women as toward slaves, such as is expressed in the common phrase, 'Tell that to women and children'" (17). In such cases, Fuller attacks linguistic practices sanctioned by general use that perpetuate stereotyped thinking.

By using quotation and paraphrase, Fuller also brings the voices of other individuals into her text. She paraphrases narratives of historical figures, classical myths, German ballads, and American Indian legends, shaping the stream of discourse into a conversation with anecdotes by different speakers. She also quotes remarks from a wide variety of literary texts, adding authoritative speakers to the narrative exemplars in support of her discussion.

Traditionally, a deliberate, planned structure is taken as evidence of artistry or rhetorical mastery and of control of one's discourse. However, when the aim is to convey immediacy and, by implication, a sincerity of unpremeditated expression, texts are not likely to exhibit traditional structures. For many analysts of Fuller's *Woman*, the structure of the text is a major concern if not an embarrassment. *Woman* does not seem to follow classical rhetorical principles of arrangement or move in linear fashion from one subtopic to the next toward a conclusion. Rather, this text again simulates conversation or extemporaneous discussion, which moves among subtopics informally with returns to previous topics and strategies of topic control that differ from traditional rhetorical practice.

Fuller's techniques of topic control display an aesthetic that emphasizes a smooth flow of discourse rather than syllogistic logical sequence. Her subtle topic shifting creates "topical cohesion" rather than structuring devices that cut up the discourse into discrete sections. Deborah Tannen's term "topical cohesion" refers to the ways speakers introduce and develop topics in conversation, creating an integrated activity out of various speakers' discourses ("Gender Differences" 168). Tannen has shown that an unfamiliar style of topic shifting in writing can give the impression of informal organization (*Conversational Style* 26–27). Fuller sometimes simulates unstructured conversation in her work with informal methods of topical cohesion, such as conversational topic introducers and topic splicing instead of highly marked topic shifts.

Fuller employs subtle topic shifting by informal metatalk, which is talking about talk (Hobbs 17–18), and by splicing topics within paragraphs. Tannen has asserted a gender difference in conversational topic shifting, observing that the boys she studied jumped abruptly from topic to topic, while girls did not (*Understand* 263). Whether or not gender was an influence, Fuller rarely makes clean breaks between subtopics in her discussion. Her topics are spliced by overlapping or interweaving two topics in the same paragraph or sentence. Moving almost imperceptibly from one topic to another creates an uninterrupted stream of discourse that reveals her conversational aesthetic. The unbroken flow also carries the reader along, allowing no convenient point of disengaging through textual breaks while transferring from one topic to the next. Thus, topic splicing contributes to a conversational style and can make a text seem more informal than one with conventional paragraph organization. In addition to subtle topic shifts, general rhetorical patterns sometimes overshadow links between subtopics. Her discussion of "the idea of woman" rests primarily on comparison and contrast, highlighting differences over time and across boundaries of nationality and gender. In some portions of the text, patterns of comparison override topic shifts. One such instance occurs when Fuller compares literature and history from diverse countries to locate illustrious women and men who influence their cultures. They exemplify the promise of a new era, which Fuller hopes will be realized in the nineteenth century (37–38). In sequential paragraphs, she first discusses British figures Queen Elizabeth and Shakespeare, who influenced their country. In the following paragraph, a new subtopic—love and marriage—is announced in the first sentence (40–41), but Fuller continues using quotations from influential British writers after Shakespeare to exemplify English ideas of marriage, making it easy to miss the topic shift in a chronological series of British examples.

Fuller's patterns of paragraphing can indicate segmental organization; short, one-sentence paragraphs often occur between—and splice—subtopics that are developed in separate groups of paragraphs. For example, a one-sentence paragraph marks her transition from the topic of women as companions for men to single women with their own lives: "In this regard of self-dependence, and a greater simplicity and fulness [sic] of being, we must hail as a preliminary the increase of the class contemptuously designated as 'old maids'" (62). Fuller often employs this structural device to conclude the previous section or announce its connection to the next. By isolating the sentence in white space, Fuller seems to simulate tonal changes and pauses one would use in making an emphatic or concluding statement in oral discourse.

In her longer transitional paragraphs, the reader may be alerted to the topic shifts within the paragraph by conjunctions and references to topics. In one instance, topic shift is marked by three devices: the conjunction "but," the phrase "delicate subject," and the defensive metatalk that follows mention of the subject, such as "let me say in behalf of Miranda and myself." In considering the obstacles that faced nineteenth-century women, Fuller discusses women's need for self-reliance, linguistic practices that stereotype women as weak, and the limited or qualified generosity of men in praising or representing women. The discussion covers eleven paragraphs and a section of constructed dialogue before the transitional paragraph, which splices the topic into the next subdivision (proper relations between the sexes). Fuller writes:

> Thus, in Schiller's Dignity of Woman, beautiful as the poem is, there is no "grave and perfect man," but only a great boy to be softened and restrained by the influence of girls. . . . Even with Richter, one foremost thought about a wife was that she would "cook him something good." But as this is a *delicate subject*, and we are in constant danger of being accused of slighting what are called "the functions," let me say *in behalf of Miranda and myself*, that we have high respect for those who cook something good, who create and preserve fair order in houses, and prepare therein the shining raiment for worthy inmates, worthy guests. Only these "functions" must not be a drudgery, or enforced necessity, but a part of life. (emphasis added, 24–25)

The subtlety of her topic shifts very likely contributed to perceptions among contemporary reviewers that her work had "no method" or that, in the words of Orestes Brownson, it could be read backwards or from the center outward as well as from the beginning without affecting the succession of ideas (19). Although Brownson could not perceive its design, scholarship on conversational structure allows us new possibilities for detecting Fuller's methods.

Fuller sometimes signals a topic shift by metatalk. These shifts are also marked by first-person pronouns that represent her presence in organizing the text. In one instance, Fuller combines first-person pronouns and an iconic image to link two topics—here, two writers—as their books are placed on a shelf. Shifting from discussing George Sand to Mary Wollstonecraft, she writes "I would put beside [Sand's work], on the shelf, a little volume, containing a similar appeal . . . made by Godwin in behalf of his wife, . . . Mary Wollstonecraft" (46). Although Fuller sometimes employs formal, direct statements about her text—"organizers" that enumerate or classify subsequent remarks—they usually announce examples rather than mark a shift between topics. Fuller chooses conversational topic introducers in shifting to a new topic and creates moments of intimacy. For example, in one topic shift, she ends an abstract discussion of ideas by breaking into a conversational voice, representing herself as involved in everyday activities as if just casually finding an example to make her point: "This morning, I open the Boston 'Daily Mail,' and find in its 'poet's corner' a translation of Schiller's 'Dignity of Woman'" (15). These methods of topic control can support both a rhetoric of personal conversation and an aesthetic of smooth discourse.

In *Woman in the Nineteenth Century*, Fuller employs both a power-based rhetoric associated with nineteenth-century masculine discourse style (common to sermons and oratory) and a rapport-based rhetoric associated with woman's discourse (in conversation). Historically, Fuller's prose can be placed in the early stages of a shift toward informal public discourse that has continued through the twentieth century (Jamieson 81–84). Nineteenth-century gender expectations were only partially involved in her choice of a conversational style. Her attraction to tenets of Transcendentalism and Romanticism as well as her individual talents and concept of self affected her discourse choices. Her style is marked by dialogic techniques that produce the effect of a multivoiced, yet smooth-flowing and spontaneous conversation, one that is impressive by its diversity, enlivened by engaging narratives, yet always related to the central topic.

Nineteenth-century women writers and speakers were often denied instruction or practice in classical rhetoric—or, like Fuller, selected some elements of rhetoric in combination with informal discourse genres. Analysis of their public discourse points out the limitations of the classical tradition for describing the entire range of public discourse in that period. We are led to question, as Joy Rouse has, what other rhetorics may have been overlooked and how the variety of rhetorics interacted with each other in that very active age of public speaking. A more complete rhetorical history of the nineteenth century can provide for greater understanding of the developments and shifts in rhetorical styles.

NOTES

1. An earlier version of this paper was presented at the 1991 Conference of South Central Modern Language Association, Fort Worth, Texas.

2. For a description of possible alternatives, see Rouse.

3. On gender, see Coates.

4. The informal elements of Fuller's discourse create her conversational (but not colloquial) effects. Informal texts can be described as interactive texts that might appear at one end of a continuum, which has highly edited texts at the opposite end (Biber 398).

5. Similarly, after her narration of a German ballad, for example, she writes: "Is not this sorrowful story of a lofty beauty? Does it not show a sufficiently high view of woman, of Marriage? This is commonly the chivalric, still more the German view" (36).

REFERENCES

Biber, Douglas. "Spoken and Written Textual Dimensions in English: Resolving the Contradictory Findings." *Language* 62 (1986): 384–414.

Brownson, Orestes A. "Miss Fuller and Reformers." *Critical Essays on Margaret Fuller.* Ed. Joel Myerson. Boston: Hall, 1980.

Buell, Lawrence. "From Conversation to Essay." *Literary Transcendentalism.* Ithaca, NY: Cornell UP, 1973. 77–101.

Campbell, Karlyn Kohrs. *Man Cannot Speak for Her.* Vol. 1. New York: Praeger, 1989.

Chafe, Wallace L. "Integration and Involvement in Speaking, Writing, and Oral Literature." *Spoken and Written Language: Exploring Orality and Literacy.* Ed. Deborah Tannen. Norwood, N J: Ablex, 1982. 35–53.

Chevigny, Bell Gale. *The Woman and the Myth: Margaret Fuller's Life and Writings.* Boston: Northeastern UP, 1993.

Cmiel, Kenneth. *Democratic Eloquence: The Fight over Popular Speech in Nineteenth-Century America*. New York: Morrow, 1990.

Coates, Jennifer. *Women, Men and Language: A Sociolinguistic Account of Sex Differences in Language*. New York: Longman, 1986.

Donovan, Josephine. "The Silence is Broken." *Women and Language in Literature and Society*. Ed. Sally McConnell-Ginet, Ruth Borker, and Nelly Furman. New York: Praeger, 1980. 205–221.

Ellison, Julie. *Delicate Subjects: Romanticism, Gender, and the Ethics of Understanding*. Ithaca, NY: Cornell UP, 1990.

Fuller, Margaret. *Woman in the Nineteenth Century*. Ed. Donna Dickenson. New York: Oxford UP, 1994.

Gates, Henry Louis, Jr. *The Signifying Monkey: A Theory of African-American Literary Criticism*. New York: Oxford UP, 1988.

Herman, Vimala. "Subject Construction as Stylistic Strategy in Gerard Manley Hopkins." *Language, Discourse and Literature: An Introductory Reader in Discourse Stylistics*. Ed. Ronald Carter and Paul Simpson. London: Unwin, 1989. 213–234.

Hobbs, Jerry R. "Topic Drift." *Conversational Organization and Its Development*. Ed. Bruce Dorval. Norwood, NJ: Ablex, 1990. 3–22.

Jamieson, Kathleen Hall. *Eloquence in an Electronic Age: The Transformation of Political Speechmaking*. New York: Oxford UP, 1988.

Kirkland, Caroline. *Western Clearings*. New York: Wiley, 1845.

Kolodny, Annette. "Inventing a Feminist Discourse: Rhetoric and Resistance in Margaret Fuller's *Woman in the Nineteenth Century*." *New Literary History* 25 (1994): 355–82.

Merish, Lori. "'The Hand of Refined Taste.'" *American Quarterly* 45 (1993): 485–523.

O'Connor, Lillian. *Pioneer Women Orators: Rhetoric in the Ante-bellum Reform Movement*. New York: Columbia UP, 1954.

Ong, Walter. *Orality and Literacy: The Technologizing of the Word*. London: Methuen, 1982.

Oravec, Christine. "The Democratic Critics: An Alternative American Rhetorical Tradition of the Nineteenth Century." *Rhetorica* 4 (1986): 395–421.

Peabody, Andrew. *Conversation: Its Faults and Its Graces*. Boston: Monroe, 1855.

Rouse, Joy. "Positional Historiography and Margaret Fuller's Public Discourse of Mutual Interpretation." *Rhetoric Society Quarterly* 20 (1990): 233–39.

Showalter, Elaine. "Miranda and Cassandra: The Discourse of the Feminist Intellectual." *Traditions and the Talents of Women*. Ed. Florence Howe. Urbana: U of Illinois P, 1991. 311–27.

St. George, Andrew. "Victorians, Conversations and Poems." *Language and Communication* 7 (1987): 303–335.

Steele, Jeffrey. "The Call of Eurydice: Mourning and Intertextuality in Margaret Fuller's Writing." *Influence and Intertextuality*. Ed. Jay Clayton and Eric Rothstein. Madison: U of Wisconsin P, 1991. 246–70.

Stowe, William W. "Conventions and Voices in Margaret Fuller's Travel Writing." *American Literature* 63 (1991): 242–62.

Tannen, Deborah. *Conversational Style: Analyzing Talk Among Friends*. Norwood, NJ: Ablex, 1982.

———. "Gender Differences in Conversational Coherence: Physical Alignment and Topical Cohesion." *Conversational Organization and Its Development*. Ed. Bruce Dorval. Norwood, NJ: Ablex, 1990. 167–206.

———. *"You Just Don't Understand": Women and Men in Conversation*. New York: Morrow, 1990.

Urbanski, Marie Mitchell Olesen. *Margaret Fuller's Woman in the Nineteenth Century: A Literary Study of Form and Content, of Sources and Influence*. Westport, CT: Greenwood, 1980.

Walker, Cheryl. *The Nightingale's Burden: Women Poets and American Culture Before 1900*. Bloomington: Indiana UP, 1982.

Wood, Mary E. "'With Ready Eye': Margaret Fuller and Lesbianism in Nineteenth-Century America." *American Literature* 65 (1993): 1–18.

"Thumping Against the Glittering Wall of Limitations":
Lydia Maria Child's "Letters from New York"

Stephanie A. Tingley

Few contemporary writers, with the exception perhaps of Stephen King or Judith Krantz, enjoy the kind of financially lucrative literary celebrity that nineteenth-century author Lydia Maria Child (1802–80) did for most of her lengthy career as a popular professional writer, for Americans nowadays usually reserve celebrity status for figures in the movie and music industries—the Madonnas, Julia Robertses, and Arnold Schwarzeneggers. Although she is perhaps best known for her activism in the antebellum abolitionist reform movement and her editing of Harriet Jacobs's slave narrative, *Incidents in the Life of a Slave Girl* (1860), Child's writing certainly had the ability to capture the hearts and imaginations of a large and enthusiastic reading public.

As early as the 1870s, critics were beginning to point out Child's significant contributions to American literature. Writer and editor Thomas Wentworth Higginson, for example, comments in a biographical sketch of his friend:

> It is needless to debate whether she did the greatest or most permanent work in any especial department of literature, since she did pioneer work in so many. She showed memorable independence in repeatedly leaving beaten paths to strike out for herself in new literary directions, and combined the authorship of more than thirty books and pamphlets with singular devotion both to public and private philanthropies, and with almost too exacting a faithfulness to the humblest domestic duties. (109)

Although much good, original research and critical commentary about Child's important contributions as a pioneering early nineteenth-century woman writer have appeared since, especially in the last decade[1], most have concentrated on her career as a novelist, particularly her 1824 novel *Hobomok*, and her work as an abolitionist and an early advocate for Native Americans.

Child's newspaper writing, usually in the form of informal sketches that might best be described as opinion pieces or personal essays, deserves more attention because Child was a pioneer in establishing an American women's tradition for essay writing.[2] Although other American writers in this pre-Civil War period also contributed personal essays to newspapers and other periodicals, Child's are among the earliest in this genre to be written with a distinctly female voice and point of view and among the first to ask readers to "identify as a woman and examine the world through a woman's eye" (Fetterley 24). This article will focus on the journalistic sketches, collectively titled "Letters from New York," that Child originally wrote for two newspapers, the *National Anti-Slavery Standard* (where she served as editor between 1841 and 1843) and the *Boston Courier*, and which were subsequently collected in two books titled *Letters from New York* (*First Series 1841–43* and *Second Series 1845*). Child's powerful and affecting prose in "Letters from New York" shows her at her best.[3]

Child clearly relished the flexibility and freedom that the journalistic sketch afforded her, for in these short personal essays Child does much of her most innovative and energetic writing. Her subjects are varied: Child offers perceptive, often witty commentary about social justice issues, gender politics, domestic life, the arts, and women's issues in nineteenth-century America. Her newspaper column gave her a place to experiment with subject matter, voice, and style—an ongoing opportunity to transcend restrictions and push against boundaries, to throw herself "against the glittering wall of limitations." Child uses this phrase in a letter tentatively dated October 1846 to editor Rufus Griswold to describe the frustration she felt during the early part of her career, when she was celebrated for her first published work, the historical novel *Hobomok*. She recalls:

> Upon the strength of it [*Hobomok*], the Boston fashionables took me up, and made a "little wee bit" of a lion of me. But I did not stay among them long enough to have much life suffocated out of me. In such company, I am like a butterfly under a gilded glass tumbler; I can do nothing but pant despairingly, or beat all the feathers off my wings, thumping against the glittering wall of limitations. (Holland and Meltzer 232)

Child's images of confinement and suffocation are powerful. She equates her situation as a woman writer with that of a butterfly fluttering futilely against the sides of a glass jar and then shifts her metaphor to one common in the work of nineteenth-century American women writers, becoming a caged bird that longs for freedom from its gilded prison.

As her comments to Griswold suggest, Child had initially created a sensation as the twenty-four-year-old author of *Hobomok*, her bestselling historical novel that takes as its controversial subject interactions between Native Americans and whites in colonial America. Child's popularity continued to grow after she authored a popular advice manual for women called *The Frugal Housewife* (1829) and served as the editor of the first successful American magazine for children between 1826 and 1833. When she published her passionate and highly controversial book-length abolitionist treatise, *Appeal in Favor of That Class of Americans Called Africans*, in 1833, however, Child fell out of favor with her public. Scorned and ignored, she lived in poverty and virtual obscurity for a number of years and continually worked on ways to rehabilitate her literary reputation, an effort at which she was unsuccessful until she was given the opportunity in 1841 to move to New York City to become the editor of the *National Anti-Slavery Standard*, the weekly newspaper of the American Anti-Slavery Society. In this publication, she began to publish weekly articles in a column she titled "Letters from New York," a project she later transferred to the *Boston Courier*, where the letters appeared biweekly.

The "Letters," popular with New York readers and widely reprinted in newspapers across the nation, restored Child's popularity and regained her an audience. In an 1840 letter to her friend Ellis Gray Loring, Child writes about how crucial she believed "Letters from New York" would be to the restoration of her popularity as a writer. She puns on her title, saying that she considered the series of newspaper essays her "letter of introduction to the literary world, where I have so long been a stranger" (Karcher 301). Child's comment about audience echoes words penned by one of her contemporaries, poet Emily Dickinson, who begins her well-known poem about a writer's relationship with her audience with the wistful (or defiant?) lines: "This is my Letter—to the World/ That never wrote to Me—" (J 441).

In her review of Child's novel *Philothea*, Carolyn Healey Dall describes the eagerness with which antebellum American readers waited for Child's latest "Letter from New York" newspaper column to appear in the *Boston Courier*:

> The counting-room of the *Courier* was filled by an eager crowd, half an hour before the proper time, on the days when they were expected. The paper came damp from the press, and many a delicate glove bore traces of the fervor with which the owner had grasped the sheet. Men read it as they walked slowly up School Street. Young women ran into Munro and Francis' bookstore for their first glimpse. These letters were read aloud at the tea-table, and the next day everybody passed their bright sayings along. (526)

Contemporary equivalents for this kind of enthusiastic audience response to a writer's work might be discussions in the office lounge of recent sporting events or what happened on a popular television drama.

In 1843 Child collected the best of these letters in book form, taking a large personal financial risk by publishing the volume at her own expense, since the publishing company that had agreed to print *Letters from New York* backed out at the last minute. The publishers feared that some of the issues that Child addressed might offend readers in the South. These fears proved ungrounded. *Letters from New York*'s first printing sold out quickly, and response from both the general public and reviewers was positive. Writing in the January 1844 issue of *The Dial*, for example, Margaret Fuller called the *Letters* "really, a contribution to *American* literature, recording in generous spirit, and with lively truth, the pulsations in one great centre of the national existence" (1).

When she began the task of selecting which letters to include in a volume designed for the mass market, Child worked to reorient and reshape her "Letters" for the general public. She recognized that she needed to select pieces that would appeal to readers who were far different from the ardent abolitionists who subscribed to the *Standard*, yet she still wanted to include her antislavery message. Carolyn Karcher describes how Child accomplished this sophisticated and savvy repackaging of her product in her cultural biography of Child, *The First Woman of the Republic*:

> In repackaging *Letters from New York* as a book for the commercial market, Child simply increased the size of the garland ["of imagination and taste"] and enveloped her antislavery message more ingeniously. Besides reducing the proportion of antislavery material, Child eliminated the letters most likely to offend readers who considered abolitionists meddlesome fanatics. . . . (302)

Despite these shifts in emphasis, Karcher adds, at least nine of the forty letters collected in *Letters from New York (First Series)*, selected from fifty-eight original columns, retained some antislavery material. This first series was such a commercial success that Child followed it up with a second collection of her newspaper essays in 1845.

Although Child's "Letters from New York" resist easy categorization by genre, the label that best suits their blend of reverie, description, philosophizing, and social critique is the "familiar essay." C. Hugh Holman and Michael Shagrue, along with most others who attempt to define what Ruth-Ellen Boetcher Joeres and Elizabeth Mittman, in their collection of articles *The Politics of the Essay: Feminist Perspectives*, have accurately described as the "slippery nature of the form" (16), credit the fourteenth-century French writer Michel de Montaigne (1533–92), the "father" of the familiar essay, as the person who coined the term "*essais*" (or "attempts") to describe the informal, loosely organized, fluid structure and style of his tentative discussions of subjects in his own prose pieces. In a critical study of Montaigne's writings, Mariel Tetel adds that the word "essay" derives from the Latin *"exagium,"* which means "a weighing, a trial, a testing or investigation of a subject" (1), but the word also describes "a thinking process, an effort to 'think oneself' and thus to create oneself" (2). Essay writers privilege the dynamic process of exploring a topic rather than any finished product. As such, Tetel argues, the essay functions as a means of self-portraiture that is, of necessity, inconclusive, for as the individual looks at both the outside world and at himself or herself, the "I" learns, changes, and grows over time as the speaker undergoes a voyage—both literal and figurative (96).

A survey of writing about the essay as a literary genre demonstrates that scholars have yet to produce a satisfactory definition of such a fluid and flexible form. C. Hugh Holman, in *A Handbook to Literature*, does as well as anyone when he defines the familiar essay as "a moderately brief prose discussion of a restricted topic" (186). More useful by far is his list of the qualities the informal essay possesses:

> [T]he personal element (self-revelation, individual tastes and experiences, confidential manner), humor, graceful style, rambling structure, unconventionality or novelty of theme, freshness of form, freedom from stiffness and affectation, incomplete or tentative treatment of a topic. (186–90)

In his introduction to the anthology *The Essay*, Michael Shagrue adds that an essay presents "a view based on the writer's thought and experience rather than on formal study." Because the essay "depends less on fact than it does on the revelation of the author's point of view," he continues, familiar essays are "tentative and discursive" prose pieces in which readers hear "a person speaking his or her mind" (1). More recently, Joeres and Mittman identify two other ways in which essays resist easy definition as a literary form: not only are essays connected with other genres like letters, journals, and diaries that are collectively labeled "personal narratives" or "private writing," but they occupy a "precarious position between the non-fictional and the fictional" (12).

Child is among the first American women writers to explore and exploit the personal essay's flexibility as a literary form. In fact, she may well have been attracted to the essay form precisely because of its "openness, its accessibility, its sense of initiated dialogue, [and] its emphasis on the particular and the concrete" (Joeres and Mittman 20). Judith Fetterley concurs, suggesting that Child and other nineteenth-century women writers may have found the personal essay, sketch, letter, newspaper article, and other episodic forms attractive because they could "experiment with artistic form . . . in genres less formalized, less pretentious, and less predetermined, and therefore, more open, fluid, and malleable to their uses" (15). Fetterley and French feminist critics have even gone so far as to suggest that the personal essay is a characteristically "female" kind of writing.[4] Child's personal essays do offer her ample opportunity to mix modes and employ some of the nonlinear, nonhierarchical writing strategies that typify much writing we label "personal" or "private," particularly writing by women.

Child exploited the flexibility of the traditional familiar essay in several ways. I hear at least three distinct and different voices—the activist/reformer, poet/storyteller, and analyst/philosopher—that alternate and interconnect, even within a single essay in the series. Child's strategy here has some interesting connections with the Russian theorist Bakhtin's notion of "heteroglossia"—his theory about the function of multiple voices in prose. Ian Marshall has explored ways in which Child's novel *Hobomok* employs multiple voices in his article in *Legacy*. In general, the style and tone of Child's journalistic sketches freely move between two poles: the utilitarian prose of a straight news story or sociological study and the lyrical, metaphor-laden creative writing characteristic of poetry and fiction.

The activist/reformer voice is strongest in those essays where Child experiments with expanding the range of subject matter available to American women writers, for she regularly takes on topics not considered fit subject matter for a "lady"[5] and approaches her subjects with a woman's eye and point of view. In her "Letters from New York," Child often comments on the ambivalence she felt toward the restrictions on subject matter imposed by her culture that insisted women writers should confine themselves to matters of home and hearth (the domestic sphere) and should only privilege or highlight cheerful, uplifting subject matter. Although some of Child's essays remain within the required parameters for acceptable subject matter because of their focus on pleasant descriptions of beautiful places in New York City and the surrounding areas or on cultural reviews that celebrate art, music, and theater in the city, many others do not. Instead, Child chooses to write about the fast-paced, ever-changing, largely unmapped and unsettled center of America's urban frontier in all its diversity.

In Letter XIII in the *First Series*, Child compares the way her memory works to the way daguerreotypes capture images on photosensitive plates. She begins her musings by asking her readers a rhetorical question:

> Is your memory a daguerreotype machine, taking instantaneous likenesses of whatsoever the light of imagination happens to rest upon? I wish mine were not; especially in a city like this—unless it would be more select in its choice, and engrave only the beautiful. (88)

Child's "photographic memory" ensures that her "Letters to New York" are filled with realistic details about life in New York City's urban jungle—the unsavory aspects as well as the pretty sights most tourists would see. In many of her "Letters," Child concentrates on social reform topics such as abolition, the plight of the urban poor (with emphasis on the suffering of women and children), the tension between crass commercialism and other human values, prison reform, capital punishment, and women's rights.

Child's "Letters from New York" put into practice her firm belief that her words, both in fictional and nonfictional genres, had the power to alter public opinions and attitudes and thus effect social and political change. During Child's long and remarkable career, she worked as both a writer and a reformer, vocations that she believed were intricately connected, as she explains in a letter to Thomas Wentworth Higginson: "My natural inclinations . . . drew me much more strongly towards literature and the arts than towards reform, and the weight of conscience was needed to turn the scale" (Higginson 140). Child fervently believed that literature could be put to the service of reform because of its power to bring abstract ideas and social problems to life for readers. In his critical study of Child's writing, *Cultural Reformations: Lydia Maria Child and the Literature of Reform*, Bruce Mills explains how Child and some of her contemporaries viewed the intersection between writing and reform:

> For Child and others seeking to reform through literature, works of the imagination served to purify the affections. Achieving eloquence in essay, conversation, letter, and fiction was not solely an artistic enterprise but, at heart, a religious action that undammed celestial waters. Words could anoint with truth, and truth would change the world. (73)

Feminist critic Fetterley argues that Child shares this belief in the power of language to trigger or inspire cultural reform with many of the nineteenth-century American women writers she includes in her anthology, *Provisions*, women who, she writes, "believed in the power of words to effect change . . . and thus produced a literature characterized by a sensitivity to and a protest against what they saw as injustice" (11).

Child's very first letter, which appeared on August 19, 1841, directly addresses the topic of "appropriate" subject matter. She points to the tension between the requirement that she write exclusively about happy topics and pleasant scenes and her tendency to take on topics that are much darker and more unpleasant when she writes: "But I am cutting the lines deep, when I meant only to give you an airy, unfinished sketch" (15). Subsequent letters continue the debate about her choice of topics. In Letter II, for example, Child makes one of her most explicit comments about her subject matter. She writes:

> The disagreeables of New-York, I deliberately mean to keep out of sight, when I write to you. By contemplating beauty, the character be-

comes beautiful; and in this wearisome world, I deem it a duty to speak genial words and wear cheerful looks. (23)

Yet in the next breath, she begins to do just the opposite. Her language here makes the transgression explicit, for she adds: "Yet for once, I will depart from this rule, to speak of the dog-killers" (23). What follows is a disgustingly graphic description of people who brutally kill abandoned pets for a living. Most of the more upbeat passages in her "Letters" are undercut with darker moments and the writer's profuse apologies to readers for being unable to keep her promise to write lightheartedly.

Child justifies and excuses her "bad" behavior by claiming that her writing inevitably reflects her own shifts in mood and changes in attitude. Because she has darker moods and moments, she argues, some of her personal essays must take on somber topics and a darker tone. In Letter II, she speaks intimately and directly to her readers about the problem: "You promised to take my letters as they happened to come—fanciful, gay, or serious. I am in autumnal mood to-day, therefore forgive the sobriety of my strain" (23). Despite this and many similar disclaimers, she regularly blames herself for her focus on gloomy and sordid city scenes, admitting to readers in Letter XVII, for instance, that "[i]n looking over some of my letters, my spirit stands reproved for its sadness" and adds:

> The fault was in my own spirit rather than in the streets of New York. "Who *has* no inward beauty, none *perceives*, though all around is beautiful." Had my soul been at one with Nature and with God, I should not have seen *only* misery and vice in my city rambles. (116)

In Letter IX from the *Second Series*, Child asks: "Why need I sigh for green fields? Does not Broadway superabound with beauty?" (96).

In fact, it was precisely the ironic contrast between the pleasant and the unpleasant in New York City that most interested Child, for her "Letters'" structure and style depend on passages that juxtapose beauty and ugliness or contrast scenes of grinding poverty with those illustrating the most blatant excesses of wealth, privilege, and conspicuous consumption. Her very first letter sets the soon-familiar pattern:

> Well, Babylon remains the same as then. The din of crowded life, and the eager chase for gain, still run through its streets, like the perpetual murmur of a hive. Wealth dozes on French couches, thrice piled, and canopied with damask, while Poverty naps on the dirty pavement, or sleeps off its wretchedness in the watch-house. There, amid the splendour of Broadway, sits the blind negro beggar, with horny hand and tattered garments, while opposite to him stands the stately man-

sion of the slave trader, still plying his bloody trade, and laughing to scorn the cobweb laws, through which the strong can break so easily. (*First Series* 13)

Child is able to comment on the drastic contrast between rich and poor and on slavery and race relations by describing the strikingly different fates of the black beggar and the slave trader who has grown rich by exploiting and abusing other human beings.

Later letters continue to develop this contrast between wealth and need. Again and again, Child asks readers to look through a woman's eyes. In Letter XIV, for example, Child describes her encounter with "two young boys fighting furiously for some coppers . . . while [n]ear by on the cold stone steps, sat a ragged, emaciated woman, whom I conjectured, from the resemblance of her large dark eyes, might be their mother. . . ." The speaker clearly identifies with the wretched woman and wants her readers to do likewise, for she exclaims, "Poor, forlorn wanderer!" (96). Seldom content to let her story speak for itself, Child makes her point explicit here:

I raised my eyes above the woman's weather-beaten head, and saw, behind the window of clear, plate glass, large vases of gold and silver, curiously wrought. They spoke significantly of the sad contrasts in this disordered world; and excited in my mind whole volumes, not of political, but of angelic economy. (97)

Here and elsewhere, Child uses the ironic contrast between these two New York Cities as an opportunity to raise her readers' awareness of social injustice and to free up a space for her own comments on American virtues, villains, and values.

In contrast to the stern, straightforward reporting of the activist/reformer, Child's poet/storyteller voice speaks in the following lyrical passage describing a moonlight walk along the Battery, which employs strategies drawn from fiction-writing and poetry:

If you deem me heretical in preferring the Battery to the Common, consecrated by so many pleasant associations of my youth, I know you will forgive me, if you will go there in the silence of moonlight, to meet the breeze on your cheek, like the kiss of a friend; to hear the continual plashing of the sea, like the cool sound of oriental fountains; to see the moon look lovingly on the sea-nymphs, and throw down wealth of jewels on their shining hair; to look on the ships in their dim and distant beauty, each containing within itself, a little world of human thought, and human passion. (Letter I 15)

The poetic impulse also dominates the opening paragraphs of this same letter. Child writes:

> "You ask what is now my opinion of this great Babylon; and playfully remind me of former philipics, and a long string of vituperative alliterations, such as magnificence and mud, finery and filth, diamonds and dirt, bullion and brass-tape, &c. &c." (13). As her sentence begins to fall into patterns that echo poetic meter, Child calls her readers' attention to her use of alliteration and metaphor in this passage.

Thus Child's series of columns titled "Letters from New York" employs both storytelling impulses drawn from fiction and pointed social commentary common to muckraking reporters. Child's skillful blending of these fictional and nonfictional strains allows her to use storytelling as a way to make her social and political commentary "come alive" for her readers. Karcher argues: "Where Child is at her most creative, she is clearly breaking out of the journalistic mold altogether and stretching her wings in the sphere of fiction" (317). Child devotes all of Letter XI, for example, to a distinct reconstruction of the story of Julia Pell, an African-American woman preacher, while in Letter XIV, Child uses her skills as a storyteller to help make vivid the plight of children living in poverty. Child's speaker describes how she met a "little ragged urchin, about four years old, with a heap of newspapers. . . ." She goes on to imagine the horrible conditions this child will find when he goes home and encourages readers to think about the horror that his daily life must be, adding: "Imagination followed him to the miserable cellar where he probably slept on dirty straw; I saw him flogged, after his day of cheerless toil, because he had failed to bring home pence enough for his parents' grog"(95). After building the picture of the boy's miserable existence for several paragraphs, Child adds an explicit social comment that generalizes from one ragged urchin's experience. The moral of the story: "God grant the little shivering carrier-boy a brighter destiny than I have foreseen for him" (96). The rest of this letter provides other examples of women and children maimed and tormented by poverty. In these and many other powerful passages, Child's essays teach as well as entertain through her skillful intertwining of highly descriptive lyrical writing and more analytical and argumentative passages.

Yet throughout her "Letters," Child continues to wrestle with the problem of reconciling her literary and reforming impulses. Often she accomplishes this by shifting to a third voice, that of an analyst/philosopher who concentrates on pointing out things that are good, beautiful, and true in even the most sordid city circumstances. A passage in Letter XIV illustrates one of Child's favorite rhetorical strategies. She pauses to describe, in lyrical, poetic language, the beauty that abounds in the most unpromising of places:

The evening was closing in, as we returned, thoughtful, but not gloomy. Bright lights shone through crimson, blue, and green, in the apothecaries' windows, and were reflected in prismatic beauty from the dirty pools in the street. It was like poetic thoughts in the minds of the poor and ignorant; like the memory of pure aspirations in the vicious; like a rainbow of promise, that God's spirit never leaves even the most degraded soul. I smiled, as my spirit gratefully accepted this love-token from the outward; and I thanked our heavenly Father for a world beyond this. (100)

Here Child manages, for a few moments, to reconcile the tension she always felt between her poetic and practical impulses, a battle that she describes in a letter to her friend Louisa Loring. Child confides: "Dear Louise, the poetic in my *nature* more than balances the practical; I cannot help it, if I would; and being *always*, from my birth to the present hour, dammed up by mean and meagre external circumstances, the sparkling stream finds vent in these little follies" (Meltzer and Holland 242).

Child apologizes to her readers in her first "letter" for switching from her reformer's voice to a more lyrical one and explains why she does so:

Therefore blame me not, if I turn wearily aside from the dusty road of reforming duty, to gather flowers in sheltered nooks, or play with gems in hidden grottoes. The Practical has striven hard to suffocate the Ideal with me; but it is immortal, and cannot die. It needs but a glance of Beauty from earth or sky, and starts into blooming life, like the aloe touched by the fairy wand. (*First Series* 17)

Child's ability to see beauty in the most unlikely places and her impulse to use specific incidents she observes and describes to make a large, abstract, and philosophical point about the nature of the universe link her to her Transcendentalist contemporaries. Child knew many in the Transcendentalist circle personally as well as through their writing. She attended one of Fuller's series of conversations for women in the early 1840s and, while she lived with her brother Convers Francis, frequently met Bronson Alcott and other members of the group. In addition, Child attended one series of lectures Ralph Waldo Emerson gave in Boston (Karcher), and we know from a letter Child wrote to her friend Augusta G. King, dated October 30, 1884, that Emerson sent her a copy of his *Essays: Second Series* (Meltzer and Holland 216). Child writes about her strong and ambivalent reaction to reading this book:

. . . Emerson has sent me his new volume. As usual, it is full of deep and original sayings, and touches of exceeding beauty. But, as usual, it

takes away my strength, and makes me uncertain whether to hang myself or my gown over a chair. What is the use of telling us that everything is "scene-painting and counterfeit"; that nothing is real; that everything eludes us? That no single thing in life keeps the promise it
makes? (216)

Echoes of Emerson's prose are the strongest in Letter XIII in the *First Series.*
Child includes such comments as "Be true to thyself. Let not the forms of
business, or the conventional arrangements of society seduce thee into false-
hood" (88); "Be true to thy friend" (92); and "Be true to the world" (93).

In Letter I of the *First Series,* Child the philosopher makes a comment that
clearly links her essay-writing project in "Letters from New York" with Transcendentalist theory and practice:

There was a time when all these things would have passed by me like
the flitting figures of the magic lantern, or the changing scenery of a
theatre, sufficient for the amusement of an hour. But now, I have lost
the power of looking merely on the surface. Every thing seems to me to
come from the Infinite, to be tending toward the Infinite. (14)

This passage is a clear and convincing articulation of a central Transcendentalist tenet: the doctrine of correspondences between the natural world and the
ideal world, where real things are hieroglyphic symbols of the spiritual realm
(Letter XXIV 166–67). In Letter XXIV, Child transforms the simple story of
seeing a little child who is able to find beauty in a small, dusty patch of grass
into a Transcendental parable:

[W]hile yet amid the rattle and glare of the city, close by the iron railway, I saw a very little, ragged child stooping over a small patch of
stunted, dusty grass. She rose up with a broad smile over her hot face,
for she had found a white clover! The tears were in my eyes. "God bless
thee, poor child!" said I: "thou hast taught my soul a lesson, which it
will not soon forget. Thou poor neglected one, canst find blossoms by
the dusty wayside, and rejoice in thy hard path, as if it were a mossy
bank strewn with violets." I felt humbled before that ragged, gladsome
child. (163–64)

Walt Whitman chooses a similar moment and employs a similar rhetorical strategy in a famous passage from "Song of Myself." Section six begins:

A child said *What is the grass?* fetching it to me with full hands,
How could I answer the child? I do not know what it is any
      more than he.

In the lines that follow, the speaker ponders a long series of possible answers to the child's question. The grass is "the handkerchief of the Lord," "a uniform hieroglyphic," and "the beautiful uncut hair of graves." In the process, the grass becomes an optimistic emblem for eternal life and hope, as it does for Child's child, for "[t]he smallest sprout shows there is really no death" (Whitman 28–29). In another early letter, Child reveals that she also shares the Transcendentalists' belief that each human being contains a spark of the divine, the Oversoul, and echoes their suspicion of organized religion's emphasis on the outward trappings of ritual and rule, telling readers in Letter II: "After all, the God *within* us is the God we really believe in whatever we may have learned in catechisms or creeds" (24). In letter after letter, Child uncovers Transcendental truths in New York's harshness and hardships.

Yet as Child herself makes clear, her relationship with Transcendentalist theory and practice is always an uneasy and ambivalent one. Although she obviously admired their impulse to "read" specific phenomena in nature as hieroglyphics, as nonverbal "signs" of larger ideas about the nature of the universe, the reform-minded and practical Child faulted these writers for being too abstract and too ethereal. In Letter II, for example, Child interrupts her essay to distance herself from the Transcendentalists by saying,

> But I must quit this strain; or you will say the fair, floating Grecian shadow casts itself too obviously over *my* Christianity. Perchance, you will even call me "transcendental"; that being a word of most elastic signification, used to denote every thing that has no name in particular, and that does not especially relate to pigs and poultry. (26)

Here Child reveals her activist's impatience with theory that is divorced from application and action. Thus she alters the Transcendentalist paradigm. Although, as Mills points out, Child "follows the path from fact to symbol often taken by Transcendentalists," she "sought to revise Transcendentalist values and images in urban and abolitionist terms; she attempted, in other words, to connect her reflections more clearly in community events and public issues" (85). When she takes on the role of analyst/philosopher, Child adapts Transcendentalist theory and practice to suit better her social justice topics and activist's agenda. In her choice of events to explicate, Child reorients the Transcendentalist process toward women's and children's issues. She reads and interprets the emblems that New York City offers her with a woman's eye, mind, and heart.

As we have seen, Child creates a variety of voices and roles for the "I" who is the controlling consciousness in her essays. In addition, she offers her readers intriguing insights into her thought processes and opinions, taking full advantage of the stylistic flexibility characteristic of the familiar essay in her

"Letters from New York." Child adapts the essay form to create a fertile space within which she can process her experiences as both woman and writer. The very act of composing her "Letters" thus becomes one mechanism by which she meditates on and interprets the "larger" significances of her personal experiences. Child experiments with ideas about audience and tests a variety of relationships with her readers. Such experiments affect both the structure and tone of her essays, which test limits and blur genre boundaries.

Child sets up an intimate relationship between "I" and "you" in her "Letters from New York," a strategy reminiscent of the personal letter in which the writer intends her comments for the eyes of a trusted relative or friend. In Letter XXVI in the *First Series*, Child explains: "I did not *intend* to write thus mystically; and I feel that these are thoughts that should be spoken into your private ear, not published in the world" (182). In addition, as Karcher notes, Child often "invites her readers to participate in a dialogue and share their private thoughts and experiences with her" (301) and often uses rhetorical questions as a strategy to draw readers into a conversation with the writer.

Thus Child creates a relationship with her readers that is simultaneously intimate and far-reaching. Fuller's review of *Letters from New York: Second Series* in the *New York Tribune* identifies two types of readers who she believes will enjoy these "pictures of New York life":

> For him who seeks sprightly, well defined and sympathetic narratives of events that lie around us all, but which few have eyes to see, or hearts to understand, without prompting, this book will be the New York Spectator. Another class will find more satisfaction in the part, a large one in the present volume, which expresses the more intimate experiences of the mind, new revelations on Music, illustrations of the doctrine of Correspondences, and a general intelligence of the mode in which the warp and woof of life have mingled, are mingling, which casts light upon the beauty and meaning of the pattern. (1)

Karcher admires the skill with which Child is able to address a mass audience in such a personal, intimate way: "Whomever Child imagined as her audience, what charmed her readers was their sense that she was speaking personally to each of them" (300). Perhaps this is because Child seems to have had one particular reader in mind as the recipient of the "Letters from New York." As she explains in a January 1842 letter to her good friend Ellis Gray Loring, "I *thought* I addressed them ["Letters from New York"] to an abstraction, but I find that you are *always* in my mind as the person addressed" (qtd. in Mills 168). Her friend Loring seemed to offer the spiritual and intellectual companionship she pined for in the city.

Child's "Letters from New York" also reveal much about her as an individual woman who is working to understand her experiences. She offers her readers frequent glimpses into how her mind works and feels free to vary her approach, subject, and tone with her ever-changing moods. In Letter XXXVII, for example, she explains:

> When I began to write these letters, it was simply as a safety valve for an expanding spirit, pent up like steam in a boiler. I told you they would be of every fashion, according to my changing mood; now a mere panorama of passing scenes, then child-like prattle about birds or mosses; now a serious exposition of facts, for the reformer's use, and then the poet's path, on winged Pegasus, far up into the blue.
>
> To-day I know not what I shall write; but I *think* I shall be off to the sky; for my spirit is in that mood when smiling faces peep through chinks in the clouds, and angel-fingers beckon and point upward. (270)

Child employs an apt and amusing metaphor drawn from the world of dance to describe her rhetorical strategies in Letter XXVIII from *Letters (Second Series)*, which takes as its subject the variety of advertisements visible in New York City. Seeing these ads triggers one of her philosophical reveries. Child admits that

> the queer advertisements in New-York papers would seem very unlikely to lead thought into such channels. Yet, I assure you, I never go hunting after such analogies. They come to me, whether I will or no. Let me start from what point I may, an invisible air-line, like that which guides the bee to her cell, brings me into music. . . . (257)

She goes on to compare the variety and changeability of her prose styles in her "Letters" to different kinds of dances:

> But you will pardon my vagaries, because you know very well that they are the unaffected utterance of my mood of mind. In good truth, I can seldom write a letter without making myself liable to the Vagrant Act. A witty Englishman once said to me, "Madam, your countrymen dance as if they did it by act of the legislature." My pen has no such gift. It paces or whirls, bounds or waltzes, steps in the slow minuet, or capers in the fantastic fandango, according to the tune within. (257)

The smallest or most unpromising experience can trigger one of her meditations on life, as she notes in Letter III: "Whence came all this digression? It has as little to do with New-York, as a seraph has to do with Banks and Markets. Yet in good truth, it all came from a painted brick wall staring in at my chamber window. What a strange thing is the mind! How marvelously is the infinite embodied in the smallest fragment of the finite!" (25). Child's rambling style and loose linking of ideas replicate something of her thought processes for her readers.

Readers of the series of "Letters" come to know as much or more about the woman who writes them as about the subject on which she writes. Child confirms this autobiographical impulse in her preface "To The Reader" in her second series of *Letters* (1844), where she claims that her essays are intended only as "an honest record of my own views and impressions, on subjects which most interest me" and confesses: "But frankly and confidingly, as children do, I show you an image of my soul, as reflected in the mirror of its passing thoughts" (ix). In several places, she admits that loneliness is a primary impetus for sharing her thoughts on paper with readers, complaining in Letter XIV that "amid these magnificent masses of sparkling marble, hewn in *prison*, I am alone. For eight weary months, I have met in the crowded streets but two faces I had ever seen before" (94). She shares her personal responses to her experiences with her readers as if they were trusted friends.

As glimpses into the writer's mind and heart, Child's essays follow no rigid argumentative or logical structure. Instead, they ramble, perhaps in an effort to reproduce the episodic, often quixotic rambles she made through the city streets in search of her subject matter. Such fluid, loosely organized prose is typical of the familiar essay as a genre, for what organizes and orders the material is the writer's consciousness rather than a strictly controlled thesis or outline. Karcher argues that "[t]he style of free association Child invented verges on stream of consciousness" (306) and adds that "[b]y inviting them [her readers] into the private recesses of her mind as it floats from one association to the next, she has also enabled her readers to discern the connections uniting the individual, social, physical, and spiritual planes" (308). The multiplicity and fluidity of form complement the variety of voices Child intertwines in her "Letters."

By experimenting with voice, audience, form, and style, Child took full advantage of the flexibility and fluidity that the genre of the familiar essay offered. Fetterley effectively summarizes Child's innovations and contributions to the personal essay as a form in her introductory remarks about Child's "Letters from New York" in *Provisions*. She observes that writing in the form of the "relatively informal 'letter home'" enabled Child to create

> a voice that was personal, conversational, and frank. She freely shares with the reader the full range of responses that "this great Babylon" evokes from her and shares as well her own internal conflicts as to what the city means. Frequently based on her rambles through the city, the letters themselves often duplicate these rambles. Exploiting the informality and consequent organizational looseness of the form she

has chosen, Child is free to let her pen follow her mind and eye. In this context, digression becomes a meaningless concept, and coherence, integration, unity result from the developing perspective through which Child views the multiplicity of experience. (163)

What is perhaps most significant and most admirable about Child's essay-writing project in "Letters from New York," then, is her talent for integrating the social reform and literary agendas, a project that James Russell Lowell pokes gentle fun at in his pen portrait of Child in his "Fable for Critics" (1848), a verse satire on American writers who were his contemporaries. Lowell writes:

> There comes Philothea, her face all aglow,
> She has just been dividing some poor creature's woe,
> And can't tell which pleases her most, to relieve
> His want, or her story to hear and believe;
> . . . .
> Yes, a great heart is hers, one that dares to go in
> To the prison, the slave-hut, the alleys of sin,
> And to bring into each, or to find there, some line
> Of the never completely out-trampled divine;
> If her heart at high floods swamps her brain now and then,
> 'T is but richer for that when the tide ebbs again,
> As after old Nile has subsided, his plain
> Overflows with a second broad deluge of grain;
> What a wealth would it bring to the narrow and sour,
> Could they be as a Child but for one little hour!
>
> (qtd. in Higginson 129–30)

By deliberately blurring genre boundaries, mixing lyrical, poetically impressionistic passages with argumentative prose passages and blending humor with pithy social commentary, Child both entertains and informs her readers. It seems only fair that Child herself have the last word about her literary aims and sense of social mission, as she does in her final letter in *Letters from New York (Second Series)*. She writes:

Those who can do nothing more, can now and then read a pleasant book to some old man stricken with blindness, or teach a coloured child to write, or some poor Irish woman to read, or some young housewife how to make bread. Children are found to improve most rapidly, and make lighter work of study, when they are alternately employed in teaching others, who know a little less than themselves. The form of the use is of small consequence. Whatever our gifts may be, the love of imparting them for the good of others, brings heaven into the soul. (Letter XXXI 286)

NOTES

1. Note particularly the work of Carolyn Karcher, Bruce Mills, Judith Fetterley, and Patricia Holland. Holland's article about Child as a professional woman writer points out that her "Letters from New York" series came out of the second of three writing peaks in the mid-1840s. Child has been the subject of four book-length biographies by Helene G. Baer (1964), William S. Osborne (1980), Deborah Pickman Clifford (1992), and Carolyn L. Karcher (1994). Karcher's biography is by far the most comprehensive and provides the broadest and deepest historical and cultural contexts for Child's writing.

2. Karcher argues that Child created a new genre in "Letters from New York" in her biography: "Along with the new vision they conjured up of urban America, Child's journalistic sketches launched what her contemporaries recognized as a new literary genre—a genre Margaret Fuller, Fanny Fern, Grace Greenwood, and Gail Hamilton would help shape" (306).

3. Higginson's laudatory profile of Child comments on the quality and importance of Child's pioneering work in her short, personal newspaper pieces. He writes:

[t]hey were the precursors of that modern school of newspaper correspondence to which women have so large a share, and which has something of the charm of women's private letters,—a style of writing where description preponderates over argument and statistics make way for fancy and enthusiasm. Many have since followed in this path, and perhaps Mrs. Child's letters would not now be hailed as they then were. Others may have equaled her, but she gave us a new sensation. . . . (Higginson 127–28)

In fact, Child and her contemporary and friend Margaret Fuller were the first American women to write regular columns for newspapers and thus serve as foremothers of contemporary female syndicated columnists like Anna Quindlen and Ellen Goodman.

4. Joeres and Mittman pursue this question in the introduction to their collection of essays on women essayists. They ask: "Do the attempts to describe the essay as an open form, a non-linear, reflective, playful medium provide an opening on the basis of the notion of *écriture feminine*?" and go on to argue that there is good evidence to suggest that the essay as a form has long been associated with the feminine or the female. They argue that "[i]n its status as a borderline genre, the essay already seems to connect with women, whose sense of marginality and not-belonging is still so present." They also note that because of

the unsystematized nature of the essay, its spontaneous and almost accidental quality, its assumed opposition to doctrinaire, disciplinary thinking, its focus on personal experience, its cultivation of diversity, its stress on particularity, its "happy inheritance of meaninglessness" (as Barbara Sichtermann puts it), its concern with knowledge that is intimately connected with the author, its emphasis on objects and the importance of things. . . . the essay is placed over and over again into a space that is uncannily feminine, at least as the qualities adhering to the "feminine" have been defined since the eighteenth century. (19–20)

5. By writing about subjects her culture considered ungenteel, Child joins a group of early American writers, many of whom were women, whose writing placed their personal experiences in social and political contexts to create a body of literature "concerned with

experiences in social and political contexts to create a body of literature "concerned with the connection between manners, morals, social class, and social value" (*Provisions* "Introduction" 9). Karcher points out the strong parallels between Child's topics and rhetorical strategies and those of Rebecca Harding Davis in "Life in the Iron Mills." Like Davis, Karcher explains, "Child . . . takes her genteel readers on a tour of the institutions designed to segregate the poor from the rich and to punish any transgressions of boundaries: prisons, insane asylums, almshouses, and orphanages" (303).

REFERENCES

Baer, Helene G. *The Heart is Like Heaven: The Life of Lydia Maria Child*. Philadelphia: U of Pennsylvania P, 1964.

Child, Lydia Maria. *Hobomok & Other Writings on Indians*. Ed. Carolyn L. Karcher. American Women Writers Series. New Brunswick, NJ: Rutgers UP, 1986.

———. *Letters from New York (First Series)*. 3rd ed., 1845. American Fiction Reprint Series. Freeport, NY: Books for Libraries Press, 1970.

———. *Letters from New York (Second Series)*. 11th ed., 1850. New York: C.S. Francis and Co., 1944.

Clifford, Deborah Pickman. *Crusader for Freedom: A Life of Lydia Maria Child*. Boston: Beacon, 1992.

Dall, Carolyn Healey. "Lydia Maria Child and Mary Russell Mitford." *Unitarian Review* June 1883: 519–34.

Dickinson, Emily. "This is my Letter—to the World" (J 441). *The Complete Poems of Emily Dickinson*. Ed. Thomas H. Johnson. Boston: Little, 1960.

Fetterley, Judith, ed. *Provisions: A Reader from 19th-Century American Women*. Bloomington: Indiana UP, 1985.

Fuller, Margaret. "Mrs. Child's Letters." *New York Daily Tribune* 10 May 1845: 1.

———. "Mrs. Child's *Letters from New York*." *The Dial* Jan. 1844: 1.

Higginson, Thomas Wentworth. "Lydia Maria Child." *Contemporaries, Vol. II of The Writings of Thomas Wentworth Higginson*. Boston: Houghton, 1900.

Holland, Patricia G. "Lydia Maria Child." *Legacy* 5.2 (1988): 45–53.

———. "Lydia Maria Child as a Nineteenth-Century Professional Author." *Studies in the American Renaissance*. Ed. Joel Myerson. Boston: Twayne, 1981. 157–67.

Holman, C. Hugh. *A Handbook to Literature*. New York: Macmillan, 1986.

Joeres, Ruth-Ellen Boetcher, and Elizabeth Mittman. "An Introductory Essay." *The Politics of the Essay: Feminist Perspectives*. Ed. Joeres and Mittman. Bloomington: Indiana UP, 1993. 12–20.

Karcher, Carolyn L. *The First Woman in the Republic: A Cultural Biography of Lydia Maria Child*. Durham: Duke UP, 1994.

Marshall, Ian. "Heteroglossia in Lydia Maria Child's *Hobomok*." *Legacy* 10.1 (1993): 1–16.

Meltzer, Milton, and Patricia J. Holland, eds. *Lydia Maria Child: Selected Letters, 1817–1880*. Amherst: U of Massachusetts P, 1982.

Mills, Bruce. *Cultural Reformations: Lydia Maria Child and the Literature of Reform*. Athens: U of Georgia P, 1994.

Osborne, William S. *Lydia Maria Child*. Boston: Twayne, 1980.

Shagrue, Michael. *The Essay*. New York: Macmillan, 1981.

Tetel, Mariel. *Montaigne*. New York: Twayne, 1990.

Whitman, Walt. "Song of Myself." *Complete Poetry and Selected Prose by Walt Whitman*. Ed. James E. Miller, Jr. Boston: Houghton, 1959.

"We Must Be about Our Father's Business":
Anna Julia Cooper and the In-Corporation of the Nineteenth-Century African-American Woman Intellectual

Elizabeth Alexander

In 1892, Washington, D.C., educator Anna Julia Cooper published *A Voice from the South*, her collection of essays considering questions of race, gender, education, and other topics. What Mary Helen Washington has called "the most precise, forceful, well-argued statement of black feminist thought to come out of the nineteenth century" was written in an Afro-America in a state of desperate flux (xxvii). Lynching, legal disfranchisement, and court-sanctioned segregation were in place and on the rise. By 1892, most of the major African-American higher educational institutions—Howard, Tuskegee, Hampton, Fisk, and others—had been founded. The Fisk Jubilee singers had traveled to Europe and raised $150,000, much of which went to further construction of the university, and T. Thomas Fortune had founded the self-help-oriented African-American League. The General Federation of Women's Clubs, which expressly excluded African-American women, was established in 1890; four million women, one million of whom were African-American, participated in the 1890 American workforce. This was the age of reform in the post-Civil War United States; by the end of the decade, American imperialism would be the order of the day.

The depression of 1893, the first Conference of Black Women in Boston in 1895, and *Plessy v. Ferguson* (1896) were just ahead. The year 1892 was one of intense contradictions for the woman activists of the emergent African-American elite. Lynching was at its highest point that year, in which the black women's club movement—led at this point by Josephine St. Pierre Ruffin, Susan McKinney, and Victoria Earle Matthews—was born. Frances Ellen Watkins Harper's novel, *Iola Leroy; or, Shadows Uplifted*, Ida B. Wells's *Southern Horrors: Lynch Law in All Its Phases* and *Oak and Ivy*, and Paul Lawrence Dunbar's first book of poems were published or at press. Booker T. Washington was nine years away from publishing *Up From Slavery*. W.E.B. Du Bois was a graduate student at Friedrich Wilhelm University in Berlin; *The Souls of Black Folk* was eleven years ahead.[1]

This is but a thumbnail sketch of the climate in which Cooper wrote *A Voice from the South*, her collection of essays written between 1886 and 1892, which primarily considers questions of race and gender, separately and as they intersect.[2] Cooper critiques the burgeoning white women's movement for its racist exclusions as well as the African-American "race leaders" for their neglect of both potential and actual contributions of women. "While our men seem thoroughly abreast of the times on almost every other subject," she wrote, "when they strike the woman question they drop back into sixteenth century logic" (75). She examines images of African people in literature by white writers and critiques the ethics behind burgeoning U.S. expansionism. Cooper viewed the arenas of politics and culture, from the grass roots to the elite echelons, as realms that needed to hear African-American women's voices in order to survive. This sentiment was common for similarly well-educated, activist African-American women of the time, for whom "Lifting As We Climb," the motto of the National Association of Colored Women, would be a credo.

Looking at *A Voice* as a whole, rather than in its parts, reveals a textual strategy taken by Cooper to find a new form to house the contemplations of an African-American female intellectual, and, by extension, a nascent African-American women's intellectual movement.[3] The essays are at once allegory, autobiography, history, oratory, poetry, and literary criticism, with traces of other forms of address. Only such a diverse structure could encompass the tensions of forging an African-American, female, demonstrably thinking self from whatever intellectual material was at hand. Additionally, Cooper's strategic use of the first person reveals the ways in which she allows her own experience—her own existence, even—to inform the rhetoric of her text as evidence for the feminist strategy she advocates. By writing her body into the texts, Cooper forges textual space for the creation of the turn-of-the-century African-American female intellectual. Such an intellectual, struggling both for self-expression and for an audience, could ill afford to exempt herself from any discursive realm in which erudition—fully bloomed or partial—was demonstrable. As such, *A Voice* becomes a symbolic representation of the body of the African-American woman of letters, newly created in the public sphere.

While Cooper uses much of the same language and knowledge as both her intellectual "fathers" (white) and "brothers" (African-American), she injects her forceful arguments with anecdotes from her own experience. Each of the essays moves in and out of the first person, fusing a received notion of political theory with the particulars of an African-American and female life. These essays stand in a new space between the first-person confessional of the slave narrative or spiritual autobiography and the third-person imperative of political essays.

Cooper's structural strategies inaugurate the idea of the African-American woman intellectual at the dawn of the twentieth century. By constructing her written self within the text, Cooper displaces the sign of "intelligentsia" (white, male) and replaces it with something unique and newly named: an African-American intelligentsia, male and female, and, in the form of Cooper herself, the African-American female intellectual working out of a fundamentally multifaceted field of reference and self-construction. In *A Voice*, Cooper creates an unprecedented self: the African-American female intellectual at the end of the nineteenth century, little more than a generation beyond slavery and two generations before the unimaginable changes to come.

* * *

The facts of Cooper's life are crucial to understanding both the historical context in which she wrote as well as how those biographical particulars inform *A Voice*. Cooper was born Anna Julia Haywood in Raleigh, North Carolina, in 1858, the daughter of Hannah Stanley Haywood, an African-American female slave, and "presumably," in Cooper's words, of George Washington Haywood, her mother's white master. Of her parents, Cooper writes,

> My mother was a slave and the finest woman I have ever known. Tho untutored she could read her Bible and write a little. It is one of my happiest childhood memories explaining for her the subtle differences between q's and g's or between b's and l's. Presumably my father was her master, if so I owe him not a sou & she was always too modest & shamefaced ever to mention him. (Hutchinson 4)

In that same account, Cooper reveals an early sense of race collectivity and duty. She describes herself as a baby in the crib as the Civil War raged nearby, an exact construction that is chronologically problematic—she would have grown beyond the crib by the time the war reached her region, and she was not, as she says, born "during" the war—but that nonetheless provides an important blueprint for ideas of self-situation she develops in *A Voice*:

> I was born during the civil war and served many an anxious slave's superstition to wake the baby up and ask directly "Which side is goin' to win de war?" "Will de Yankees beat the Rebs + will Linkum free de Niggers." I want to say that while it may be true in infancy we are nearer Heaven, if I had any vision or second sight in those days that made my answers significant to the troubled souls that hung breathlessly on my cryptic answers, such powers promptly took their flight with the dawn of intelligent consciousness. (Hutchinson 4)

In this passage she chooses to present herself as a prophet of sorts chosen by "troubled" fellow slaves. In *A Voice*, Cooper professes great admiration for Harriet Beecher Stowe's "power . . . humility and love" (186), and here she, like Stowe, renders slaves as naifs governed by "superstitions." Cooper's tone here and in parts of *A Voice* with regard to her relationship to those for whom she has chosen to lift her voice may make today's readers uncomfortable. Yet she both places herself squarely within the slave community and acknowledges her own privileged status that at times sets her apart in terms of knowledge and language. Her narration also illustrates the war Cooper will fight in *A Voice* between intuition, or so-called women's knowledge, and the "book learning" that in the nineteenth century was the legacy of men, most specifically white men. She posits herself as having access, whether or not it is exercised, to both intuition, the gift that "Heaven" has bestowed on women and non-elite African-Americans, and "intelligent consciousness," the legacy earned by her relentless pursuit of book learning and the subsequent status it afforded her. This yoked notion of class privilege and duty, even within a slave community, is an intrinsic part of Cooper's vision of her life and work. In her own eyes, from that first moment in her cradle she is someone with a message for the masses, however discomfiting that notion of her own position might be to her readers. Cooper also presents herself as having possession of more than one language, however crudely rendered (we will see others later in her work); she moves easily into her remembered slave dialect of those "troubled souls" at the same time that she is fluent in elegant standard written English. These presented aspects of herself are not necessarily contradictory; she simply reads complexity and multiplicity into her own situation. Cooper, too, was a slave at this point; within the black bonded, Cooper sees herself as separate from them as well as part of them. The notion of speaking for "her" people, however, poses a continual problem in *A Voice*, not least of all in questions of tone.

In 1868 Cooper attended the newly opened St. Augustine's Normal School and Collegiate Institute. The school was formed under the auspices of the Protestant Episcopal Church to serve newly freed slaves. A curious condition of admission, given the recent end of the war, was some prior academic training; we can infer from that as well as from Cooper's autobiographical account that Cooper's mother encouraged her daughter's education from a very young age. Cooper's account in *A Voice* of her time at St. Augustine's chronicles a struggle to reap the same educational benefits as her fellow male students. Cooper's personal papers reveal little more about her encounters with educational obstacles, but they do manifest, from her earliest articulation of her life's goals, a dogged desire akin to a bona fide calling to be an educator.[4]

In 1877 the then Annie Haywood married George Cooper, who was a candidate for the ministry at St. Augustine's. He died just two years later, and Anna Julia Cooper, in pursuit of a career in teaching, wrote to Oberlin College requesting admission, tuition, and employment.[5] In one of her letters requesting admission to the school, she wrote that at St. Augustine's she had studied:

> beside the English branches, Latin: Caesar, seven books; Virgil's Aeneid, six books; Sallust's Cataline and Jugurtha; and a few orations of Cicero;—Greek: White's first lessons; Goodwin's Greek reader, con-

taining selections from Xenophon, Plato, Herodotus and Thucydides; and five or six books of the Iliad; —Mathematics: Algebra and Geometry entire. (Gabel 19)

Cooper received her B.A. from Oberlin in the class of 1884, which included two other African-American women, Mary Church (Terrell) and Ida Gibbs (Hunt). Cooper then received an M.A. in mathematics from the same college in 1887. She went on to be a teacher and principal of the M Street High School, later to become Dunbar High School, in Washington, D.C. In 1930 she became the second president of Frelinghuysen University in Washington, a group of schools created "to provide social services, religious training, and educational programs for the people who needed them most" (Hutchinson 157). Its students were adults who worked during the day. The school for a time operated out of Cooper's home at 201 T Street, N.W. Perhaps the highlight of Cooper's life of scholarship and teaching came on December 29, 1925, when, in a ceremony chaired by Alain Locke at Howard University, Anna Julia Cooper was awarded a Ph.D. from the Université de Paris (Sorbonne). Her dissertation, "L'attitude de la France à l'égard de l'égalité des races" (The attitude of France on the question of slavery between 1789 and 1848), was written in French. She was sixty-seven years old and the fourth African-American woman to earn a Ph.D.

This extensive discussion of Cooper's life is important because of the ways in which these very facts, up to 1892, are used in *A Voice*. Like her contemporaries and many African-American writers who would follow, Cooper wrote out of the impulse to present a unified, serviceable vision of a future for African-Americans as well as out of a simultaneous resistance to a static, monolithic view of what it was to be black, and, specifically, to be a black woman. Attacking racial stereotypes was an important part of Cooper's written agenda, though some of her own arguments about male and female "nature" were extremely essentialist.

Cooper's continual commitment to educating others who did not have the elite education that she did is a key element in *A Voice* and her life. The fervor of that commitment also illuminates some of the class politics and issues in her life and work. I say "class" advisedly and specifically to refer to how Cooper's privileged educational opportunities allowed her to be part of a specific class of worker. Cooper saw herself and her peers as a class apart in the sense that they felt bound to "uplift" the "masses," but also as inextricably of and devoted to her fellow African-Americans. Was Cooper's tone condescending or was it pragmatic, given the realities of who was able to be educated in those postslavery years and the hopes of many African-Americans for what education might bring? This attitude was most famously articulated several years later in W.E.B. Du Bois's 1903 article "The Talented Tenth," in which he wrote:

Men of America, the problem is plain before you. Here is a race transplanted through the criminal foolishness of your fathers. Whether you like it or not the millions are here, and here they will remain. If you do not lift them up, they will pull you down. Education and work are the levers to uplift a people. Work alone will not do it unless inspired by the right ideals and guided by intelligence. Education must not simply teach work—it must teach Life. The Talented Tenth of the Negro race must be made leaders of thought and missionaries of culture among their people. No others can do this work and Negro colleges must train men for it. The Negro race, like all other races, is going to be saved by its exceptional men. (Du Bois 861)

Du Bois, like Cooper, is alternately inspiring and condescending here. He was also in specific debate with Booker T. Washington's more "pragmatic" approach to training African-Americans, and to do full justice to the complexities of that relationship and to African-American class politics at the turn of the century would move far beyond the reach of this article. The important point, however, is that Cooper's zeal for education veers into something more interesting, complex, and ultimately perhaps more discomfiting than noblesse oblige; rather, it is a righteous fervor born of the urgency of her times and the situation of her race that, while it made her veer at times into condescending language and thought, nonetheless has its own logic and integrity.

Producing books had powerful significance for African-Americans at this point in history, as Henry Louis Gates, Jr., explains: "Deprived of formal recognition of their subjectivity in Western arts and letters, in jurisprudence, and in all that signals full citizenship, African-Americans sought the permanence of the book to write their rhetorical selves into language. I write therefore I am" (8). In *Writing a Woman's Life*, Carolyn Heilbrun posits a theory similar to Gates's about why women authors write. She describes why she herself began to write detective novels:

I believe now that I must have wanted, with extraordinary fervor, to create a space for myself. This was, physically, almost impossible. . . .
If there was no space for a woman in the suburban dream house, how unlikely that there would be space in a small city apartment. So I sought, I now guess, psychic space. But I also sought another identity, another role. I sought to create an individual whose destiny offered more possibility than I could comfortably imagine for myself. (113–14)

For the purposes of considering the autobiographical element in Cooper's essays and exploring the personal stake involved in the philosophy propounded there, Heilbrun's comments are helpful. She points out that writing in genres not identifiably autobiographical nonetheless can bear autobiographical impulses. Cooper writes *A Voice* at an exquisite moment in history and with great self-consciousness of when and wherefore she writes:

> The race is just twenty-one years removed from the conception and experience of a chattel, just at the age of ruddy manhood [sic]. It is well enough to pause a moment for retrospection, introspection, and prospection. We look back, not to become inflated with conceit because of the depths from which we have arisen, but that we may learn wisdom from experience. We look within that we may gather together once more our forces, and, by improved and more practical methods, address ourselves to the tasks before us. . . . But this survey of the failures or achievements of the past, the difficulties and embarrassments of the present, and the mingled hopes and fears for the future, must not degenerate into mere dreaming nor consume the time which belongs to the practical and effective handling of the crucial questions of the hour; and there can be no issue more vital and momentous than this of the womanhood of the race. (27)

This presages the ways in which, for Cooper, "experience" is crucial to the theorization of a race- and gender-based critique of America. As Hazel Carby points out, the challenges faced by African-American women seeking expression in either spoken or written realms are dual: "In order to gain a public voice as orators or published writers, black women had to confront the dominant domestic ideologies and literary conventions of womanhood which excluded them from the definition 'woman'" (6).

Any African-American tradition begins against that backdrop as well as against a long history of denied literacy in which the legally forbidden word represented a kind of freedom. As Gates writes,

> The command of a written language, then, could be no mean thing in the life of a slave. Learning to read, the slave narratives repeat again and again, was a decisive political act; learning to write, as measured against an eighteenth-century scale of culture and society, was an irreversible step away from the cotton field toward a freedom larger even than physical manumission. (4)

It was necessary, then, for African-American writers to construct an autobiographical stance that would say "I am here" in a hostile environment. The "I am here" occurs simultaneously with "Who I am" as critics define themselves in relationship to the cultural condition they see and describe. Autobiography, then, as Valerie Smith puts it, is "process, rather than genre" (19), a mode of thinking and therefore a theory of reading as well.

* * *

In a key section of *A Voice*, Cooper describes herself traveling through "a land over which floated the Union Jack" (88), testing her hypothesis that "there can be no true test of national courtesy without travel" (93). The episode reaches its fullest intensity at the moment Cooper arrives at a rundown railroad station and looks toward the bathrooms: "I see two dingy little rooms with 'FOR LADIES' swinging over one and 'FOR COLORED PEOPLE' over the other; while wondering under which head I come" (96). Where does Cooper's body, both a "lady" (which encompasses gender and class) and "colored" (which encompasses race and humanity) belong? She is resistant to the direct challenge here presented to her fully coherent self. How can she exist in this physical space? To choose either door erases some crucial part of her identity, yet to embrace both and act upon them renders her a literally impossible body in her time and space. Pointing to the injustice of no-space for the African-American female body, Cooper mutters "under my breath, 'What a field for the missionary woman'" (96). She is the said missionary woman, facing the challenges to self-definition that mark the most intimate aspects of her daily life.

Cooper does not tell us what happens next; the story's strength is rhetorical. But this episode poses the most fundamental questions of selfhood and the resistance to misdefinition, of public spaces in which the black woman can exist and speak. Carby reads the everyday lives of Cooper and her peers as "a confrontation of the division between the inviolability of elitist conceptions of womanhood and that which it denied" (104). She sees the episode in the train station as summarizing "the Janus face of the conventional definition of womanhood" (105). It also suggests a possible answer for why region—rather than race, gender, or other aspects that shape identity—is emphasized in Cooper's title, *A Voice from the South*. By claiming the South as her space, Cooper latches onto region as that which is, in a sense, beyond the arguments that threaten self-definitions of personhood. In other words, Cooper places herself squarely in North Carolina and Washington, D.C., from which she comes, an integral part of the history of the U.S. South, a voice to be heeded as any other. Perhaps there is an unambiguous, physical certainty to terrain, unambiguous because as such it has meaning to white America as well. Perhaps also an invocation of region elides class distinctions between African-Americans, positing the South as an equalizing master-text for black experience.

Cooper posits an African-American woman's lived experience as evidentiary, just as are the written words of the many white male writers with whom she engages in *A Voice*. She accomplishes this in two ways. First, she continually marks the orality of the text with phrases such as "I confess" and "I would beg" (24). Other first-person phrases with which Cooper opens paragraphs and statements include: "I see not why" (31), "we must confess" (33), "I do not imagine" (42), "so far as I am informed" (43), "now I would ask in all earnestness"

(45), "now please understand me" (59), "all I claim" (60), "I grant you" (68), and so forth. Second, she opens many paragraphs with rhetorical questions and acknowledges an imagined opponent's responses. The first-person responses are particularly interesting because of how they refer to the physical presence of Cooper herself as speaker. They are self-effacing and might thus cleverly disarm her detractors. These moments also offer a critical clue that Cooper saw her audience as made up of African-American men, white women, and white men, as well as of educated African-American women like herself. She reminds her readers that they are in the process of being persuaded, and, in fact, that these essays were delivered orally, both before and after publication of the book.

Cooper places herself as an active, visible agent in the writing of the book. She liberally uses the first person and temporalizes her words throughout the text. For instance, she will say "a few weeks ago" (53) before an illustrative anecdote. This creates a sense of process in the narrative, of someone in the midst of living her life and recording her reactions to it. Cooper places herself in the active present tense; the book reads not like a moldering tome but as work in the process of being written with a definite sense of source and agency. Cooper manifests, as she writes the existence of that entity, "the black woman intellectual." For example, she writes: "My readers will pardon my illustrating my point and also giving a reason for the fear that is in me, by a little bit of personal experience" (76). She claims that she is presenting "a simple unvarnished photograph" (78), although clearly choices and omissions are at play in any autobiographical statement. Still, Cooper says that what she gives a reader is "a little bit of personal experience" to illuminate larger truths.

Cooper reminds her readers frequently that she lives and moves within a physical body with sensations and needs. This biological self-naming is a powerful weapon in her arguments for racial equality. For example, she writes, "When I seek food in a public cafe or apply for first-class accommodations on a railway train, I do so because my physical necessities are identical with those of other human beings of like constitution and temperament" (111). The "I" is a physical "I." She once again has marked, or, specified, her body as classed; in this passage her upper-class (black) status is encoded in her physical self.

Cooper has chosen as her governing metaphor the corporeally situated image of the unheard voice of the African-American woman. More important than what the African-American woman is saying is that she is speaking it in the public sphere and that it must be heard. Using the voice is a physical act, one that first announces the existence of the body of residence and then trumpets its arrival in a public space. The physicality of that metaphor asserts corporeal presence in the space of imagined absence.

The spoken quality of Cooper's text is crucial to understanding her own narrative strategizing, as the essays in *A Voice* were originally given as speeches.

For example, Chapter 1, "Womanhood a Vital Element in the Regeneration and Progress of a Race," was presented to a convocation of "colored clergy" (9) of the Protestant Episcopal Church in Washington, D.C., in 1886. She would have presented this to an audience, then, of all African-American men. This orality encodes the fact of her body in public speech in the book. The African-American female body is thus a concurrently speaking and thinking body that remains intact even when consciousness appears fragmented, such as the potentially fractious moment for Cooper at the train station rest room. The physical, gendered presence of Cooper in this text illustrates her key point that it is up to African-American women intellectuals to make a literal space within which they can exist.

The preface to *A Voice*, in which Cooper sets forth "Our Raison D'être," offers the most extensive exploration of the metaphor of the voice as a blueprint of sorts for the rest of the book. She begins:

In the clash and clatter of our American Conflict, it has been said that the South remains Silent. Like the Sphinx she inspires vociferous disputation, but herself takes little part in the noisy controversy. One muffled strain in the Silent South, a jarring chord and a vague and uncomprehended cadenza has been and still is the Negro. And that muffled chord, the one mute and voiceless note has been the sadly expectant Black Woman,

> an infant crying in the night,
> an infant crying for the light;
> and with *no language but a cry.* [i]

Cooper distinguishes between an actual voice and "clash and clatter," "vociferous," and "noise." A "cry" is different from "language"; it is not mere sound or singing but rather meaning yoked to the physical presence of the voice itself. Therefore, it is not sufficient for Cooper simply to mark a space with sound, but, rather, with sound in a certain, intelligible fashion, as we see her striving to do throughout the text.

Cooper frequently uses other corporeal metaphors when discussing the experience of learning; even the intellectual life is experienced in physical terms. Take, for instance, when she describes the world of thinking men who have failed to incorporate (literally and metaphorically) women's perspectives:

The world has had to limp along with the wobbling gait and one-sided hesitancy of a man with one eye. Suddenly the bandage is removed from the other eye and the whole body is filled with light. It sees a circle where before it saw a segment. The darkened eye restores, every member rejoices with it. (122–23)

The part once again stands in for the whole; the eye is the key member on which the overall health and completion of the body hinges, just as Cooper and her ilk stand in for the whole of African-American struggle. The refusal to see the body as divisible, head from heart or intellect from physicality, is further expounded when she sarcastically imagines, "What a travesty of its case for this eye to become plaintiff in a suit, *Eye vs. Foot*" (123). She then makes her analysis even clearer: "Why should woman become plaintiff in a suit versus the Indian, or the Negro or any other race or class who have been crushed under the iron heel of Anglo-Saxon power and selfishness?" (123). The metaphor of the body works well to describe the divide-and-conquer strategy of white patriarchal dominion. This essay was presented in Chicago in 1893 at a gathering of African-American intellectuals protesting their exclusion at the Columbian Exposition. Women's perspectives are literally incorporated; the body without them is incomplete.

When she tells the story of the African-American woman sculptor Edmonia Lewis, whom she knew at Oberlin and describes as "my friend" (113), she does so to illustrate how, despite talent and training, African-American women's bodies are still kept out of the halls of learning for which some so desperately yearn. Lewis sent an application for admission to the Corcoran School of Art in Washington, D.C. The application was evaluated, "pronounced excellent" (113), and Lewis was admitted, but when she showed up in that selfsame black and female body, "*in propria persona*" (114) as Cooper puts it, all promises were revoked. The school superintendent then "told her in plain unartistic English that of course he had not dreamed a colored person could do such work, and had he suspected the truth he would never have issued the ticket of admission" (114). This is what Cooper herself is up against, and she knows that; hence, stories are told at a careful distance that separates her from the reality of her body long enough to make her way in the door. There is a constant tension between those distances; Cooper is giving these speeches to audiences that might not always have been sympathetic to her.

The use of sarcasm is another way that Cooper weaves more than one voice into the text. In arguing for higher education for women, Cooper in "her own" voice goes into a swiftly moving paragraph that runs from her own position to that which "men believed" about women's intelligence:

that higher education was incompatible with the shape of the female cerebrum, and that even if it could be acquired it must inevitably unsex women destroying the lisping, clinging, tenderly helpless, and beautifully dependent creatures whom men would so heroically think for and so gallantly fight for, and giving in their stead a formidable race of blue stockings with corkscrew ringlets and other spinster propensities. (65–66)

Again, it is the continual demonstration of her own "reason"—that she is capable of holding more than one thought and perspective in her mind at a given moment—that is at work in this passage. As much as this is wise and strategic, however, Cooper never abandons her own position; the passage is immediately followed by a one-line paragraph, "But these are eighteenth century ideas" (66), and is preceded by the pronouncement that exemplifies Cooperian philosophy at its most succinct: "'We must be about our Father's business'" (65). She puts this phrase in quotation marks; she assumes her readers will know she cites Jesus speaking to the disciples in the Bible. But she is also quoting herself at her most powerfully epigrammatic, making herself the authority on the subject at hand.

Cooper goes on to prove herself an expert, wielding the philosophy of the white fathers and African-American brothers of literature and philosophy throughout the book. The presence, in her own adopted voice, of the counterattack on her own clearly stated position of advocacy of women's education shows Cooper as a product of multiple traditions and points of view but nonetheless unified in her position. It "earns" her the rhetorical space—she was out to convince audiences, not merely to speak to them, both orally and on paper—to make such impassioned statements as this:

> The ideal of the day was that "women must be pretty, dress prettily, flirt prettily, and not be too well-informed;" . . . that she had no God-given destiny, no soul with unquenchable longings and inexhaustible possibilities—no work of her own to do and give the world—no absolute and inherent value, no duty to self, transcending all pleasure-giving that may be demanded of a mere toy; but that her value was purely a relative one and to be estimated as are the fine arts—by the pleasure they give. (64–65)

The "no" she places before each phrase is but a rhetorical sleight of hand; the real energy and force of this passage lies in the self-description of women with "unquenchable longings and inexhaustible possibilities . . . absolute and inherent value." Cooper needs that facility of voice in order to be able to perform the persuasive tricks she does and to encode her own complex intellectual inheritance. She takes what she needs, offering critiques and then using the wisdom she gleans unapologetically. She cites Macaulay, Emerson, Tacitus, Ovid, Longfellow, Thackeray, Lessing, Voltaire, Fenelon, a Dr. Maginn, Whittier, Carlyle, Milton, and Lowell—all referred to by the shorthand of a single name, demonstrating the author's easy familiarity with these writers and presumptions that her audience will know of whom she speaks as well as a valorization of their words. Cooper criticizes these writers but readily engages them at the level of intellectual sparring between equals: if their words do service to her textual aims, they are quoted; if she needs to take issue, then she does. This is what it means for Cooper to "be about our Father's business."

Cooper does much to establish the presence of African-Americans and women in history and on the public landscape, even when they are unheard and unlistened to. This was common practice at a time when the simple accounting of "race leaders" was crucial work that made those bodies exist in a vacuum. Mrs. N.F. Mossell's *The Work of the Afro-American Woman*, published in Philadelphia in 1894, chronicles the accomplishments of professional, white-collar African-American women. It is a compendium that seems to be attempting to list everyone: writers, educators, musicians, missionaries, businesswomen (undertakers, farmers, inventors, innkeepers, even women in the sandhauling business), all of whom, as Joanne Braxton has noted in her introduction to *The Work*, were "engaged in the uplift of the race" (xxxi). Listing their names and what they have done asserts that the intellectual and professional terrain has been marked by the presence of African-American bodies. Although Mossell's book is more conciliatory in tone than is Cooper's, the latter cleared important space for *The Work*'s chapters, such as "A Sketch of Afro-American Literature," "Our Afro-American Representatives at the World's Fair," and "Caste in Universities," and for Mossell's movement from analytical essays to her own poetry—in short, a literary space that could contain any number of different voices and modes necessary for making the point. This book and other turn-of-the-century African-American texts such as D.W. Culp's *Twentieth Century Negro Literature* (1902) speak to Cooper's message: that the accomplishments of each African-American reflect on the group as a whole and that this nascent "talented tenth" synecdochically might represent bringing along those who have not yet had the opportunity for similar accomplishment. Cooper was certainly an elitist when it came to her sense of having been chosen for duty. But she was realistic about the opportunities she did have and hoped to use them for the good of someone other than herself. Perhaps this small class of people was struggling to prove even to themselves that there was such a thing as a viable, empowered African-American intelligentsia in a world that continually asserted otherwise.

Cooper actively works to restore "the vitalizing, regenerating, and progressive influence of womanhood on the civilization of today" (18), knowing that by doing so she is making rhetorical and physical space for herself and for her work as an extension of herself. She names "Ruth, Naomi, the Spartan woman, the Amazons, Penelope, Andromache, Lucretia, Joan of Arc, Petrarch's Laura . . . Sappho, Aspasia, Madame de Maintenon, and Madame de Staël" (48–49). She quotes Frances Ellen Watkins Harper's poetry and invokes other African-American women such as Sojourner Truth, Amanda Smith, Charlotte Forten Grimke, and Hallie Q. Brown (141), women who represent all *shades* of belief and as many departments of activity but have one thing in common; their sympathy with the oppressed race in America and the consecration of their several talents in whatever line to the work of its deliverance and development. (142)

Cooper makes for herself as much as for any reader a paper community of like-minded (and diverse-minded, as she points out) women thinkers, both to support her very existence as well as to keep her company in her difficult enterprise. Each of these women exists in writing, but Cooper invokes them like a griot who holds the whole tradition of her people in her head to be passed along orally.

Cooper's African-American intellectual sisters do not have the same written legacy as the white men from whom she quotes—Frances Harper's *Iola Leroy* came out in the same year, and Hallie Q. Brown's *Homespun Heroines* and Amanda Smith's autobiography would not be published until several years later. To treat their thoughts with the same respect and give them the same rhetorical space, Cooper can but invoke their thoughts and their existence, as she cannot yet quote from many of their books. Of her community, she states:

> To be a woman of the Negro race in America, and to be able to grasp the deep significance of the possibilities of the crisis, is to have a heritage, it seems to me, unique in the ages. In the first place, the race is young and full of elasticity and hopefulness of youth. All its achievements are before it. It does not look on the masterly triumph of nineteenth century civilization with the *blasé* world-weary look which characterizes the old washed out and worn out races which have already, so to speak, seen their best days. . . . Everything to this race is new and strange and inspiring. There is a quickening of its pulses and a glowing of its self-consciousness. Aha, I can rival that! I can aspire to that! I can honor my name and vindicate my race! . . . Not the photographer's sensitized plate is more delicately impressionable to outer influences than is this high-strung people here on the threshold of a career. What a responsibility then to have the sole management of the primal lights and shadows! Such is the colored woman's office. She must stamp weal or woe on the coming history of this people. May she see her opportunity and vindicate her high prerogative. (144–45)

She moves in and out of identifying with "the race," speaking to, about, and of it at the same time. When she introduces the bodily metaphors of quickening pulses, she brings in the first person; even though this is a projected first person, it functions in this text, with its multipurpose "I's," to remind us of who speaks. This passage demonstrates how her own sense of mission is inextricable from a collective sense of mission. She speaks simultaneously in third-person rhetoric: she can see, from a distance, the great gifts of African-American people and their position in history at the same time that she speaks with privileged information that would not be accessible to an outsider. In that shifting "I," she simultaneously makes a space for the community to exist and from which she can speak.

When the text opens, Cooper's "I" is at its furthest distance from her lived experience, used as a rhetorical tool expressing conventional formality toward readership—"I confess," "I would beg" (24), and the like. As we will see later, when "I" is used forcefully in what is perhaps Cooper's most famous passage, she places that "I" in quotation marks, no longer explicitly the speaking narrator but someone quoted. She speaks of simultaneous singularity and collectivity, a multiplicity of voices and perspectives at play at once. The frontispiece of her book lists "a Black Woman of the South" as the author. She is not anonymous—her name appears on the copyright on the next page as "Anna Julia Cooper"—but, rather, "a Black Woman of the South" is actually her name on the frontispiece. She is singular, "a" black woman, but she is also, by lack of a proper name, representative of many. "A Black Woman of the South" is Cooper's alter ego, her *nom de plume* within the text into which she can insert her lived experience at a point in an argument where she feels that very experience might be discredited. In calling the first section of the book "Our Raison D'être," she again presents herself as part of a group as she defines the group's very reason for existing.

Cooper is not writing about a reason for writing or for speaking but for actually existing. She also demonstrates right from the start her ability to wield French phrases. This is both a way that she can show off her education in a time when African-Americans felt the need to prove themselves able to read and write and think at all, let alone in foreign languages, as evidence of their educational attainment, and, by extension in Cooper's case, her "fitness" to serve as an uplifter for the race.

Here, in her best-known statement, Cooper addresses the question of the collective further: "Only the BLACK WOMAN can say 'when and where I enter, in the quiet, undisputed dignity of my womanhood, without violence and without suing or special patronage, then and there the whole *Negro race enters with me'*" (31). Cooper articulates a philosophy that runs directly counter to the notion of the singular intellect or genius. For her, genius works in service to the race. Again, she constructs a physical metaphor to describe the fruits of metaphysical inquiry, painting an idea of "the whole Negro race" as bodies moving into a literal space where before they have been tangibly unwelcome. "BLACK WOMAN" is in large, bold, capital letters, its body standing taller and stronger than anything else in the sentence, asserting its right to space. She tempers the statement, again I would argue, for a skeptical audience, by invoking the idea of ladylike-ness; she will not go through the courts; she will go without "violence"; she asks for no "special patronage," but she will assert her presence. Cooper may not be realistic about the privileges her class status and attainment have offered her; as we have already seen, the "masses" of African-Americans she refers to earlier are a group who in her words "wrought but they were silent," and silence is a distinctly different state from speaking but not being heard. Nonetheless, if Cooper has found her individual voice, she seems intent on making it work to the service of a larger racial good.

Perhaps the most noteworthy narrative strategy of that chapter involves the use of quotation marks. Whom, exactly, is she quoting? Several years later, as Mary Helen Washington observes, Du Bois quotes that very same passage— "only the black woman can say 'when and where I enter'"—and attributes it not to Cooper specifically but merely to "one of our women" (Washington xli–xlii). Who is "the black woman" quoted in this passage who speaks these eloquent words? It is Cooper herself. She is quoting herself, her own earlier spoken words, within this written text. This sets the quotation apart from any spoken version of the work, where no one would know, unless she said who was speaking, that she was moving into a different voice. It is important, then, to remember the oral dimension that is ever present in Cooper's work. If someone else said those words, she would have needed to quote them more explicitly. Even Du Bois said more, though not enough, when he attributed it to "one of our women." She has already told us, on the frontispiece, that she is a "Black Woman of the South." By putting the words in quotation marks, she valorizes and sets off the import of the words just as she does when she sets off a passage from Milton. She is making that which has existed only as spoken wisdom part of the written, quoted record. In this moment we see her clever, hesitant relationship to the use of the first person in the text. For these are her own words that she wishes to emphasize by quoting them. Yet it is as though she knows her own author-ity is under siege before she writes a single word, so she elides her first-person perspective into a clue-laden, newly created hybrid or collage of third and first person. She sits simultaneously in both narrative positions at once, inhabiting them as need be to state her case most persuasively.

Just two pages later, we see the first instance in which she unambiguously employs an extended first-person meditation and her own lived experience as persuasive empirical evidence. She prefaces the story of her time as a student at St. Augustine's with an elaborate asking of permission from the reader for the right to insert her body in the space of empirical evidence: "My readers will pardon my illustrating my point and also giving a reason for the fear that is in me by a little bit of personal experience" (76). She then tells how there was literally no space made for her in the classroom in St. Augustine's. She makes a space in the text for her story, which is a story of educational exclusion in which space was made for "ministerial candidates (many of them men who had been preaching before I was born)," while Cooper, an "ambitious girl," feels constantly "a thumping from within unanswered by any beckoning from without" (76). Once again, spiritual and intellectual longing is physically palpable; it is the body as well as the mind that experiences this spacelessness. When she is finally able to study Greek, which she wants desperately to do, she again gains a seat in the classroom and therefore a space in the text to unleash the depths of feeling. She quickly loses, at this very moment, the colloquial "I" we have just seen, but not without tingeing it with sarcasm, her clue to the reader as to how to read her tale: "I replied—humbly I hope, as became a member of the female species—that I would very much like to study Greek, and that I was thankful for the opportunity" (77). She then drops the "I" and unleashes her torrent:

> A boy, however meager his equipment and shallow his pretensions, had only to declare a floating intention to study theology and he could get all the support, encouragement, and stimulus he needed, be absolved from work and invested beforehand with all the dignity of his far away office. While a self-sup[porting] girl had to struggle on by teaching in the summer and working after school hours to keep up with her board bills, and actually to fight her way against positive discouragements to the higher education; till one such girl one day flared out and told the principal "the only mission opening before a girl in his school was to marry one of those candidates." He said he didn't know but it was. And when at last that same girl announced her desire and intention to go to college it was received with about the same incredulity and dismay as if a brass button on one of those candidate's coats had propounded a new method for squaring the circle or trisecting the arc. (77–78)

In short, Cooper here presents the facts of her own life, minus the "I" that marks her as Anna Julia Cooper but also as an African-American, female, and therefore narratively unstable. From her first educational experience, she has been deemed unworthy of learning, as intellectually capable as a brass button. The space of persuasive rhetoric has remained inhospitable to African-American women. The realm of "truth," of third-person empiricism, has not been the domain allocated to African-American women. Cooper temporarily erases her black and female body so that she might make a space for it, slightly refigured, in a hostile domain.

It is in the process of travel that we see her, for the first time, engaged in the act of intellectual contemplation and writing, the distillation of her own lived experiences into words. "I see" from the window, she tells us, teenaged boys working on a chain gang (95). Her response:

I make a note on the flyleaf of my memorandum, *The women in this section should organize a Society for the Prevention of Cruelty to Human Beings, and disseminate civilizing tracts, and send throughout the region apostles of anti-barbarism for the propagation of humane and enlightened ideas.* (95–96)

This is written at the same time in which Ida B. Wells is just beginning to travel the country protesting lynching. An African-American woman traveling is one thing, but for her to be traveling and working and for that work to be committed to social change is a risky situation indeed. Cooper's showing herself in the act of writing while traveling accomplishes several things. First, it "lets on" to her readers—for here she moves fully into the first person—that these stories we have been hearing are from her own personal experience. Second, she writes a space for herself and her type: the working African-American woman writing and traveling through the South with neither husband nor father, nor other companionship—simply herself and her intellect. It puts the body in that space, writing.

In *The Alchemy of Race and Rights: The Diary of a Law Professor*, Patricia J. Williams describes how she hopes her life's mission and vision can be manifest in her written work:

> [I am] trying to challenge the usual limits of commercial discourse by using an intentionally double-voiced and relational, rather than a traditionally legal black letter, vocabulary. For example, I am a commercial lawyer as well as a teacher of contract and property law. I am also black and female, a status that one of my former employers described as being "at oxymoronic odds" with that of commercial lawyer. While I certainly took issue with that particular characterization, it is true that my attempts to write in my own voice have placed me at the center of a snarl of social tensions and crossed boundaries. . . . I think, moreover, that there is a paradigm at work: a paradigm of larger social perceptions that divide public from private, black from white, dispossessed from legitimate. . . . I am trying to create a genre of legal writing to fill the gaps of traditional legal scholarship. . . . Thus . . . I hope that the gap in my own writing will be self-consciously filled in by the reader. . . . To this end, I exploit all sorts of literary devices, including parody, parable, and poetry. (6–8)

A lawyer (public) publishing a diary (private); an African-American woman writing the law in which for so long she was misrepresented; these are the oxymoronic truths of African-American women writing in the public spaces of theory.

Cooper inscribes her body and valorizes individual experience as evidence subtly placed but as compelling and valid as any other text, thus rewriting the history of perception with her own body. Furthermore, Cooper chronicles the unchronicled logic of her own intellectual processes at the point in history when her body was only newly her own legally. Yet for Cooper, the individual ideal does not exist without a group ideal, even when the two oppose each other in degrees. In short, the self-presented vision of the turn-of-the-century African-American person of letters cannot exist without a concurrently articulated sense of place in the culture at large. *A Voice* is the work of an individual who necessarily is, in Du Bois's words, "bone of the bone and flesh of the flesh" of the group of which she writes (360).

Cooper states that her words are to represent "that muffled chord, the one mute and voiceless note [of] the sadly expectant Black Woman" (i). From that first moment, she aligns her self with a group larger than just herself. She exhorts her readers to recognize a "raison d'être" not only for being but for writing about these very subjects that concern the widening of opportunities and visions for African-American people:

> It is not the intelligent woman vs. the ignorant woman; nor the white woman vs. the black, the brown, and the red,—it is not even the cause of woman vs. man. Nay 'tis woman's strongest vindication for speaking that *the world needs to hear her voice.* (121)

Thus the "auto" of autobiography no longer means "one" in the literal sense, just as here Cooper conflates the very notion of single authorship with collective voice and responsibility. As Cooper creates her self in writing, she forges a space for the African-American woman intellectual, working and thinking at the turn of the century.

NOTES
1. These dates and events are compiled from Franklin, Davis, Giddings, Jones, and Carby.
2. The span 1886 to 1892 is Gabel's estimation of the time in which the essays from *A Voice* were written. I have not been able to verify precisely when each was composed and for which occasions. Several of these essays were first given as speeches, and Cooper continued to present them orally throughout the 1890s.
3. See Giddings, Carby, Harley, and Terborg-Penn's *The Afro-American Woman: Struggles and Images,* in particular, for detailed discussion of the African-American women's intellectual climate in which Cooper wrote. For the writings of some of these women, see Culp, Matthews, Brown, and Mossell.
4. Anna Julia Cooper papers, Moorland-Spingarn Research Center, Howard University, Washington, D.C.
5. Mary Helen Washington correctly points out the ironic effect widowhood had on Cooper's career. Married women, African-American and white, were not allowed at that time to be teachers. Thus, widowhood freed Cooper to pursue teaching, which would be her greatest life's work (xxxii).

REFERENCES

Brown, Hallie Q. *Homespun Heroines and Other Women of Distinction*. 1926. New York: Oxford UP, 1988.

Carby, Hazel. *Reconstructing Womanhood: The Emergence of the African-American Woman Novelist*. New York: Oxford UP, 1988.

Cooper, Anna Julia. *A Voice from the South*. 1892. Introduction by Mary Helen Washington. New York: Oxford UP, 1988.

Culp, D.W., ed. *Twentieth Century Negro Literature; Or, a Cyclopedia of Thought on the Vital Topics Relating to the American Negro, by One Hundred of America's Greatest Negroes*. Atlanta, Napierville, IL, and Toronto: Nichols, 1902.

Davis, Angela. *Women, Race, and Class*. New York: Random, 1981.

Du Bois, W.E.B. "The Talented Tenth." 1903. In *W.E.B. Du Bois: Writings*. New York: Library of America, 1986.

———. *The Souls of Black Folk*. 1903. In *W.E.B. Du Bois: Writings*. New York: Library of America, 1986.

Franklin, John Hope. *From Slavery to Freedom: A History of Negro Americans*. New York: Knopf, 1967.

Gabel, Leona C. *From Slavery to the Sorbonne and Beyond: The Life and Writing of Anna J. Cooper*. Northampton, MA: Department of History of Smith College, 1982.

Gates, Henry Louis, Jr. *Figures in Black: Words, Signs, and the "Racial" Self*. New York: Oxford UP, 1986.

———. "The Hungry Icon: Langston Hughes Rides a Blue Note." *Voice Literary Supplement* July 1989: 8–13.

Giddings, Paula. *When and Where I Enter: The Impact of Black Women on Race and Sex in America*. New York: Bantam, 1984.

Giddings, Paula, Hazel Carby, Sharon Harley, and Rosalyn Terborg-Penn, eds. *The Afro-American Woman: Struggles and Images*. Port Washington, NY: Kennikat, 1978.

Harper, Frances Ellen Watkins. *Iola Leroy; or, Shadows Uplifted*. 1892. 2nd ed. College Park, MD: McGrath, 1969.

Heilbrun, Carolyn. *Writing a Woman's Life*. New York: Ballantine, 1988.

Hutchinson, Louise Daniel. *Anna J. Cooper: A Voice from the South*. Washington, D.C.: Smithsonian Institution, 1981.

Jones, Jacqueline. *Labor of Love, Labor of Sorrow: Black Women, Work, and Family, from Slavery to the Present*. New York: Random, 1985.

Matthews, Victoria Earle. "The Value of Race Literature." *Massachusetts Review* 27(2) (1986): 169–81.

Mossell, Mrs. N.F. *The Work of the Afro-American Woman*. 1894. Freeport, NY: Books for Libraries, 1971.

———. *The Work of the Afro-American Woman*. 1894. Introduction by Joanne Braxton. New York: Oxford UP, 1988.

Smith, Valerie. *Self-Discovery and Authority in Afro-American Narrative*. Cambridge, MA: Harvard UP, 1987.

Washington, Booker T. *Up from Slavery*. 1901. New York: Doubleday, 1902.

Washington, Mary Helen. Introduction. Cooper xxvii–liv.

Wells, Ida B. *Oak and Ivy*. Dayton, Ohio: United Brethren, 1893.

———. *On Lynchings: Southern Horrors, a Red Record, Mob Rule in New Orleans*. 1892. Salem, NH: Ayer, 1990.

Williams, Patricia J. *The Alchemy of Race and Rights: Diary of a Law Professor*. Cambridge, MA: Harvard UP, 1991.

"I Thought From the Way You *Writ*, That You Were a Great Six-Footer of a Woman":
Gender and the Public Voice in Fanny Fern's Newspaper Essays
Laura Laffrado

"I think now that there are layers within layers of significance to a woman's decision to write under a pseudonym, but the most important reason for her doing so is that the woman author is, consciously or not, creating an alter ego as she writes, another possibility of female destiny."

(Carolyn Heilbrun, *Writing a Woman's Life* 110)

"One day I read a quote: 'If a woman told the truth about her life, the world would split open.' I found a stage, where I began to tell the truth about my life—because I couldn't tell the truth off stage. And very quickly, the world began to blow apart."

(Roseanne Barr, *Roseanne: My Life as a Woman* 202)

Fanny Fern first spoke not in the private moment when Sara Payson Willis finished an essay and chose the flowery, mocking pen name, but in the public moment on September 6, 1851, when that essay, "The Little Sunbeam," was published in the Boston *Olive Branch*. Until Willis's identity was revealed four years later, readers repeatedly wondered aloud and in print about whether Fanny Fern was a man writing under a woman's name or an "unfeminine" woman writer. Even after her identity was made public, false photographs of Fanny Fern were sold, other women were identified as Fanny Fern, impostors toured the lecture circuit under the name, and, for the rest of her career, readers wrote requesting details of Fanny Fern's appearance.

Feminist criticism of the past few decades has examined the writing of women's lives. Carolyn Heilbrun, Mary Mason, Sidonie Smith, and Patricia Meyer Spacks, among others, have viewed women's autobiographies as fundamentally different from men's autobiographies. Shari Benstock, touching on Derrida's study of the relation of genre and gender, concisely states the issue, "The very requirements of the genre are put into question by the limits of gender . . . genre itself raises questions about gender" (20). A woman's "proposal to be a writer in itself reveals that female identity is not naturally what it has been assumed to be" (Jehlen 585). The long-lasting and complex public reaction that "Fanny Fern" immediately provoked can be read as a sign of cultural uneasiness with the possibility that a woman's identity might exist and even thrive outside patriarchally-sanctioned locations of home and church.

In a wide-ranging discussion of Fanny Fern and popular feminine discourse Lauren Berlant writes, "Sentimental female autobiography thus raised the possibility that under the 'woman' lurked something horrible, a residual 'female' whose knowledge and desire was not entirely caught up in the patriarchal domestic economy" (437). In this sense, women's writing could be read as what Nancy K. Miller has seen as "a defense and illustration," a negotiation of conventional ideas about women and "a poetics calling for another, freer text" (263).

The poetics of women's autobiography may be useful in considering the poetics of women's newspaper essay writing. Fanny Fern's position as a woman modifies the newspaper essay project in several ways. The female public voice engenders fictions of self-representation (the "I"), relies on an imagined audience, and, as Sidonie Smith argues, enables the woman writer to "establish the discursive authority to interpret herself publicly in a patriarchal culture" (45). However, unlike women's autobiography—and perhaps the most salient difference between the genres—the women's newspaper essay is not ultimately bound by some "iconic representation of continuous identity" (Smith 47). The weekly publication of the newspaper essay—its scheduled, familiar discourse— promotes the woman writer's repeated redefinitions and reconfigurations of the self.

Additionally, due to the location where gender and this particular genre meet, the American women's newspaper essay partakes of strains of public and private. Fictions of the "I" and the imagined audience are used to draw on what Foucault would later see as private writing, genres where writers are encouraged to "reveal" the self. Gender and the public voice thus intersect, encouraging the woman writer to confess to various representations of the self. The reader is encouraged by these confessions to believe that his or her reading of the writer is correct. At the same time, though, any one "true" reading is resisted by the various fictions of self-representation. In the case of Sara Willis, the primary rhetorical representations of Fanny Fern are seen in her representaion of Fern's self as a person and her representation and manipulation of Fern's self as manifest in voice.

Only after a series of tragedies did Sara Willis turn to the newspaper essay—the public voice—and to Fanny Fern. The deaths of her younger sister, mother, eldest child, and husband between 1844 and 1846 and the refusal of her relatives to provide financial or emotional support led to a disastrous second marriage and her attempts to support herself and her two children by trying to obtain a position as a schoolteacher and by working as a seamstress. Thus Willis first explored a range of gender-specific methods—family support, remarriage after being widowed, teaching, and sewing. For the rest of her life, Fern would associate "her writing with other more typical women's work: that of housewives, seamstresses, prostitutes" (Berlant 431). The conventional cultural ways that Willis attempted, considered appropriate to middle-class, white women's status, are also private ways. Once the private and gender-specific methods had failed disastrously and repeatedly, Willis turned to the public and androgynous. Fanny Fern was public where Willis was private, outspoken where Willis was supplicating, popular where Willis was shunned, viewed as masculine where Willis was viewed as feminine, and able to effect change where Willis was impotent.

For Willis, Fanny Fern was a fictional representation of a self, authorized to speak publicly to a series of imagined readers. Her weekly column—instituted in September 1852, fifteen months after her first essay was published—allowed her to address topics of cultural significance, to revise expectations about appropriate female speech and behavior, and to write anonymously and androgynously. Just as "an autobiographer may shift the grounds of self-representation and respond to cultural expectations about appropriate female speech and behavior" (Smith 54), so Fanny Fern's newspaper essays ranged from the sentimental to the sarcastic, the stereotypically feminine to the stereotypically masculine, each essay rhetorically promoting the self represented by that particular topic in that particular essay.

Changes in reading and writing accompanied the mid-nineteenth-century rise of the newspaper as a popular format. A growing urban population and increased readership resulted in sharp competition among newspaper publishers for readers and writers (the latter to help attract the former). Women writers, who were not automatically denied access to a lower-status format like the newspaper and who were seen as potential magnets for female readers, found increased publication possibilities. These women writers were, like Willis, eager to publish, to earn a regular income by their writing, to engage "the contested conditions of public enunciation under which Fern and many of her sister writers labored and profited" (Berlant), and thus to deliver whatever newspaper publishers wanted from their writers for their readers. Their resulting newspaper essays tailored the more elite essay genre of journals and periodicals to reflect newspaper characteristics of popularity, brevity, regular publication, and familiarity.

The newspaper essay genre was particularly suited for Willis's sensibility. Its length allowed for brief, topical commentary without extensive research or writing time. Its regular publication invited response to a range of current topics. And newspaper publication encouraged the development of a recognizable voice to appeal to a paper's readership in a time of competitive circulations. Willis was repeatedly able to increase the amount she earned through her writing because of the familiarity of Fern's voice to readers. When Robert Bonner, owner of the sensationalistic *New York Ledger*, hired Willis at an unprecedented $100 per column to write exclusively for his newspaper, "he . . . paid $2,000 for a full page advertisement in the [rival] *New York Herald*"; the advertisement featured one sentence printed repeatedly down the entire page, "Fanny Fern writes only for the *Ledger*" (McGinnis 6). Bonner then publicized Fern's salary to his readership, reinforcing the emotional and monetary significance of the well-known female public voice. Readers responded to this promotion "for years . . . mobb[ing] the offices of the *Ledger* on the day the paper came out, eager to be the first to see what Fanny Fern had to say" (Warren xxxi).

Her familiar voice enabled the woman newspaper essayist to expand the boundaries of the genre to include commentary on social issues, reviews of contemporary writers, and details of the writer's personal life. In various newspaper columns over the years, Fern supported rights of women and children, praised Whitman's *Leaves of Grass*, criticized social hypocrisy, and wrote a wide range of autobiographical essays. Whatever the subject, the nineteenth-century American women's newspaper essay required a polemical, familiar voice speaking to imagined male and female readers of the prevailing culture. This emphasis on voice enabled Willis and other nineteenth-century American women newspaper essayists to use their medium to explore scenarios of self-representation. In woman's autobiography, the process of "self-interpretation emerges rhetorically from the autobiographer's engagement with the fictive stories of selfhood" (Smith 47); in the woman's newspaper essay, the process of self-representation emerges rhetorically from the woman writer's engagement with the fictive stories of selfhood created by the dialogue between Willis and her readers' images of Fanny Fern.

The autobiographer's collaboration, then, is between the created self and the constructed, imagined culture. For Willis, the construction is between her voice and real readers. Willis periodically writes essays concerning readers' conjectures on her gender, appearance, dress, and values. Joyce W. Warren quotes "a subscriber to the *Olive Branch* [who] wrote a poem" that appeared in the newspaper's April 10, 1852, edition and began:

Oh mirth-provoking Fanny,
Pray tell me if you will,
What sort of being you really are,
And whether a Jack or a Jill
(*Fanny Fern* 101)

In "Some Gossip About Myself," Willis responds to a similar request, writing, "A correspondent inquires how I look? Am I tall? have I dark, or light complexion? and what color are my eyes?" (*Ginger Snaps* 185). Such essays invariably play on expectations that, if Fanny Fern is a woman, then—because of her role as a woman writer and the tone and content of that writing—she must be abrasive, ill-dressed, overdressed, frivolous, a poor housekeeper, and, above all, masculine. Responding to the reader, Fern writes, "I should be very happy to answer these questions, did I know myself. I proceed to explain why I cannot tell whether 'I be I'" (*Ginger Snaps* 185). She goes on to tell of her amusement at attending the opera and overhearing a man point out a woman whom he identifies (erroneously) as Fanny Fern, telling his companion he knows Fern "intimately" and saying, "Observe how expensively she is dressed. See those diamonds, and that lace! Well, I assure you, that every cent she has ever earned by her writings goes straightway upon her back" (*Ginger Snaps* 185). The gossipy speaker rhetorically attempts to disempower Fern's voice with the "assurance" that she uses that voice solely as a means to an economic, gender-specific, and frivolous end.[1] By implication, to know Fanny Fern confers social status; this particular recognition asserts private knowledge, an explanation for the voice's existence ("every cent she has ever earned by her writings goes straightway upon her back"). That such a voice should provoke explanation suggests its strength, a strength here resisted by false explanation and triviality. Ironically, Willis can afford to be amused at this commentary because Fern's voice *is* so strong—the same reason the speaker is compelled to offer his false explanation. The *Musical World and Times* used this same strength of voice to defend Fern, writing that many had argued

> that the writer of such searching, forcible, and, withal, common-sense articles as sometimes came from the unknown pen, must be a man;— the public being unwilling to give femininity credit for the power and courage necessary for their production. (Warren, *Fanny Fern*, 101)

Further, in "Some Gossip About Myself," Willis writes,

> Again—in a list of pictures announced to be sold lately, was one labelled "Fanny Fern." Having lost curiosity concerning that lady my-

self, I did not go on a tour of inspection; but a gentleman friend of mine who did, came back in high glee at the manner in which the purchaser thereof, if any should be found, would be swindled—as "I was *not* I" in that case either. (186)

She offers the first representation of herself as a woman misidentified as Fanny Fern; the second representation is a photograph of another woman. These passages are not misdescriptions of Fern, but rather substitutions. The substitutes displace representation of the "real" Fanny Fern and so provide a means for Fern to engage in self-representation without necessarily defining that self in some permanent way. By citing incidents of *mis*representation, representation of the self remains fluid. Self-representation then results from the woman newspaper essay writer's engagement with fictive stories of selfhood imagined of her by her readers.

Finally, a reader meets Willis herself and,

after breathlessly inspecting me, remark[s], "Well, now, I *am* agreeably disappointed! I thought from the way you *writ*, that you were a great six-footer of a woman, with snapping black eyes and a big waist, and I *am* pleased to find you looking so soft and so femi-*nine*!" (*Ginger Snaps* 186–87)

Again, Willis is amused. And again, Fern's voice and appearance are conflated. Fern's voice leads the observer to assume that she will appear as "strong," that is, as masculine, as her writing. His "breathless inspection" implies his Amazonian expectations, while his "agreeable disappointment" links him with the speaker at the opera, relieved to be able to categorize that public voice as privately gender-specific. Whether speakers view another woman, a photograph of another woman, or Sara Willis herself, their expectations of Fern's appearance are at the intersection of gender and public voice.

Willis confesses that such experiences make it impossible for Fern to represent herself truthfully to her correspondents: "You will see . . . how impossible it is, for such a chameleon female, to describe herself" (186). This is not Willis's inability to describe Willis, but Willis's inability to describe Fern, "a chameleon female." Fanny Fern is a public construct. When various readers imagine, describe, or identify her appearance in different ways, such misrepresentations can be recorded, mocked, dismissed, or refuted. But, according to the essay, because of such misrepresentations, there can be no true self-representation because each misrepresentation becomes an aspect of Fern's self. She is "a chameleon female" *because* she is so often misrepresented. Misrepresentations are vital elements of her linguistic self-representation, and thus any one self-representation, any "true" self-representation, is impossible—as impossible as permanently describing a chameleon in any one color.

Throughout her essays, Fern is represented by comparisons, sometimes those made by others, sometimes by Fern herself. In "A Sermon to Plymouth Pulpit," for instance, Fern compares her attitude on a controversial issue (the subject of sweets for children) to the attitude of

> a rampant female at a public meeting the other night, who was scolding her husband for not getting her a better seat. The distressed man laid his hand on her arm, saying, "Hush! here's Fanny Fern; she will hear you." With distended nostrils, that admirable woman replied, "I don't care for six hundred Fanny Ferns!" (*Ginger Snaps* 63)

Here Fern represents herself as another woman, "a rampant female" who scornfully refuses to lower her voice (with all the significance of that act) because of Fern's presence. Again, Fern is represented by comparison. This time, however, the comparison is made by Fern herself, who slyly promotes the woman's implication that there could be six hundred representations of Fern and who happily compares her attitude to that of a woman who, as a matter of her own self-representation (seen in her refusal to "hush"—to present herself differently so that her voice will not be heard) scorns the opinion of one or six hundred Fanny Ferns.

These misrepresentations and substitutions continue throughout the essays, sometimes offered by readers and quoted by Fern, sometimes offered by Fern herself. In "Peeps from Under a Parasol," after describing various news personages of the day, she writes, "And here by the rood, comes FANNY FERN! Fanny is a woman. . . . she might be prettier; she might be younger. She might be older; she might be uglier. She might be better; she might be worse. She has been both over-praised and over-abused" (Warren 272). Again, the passage, playing on various misrepresentations of Fern, insists on redefining and reconfiguring the self as ambiguous.

"A Rainy Day" shows Fern receiving a letter from a reader saying that Fern is actually the wife of the newspaper's editor: "Mrs. Robert Bonner alias Fanny Fern! How will Mrs. Bonner like that and what will be the predominant expression on Mr. Fern's physiognomy?" (*New York Ledger* 20 Feb. 1858), while in "Some Hints to Editors"—an essay about "when editors review a woman's book . . . they so often fall into the error of reviewing the *woman* instead" (*Ginger Snaps* 98)—she writes,

> True, black hair has often been awarded me, instead of light, by these scribblers, "who were on very intimate terms with me," and I have measured six feet in height instead of four and a half; and I have "a stylish carriage and footmen". . . half the things which they have asserted I "waste my earnings upon" would be agreeable to possess. (101–102)

In these essays as in others, Willis repeatedly shows the intersection of voice and gender provoking conjectures about the woman writer's talent (to be this successful, she must be the owner's wife), appearance, and frivolous spending habits. All intend to undercut Fern's abilities (if she is successful, it is because she is married to the right man; if her earnings are high, she must spend them foolishly). Willis defeats these intentions by commenting on the stereotypical ways that readers and reviewers misrepresent the woman essayist. Her frank tone and specific examples reveal the culturally biased misrepresentations while representing the woman essayist in yet another narrative of selfhood.

Even advertising campaigns for Fern's books of essays and novels (*Ruth Hall, Rose Clarke*) capitalized on Fern's multiplicity of representations. Ranney's, a New York bookstore, placed an advertisement titled "Fanny Fern Blown Up But No Bones Broken" in the February 27, 1858, edition of *Harper's Weekly*:

> People start in great amaze,
> From their eyes they wildly gaze,
> Crying as they hurry past,
> "Fanny Fern is gone at last!"
> Keep cool, people—'tis not so—
> Fanny Fern is still the go [sic].
> 'Twas a Fanny Fern afloat,
> Name bestowed upon a boat.
> Read the choicest works of Fanny
> Get a book and gift from Ranney.
> (McGinnis 20)

Such substitutions became common as Fern's fame grew. In a December 10, 1864, essay replying to a reader's criticism of Fern's self-description as "famous," Fern cited the various things that had been named in her honor ("a mud-scow and a hand-cart, a steamboat and a hotel, a perfume and a score of babies, not to mention a tobacco and music") to argue for the legitimacy of that representation (Warren xxxii).[2] The wide-ranging list of Fanny Fern namesakes supports her self-described fame while also underscoring the permutations of signifier and signifieds provoked by the voice of the well-known woman writer.

Just as these representations of selfhood center largely on gender, so does the tone of the essays, which varies from sentimental to political. Willis often uses the popularity of women's sentimental writing to her advantage, as in many of the more sentimental essays in her first collection, *Fern Leaves from Fanny's Portfolio*, perhaps her most well-known book. For instance, "Thanksgiving Story" begins, "'Mary!' said the younger of two little girls, as they nestled under a coarse coverlid, one cold night in December, 'tell me about Thanksgiving-day before papa went to heaven. I'm cold and hungry, and I can't go to sleep'" (*Fern Leaves* 59). "Nestled," "coarse," "papa," "heaven," and two cold, hungry children signal the sentimental essay to come. The implications of the woman writer as not only a mother but a mother forced by harsh economic circumstances to turn to writing to feed her children after her husband's death invokes a female script cherished by nineteenth-century Americans: the domestic, private, delicate woman whose fiercely maternal feelings force her—as nothing else could—to reveal herself publicly. Thus the essay immediately plays on readers' expectations of the proper province and concerns of the woman writer.

The beginning of "Hints to Young Wives," however—"Shouldn't I like to make a bon-fire of all the 'Hints to Young Wives,' 'Married Woman's Friend,' etc., and throw in the authors after them?" (*Olive Branch*, 14 Feb. 1852)—confounds those gender-specific expectations in tone and subject. Moreover, the texts (and authors) Fern wishes to burn are those that promote the very expectations she plays on in her sentimental essays. Susan K. Harris notes that in Willis's novel, *Ruth Hall*, "Fanny Fern alternates between sentimental and acerbic language all in the interest of defending women's right to be economically independent" (57). I would argue further that, in the newspaper essays, Fern moves between the sentimental and acerbic in the interest of defending women's right to be independent in all ways, economic and otherwise, that is, to have a recognizable, even accepted voice that ranges within and beyond gender-specific audience expectations. As Lauren Berlant writes, "By providing a formal structure of identification through the example of her own 'personal journalism,' the expression of Fern's personality becomes the model for that kind of individuated expression she aims to enable the reader to imagine in herself" (445). That this strategy had its success can be seen, for example, in the response of a woman reader from Salem who wrote "that she did not care about Fern's identity: 'I know what you are to *me* . . . a kind, loving sister, with a flashing smile that breaks through the drolleries, making me long to shake hands with you'" (Warren, *Fanny Fern,* 100) and in the "editorial from a Virginia paper" that also rises above questions of gender expectations:

> It makes not one iota of difference whether Fanny Fern is a *he* or a *she*, it cannot be denied that she (we call her *she* in virtue of her *nom de plume*) has written some of the most beautiful fragments and "prose poems" in her piquant off-hand style, to be found in the English language, to say nothing of the dashes of genuine humor which some of them contain. Crusty, crabbed and sour anatomical specimens of editors may say what they please, Fanny Fern is, and will continue a popular writer, for she writes from the *heart*, and it will reach the hearts of those who read. (Warren, *Fanny Fern,* 100–101)

The shift in tone in the essays thus serves the broader interests of expanding readers' definitions of the woman newspaper essayist's voice.

The fictive stories of selfhood and changes in Fern's tone show Willis engaged in self-revision and self-interpretation of the woman essayist's voice. Just as "female autobiographers know that they are being read as *women*" (Miller 262), Willis knows readers wish to read Fern as a woman. Willis's creation of the feminine and yet ironic name Fanny Fern begins her rhetorical acknowledgment of "the fact of her femininity as a social reality" (Miller 263), of newspaper readers' gender expectations of the woman essayist. Subsequent columns continue her play on those expectations by shifts in subject matter and tone. At times, Fern meets her readers' gender expectations fully; at other times, she contradicts them. The changes in subject matter and tone of her columns from sentimental to political to literary and back show Willis suggesting revisions of the voice of the woman essayist to her readers.

Such changes also show Willis engaged in self-interpretation of that voice. Unlike the female autobiographer, the female newspaper essayist may repeatedly interpret and reinterpret the female public voice (the "I"). The weekly publication of the newspaper essay combined with the familiarity of Fern's voice encouraged repeated redefinitions and reconfigurations of the self. Her imagined audience lends Willis the authority to interpret the role of the woman essayist in a patriarchal culture.

III

Using Priscilla's appearance as the Veiled Lady in *The Blithedale Romance*, Richard Brodhead argues that "what the Veiled Lady is most essentially is an image of woman as public performer," one that can reveal the American mid-nineteenth century as a "time of the emergence of some women—specifically women in the entertainment sector—to an exaggeratedly public life" (276). Thus, "the Veiled Lady is a lady, but in being *veiled* she is made into a lady who does not appear in public" (274). Brodhead sees nineteenth-century American women writers such as Sara Payson Willis, Mary Virginia Terhune, and Emily Chubbuck as Veiled Ladies, "their regular use of pseudonyms [as] the literary equivalent of that highly public erasure of oneself in public embodied in the Veiled Lady's veil" (278). Such authors, like the Veiled Lady, can then "perform" publicly, while their pseudonyms cover them, allowing them to appear as a public self and yet remain a concealed private self.

Such veiling was suggested when Mason Brothers, publishers of Fern's first novel *Ruth Hall*, "ran ads that asked, 'IS *RUTH HALL* AUTOBIOGRAPHICAL?'" (Brodhead 286), tempting readers to look behind the veil of the public Ruth Hall to see the private Fanny Fern (and, by implication, the even more private Sara Payson Willis). The very familiarity of Fern's voice to the reading public gave the advertisement its appeal. Readers who were tantalized by the multiplicity of Fern's representations in her newspaper essays were now invited to consider a "true" representation of Fern masked in a fictional, perhaps confessional, account.

The essays of other women writers of the time, such as Rose Terry Cooke, Mary Virginia Terhune (Marion Harland), and Emily Chubbuck, later Emily C. Judson (Fanny Forrester), partake of this same engagement with self-interpretation of the woman essayist's role. At various points in their careers, these women viewed their public essays as separate from their private authorship of those essays. They thus recognized the essay as a genre where a self could be revealed, even confessed to, without that self becoming the one permanent public and private self that the author would then have to inhabit. The sometimes complex intersection of gender and public voice allowed for a public confession of a self without any accompanying private exposure—hence, a public yet private confession. Depending on the writer, this seeming paradox is viewed as an amusing opportunity for parody, an absolute necessity for the private self, or even a shrewd method by which to promote one's career.

Rose Terry Cooke, best known for her short-story contributions to the *Atlantic Monthly*, wrote as Matilda Muffin in "The Memorial of A. B. or Matilda Muffin," an essay that appeared in the February 1860 issue of the *Atlantic*, recording how readers misidentified her:

> Somebody told me she was a lady living on the North River, very wealthy, very haughty, and very unhappy in her domestic relations. Another said she was a young widow in Alabama, whose mother was extremely tyrannical, and opposed her second marriage. A third person declared to me that A.B. was a physician in the navy,—a highly educated man, but reduced in circumstances.

Like Willis, Cooke points to readers' desire to identify women essayists in terms of gender and public voice. The two female substitutes offered are both in unhappy situations, while the male substitute is "reduced in circumstances" (as may well also be the case for the "young widow"). The readers' misidentifications of Matilda Muffin reveal their muddled gender stereotypes (women write for emotional and economic reasons, men for economic reasons alone); more significantly, they reveal their implicit understanding of the woman essayist writing to escape an oppressive or monologic representation of the self and to write as a different self.

Cooke's realization of her readers' assumption that all writers, regardless of pen name, are male is clear as she continues,

I called myself a woman in the very next contribution, for fear of the united wrath of the stronger sex, should I ever be discovered to have so imposed upon the public; although I know several old women who remain undiscovered to this day, simply because they avail themselves of a masculine signature. (188)

The choice of "old" women, "to this day," and "simply" make explicit that the woman essayist can write whatever and however she likes as long as a male "signature" (as opposed to any fuller representation of gender identity) is used. Cooke's tongue-in-cheek creation of Matilda Muffin (a light mockery of the varying degrees of irony and femininity found in pseudonyms of popular women writers such as Fanny Fern, Fanny Forrester, and Grace Greenwood) and the conjectures about Matilda's identity reveal Cooke's rueful recognition of the public yet private confessions of the woman essayist. Cooke points to readers' misrepresentations, then leaves the reader to decode their prejudices, Matilda Muffin, and Cooke's representation of herself as Matilda Muffin; however, she ultimately declines, as does Fanny Fern, to provide any "true" representation.

Mary Virginia Terhune, highly successful nineteenth-century author of "more than twenty-five novels . . . innumerable stories, essays, and sketches that appeared in magazines, journals, and newspapers" (Kelley 17), began her own interpretation of the role of the woman essayist early in her career, writing a series of articles on religion under the name Robert Remer (Kelley 131). When she was nineteen, friends "discovered that Terhune was the author"; she then wrote to a friend,

My surprise was only equalled by my mortification and wounded feeling. . . . I do not expect others to understand the feelings which induce me to keep this secret, but you may perhaps think they are weighty, when I tell you, that I would rather anything else that my bosom guards in silence should have been proclaimed. (Kelley 131)

To the nineteen-year-old Terhune, the role of the woman essayist was private and secret, hidden behind a male signature. When her identity was found out, her "mortification" was the result of her being exposed, that is, of being revealed as a woman revealing herself in public. That she "would rather anything else that my bosom guards in silence should have been proclaimed" suggests the tension between the public voice of the woman essayist—that representation of the self—and the private, "guarded" self. The misrepresentation she offers as Robert Remer is mirrored by the misrepresentation she fears once her private identity as a woman essayist is made public.

Terhune later wrote permanently under the name Marion Harland, though still with marked ambivalence. As Mary Kelley notes,

After forty years as a national best-selling author . . . she replied to a letter inquiring about her use of a pseudonym. "My reason for choosing a 'pen name' at all," explained the sixty-two-year-old woman, "was the desire of a young writer to screen her personality from even her intimate friends."

She continued that she had had "a hazy idea of, in some degree, preserving my identity to myself" (Kelley 132). To wish to "screen her personality" and "preserve her identity" while still writing publicly and successfully shows Terhune over the course of her long career resisting the monolithic representation of the public woman writer. Her "hazy idea" and "in some degree" suggest a partial recognition of the self-representations available to the regularly published woman writer. Thus, Marion Harland could write publicly, prolifically, and passionately for decades and, despite whatever selves were revealed, whatever thoughts confessed, Terhune could still "preserve" her "identity" from her intimates for her most private self.

Fanny Forrester (Emily Chubbuck), initially a writer of "pious Sunday school tales that found a small but dependable market" (Wood 11), began teaching school and writing to support her impoverished family when her father failed to earn a living. When she shrewdly attempted to broaden her audience and market with submissions to the *New York Mirror*, she misrepresented herself and "coyly explained that, although her friend 'Bel' had urged her to pretend poverty to win sympathy, she has decided to tell the 'truth'—she is a charming young thing who simply wants a little cash for a new hat!" (Wood 11). Forrester does provide some truth in her self-representation, but that truth is presented as a lie a "friend" urged her to tell. Her "true" self-representation is itself a false confession. She "confesses" to considering a "lie" (which would have been the truth of Emily Chubbuck's situation) and "confesses" to the "truth"— that is, to a false representation of the self. Playing on "the confession as one of the main rituals we rely on for the production of truth" (Foucault 58), Forrester uses the confession to both mask and unmask herself as a woman essayist.

Across genres, then, in mid-nineteenth-century America, the intersection of gender and public voice resulted in a sharp and sometimes deeply desired division between women's private and public selves. The voices of women newspaper essayists in particular revealed ambiguous body contours under their pseudonymous "veils." Their scheduled, familiar discourse and the fictive stories of selfhood imagined by their readers promoted their use of this schism to explore, develop, and articulate various representations of the self.

IV

In autobiography, "there have always been women who cross the line between public and private utterance, unmasking their desire for the empowering self-interpretation of autobiography as they unmasked in their lives the desire for publicity" (Smith 44). In the nineteenth-century American woman's essay, the writer can cross the line between public and private utterance and use the genre for self-interpretation, but, unlike the autobiographer, the essayist can simultaneously unmask and mask the self—that is, repeatedly represent and revise her voice. Separation between the woman writer's public and private voice was not, as use of the newspaper essay by Willis and others suggests, arbitrary and binary, though nineteenth-century American women writers may have felt it as such in their attempts to find a voice in a repressive patriarchal culture. Rather, there exists a whole spectrum of self-representation occupying the space between public and private voice.

Nineteenth-century readers, reviewers, and writers—men and women—insisted that women's writing uphold certain selective "truths" about women and their place in culture. Emily Chubbuck thus knew that a young daughter teaching and writing to feed her father and siblings was less "true" than Fanny Forrester, "a charming young thing who simply wants a little cash for a new hat!" Earlier in the century, well-known editor Sarah Hale had insisted on "truths" of women's writing,

> caution[ing] aspiring poetesses in her *Lady's Magazine* [that] "the path of poetry like every other path in life, is to the tread of woman, exceedingly circumscribed. She may not revel in the luxuriance of fancies, images, and thoughts, or indulge in the license of choosing themes at will, like the Lords of creation." (Wood 5)

Feminine discourse as seen in the nineteenth-century American woman's newspaper essay thus became a location in which the woman essayist could both reveal herself through her writing and confess, at times, to being the woman her culture thought she should be. Foucault's discussion of the development of the confession and its production of truth leads to the individual being "authenticated by the discourse of truth he was able or obliged to produce concerning himself" (58). The woman essayist produced her confessions, her discourses of truth, to authenticate, transform, and disguise concepts of self and gender. And for her readers, "one woman's disclosure of the frustrations of everyday life ennobles the lives of other women: moreover, the complaint installs woman's writing as a part of an ongoing pedagogy about how to negotiate the contested life of femininity" (Berlant 445).

Though Willis went on to write novels and to have her identity revealed to her reading public, she wrote essays until just before her death. The editorial on her death in the *New York Ledger* reads in part:

Who was Fanny Fern? began to be the question of the day. The secret of her identity was so well guarded that the most inquisitive could not get track of her and the myriad suppositions, guesses, announcements, denials and discussions which were published on the subject greatly enhanced the public interest. (9 Nov. 1872)

Gender and public voice dominate her obituary. The editorial concludes by quoting a letter of hers to Robert Bonner, her editor. Instead of choosing a sample of her voice from her many newspaper essays, her novels, or any of her published, public writings, a letter—a brief, private note dashed off to Bonner—is quoted. The editorial thus ends with Willis's private voice in a letter she has—appropriately—signed with her public name, "Fanny Fern."

Long after Fanny Fern has ceased to be a pseudonym—when Sara Willis (by then Parton) signed personal letters Fanny Fern, sued for and won exclusive rights to the name and thus when the anonymity and androgyny of the genre no longer served her—Parton continued her life- and career-shaping genre choice. It enabled her, as it always had, to write publicly yet privately, to confess to and reveal the self. Willis, after all, grew to know her self through writing Fern's weekly essays. The habit of confessing becomes a necessity for moving on in one's life. Once no longer fully veiled, she continued—as she must have—to reveal. Ultimately, the genre's project is her project, as she used the newspaper essay to reflect and transform concepts of self and gender, feminine discourse, and public voice.

I am grateful to the Bureau for Faculty Research at Western Washington University for a generous summer research grant which enabled me to complete my work on this essay. I would also like to thank Rick Emmerson for his support, and Ning Yu and Bill Lyne for their helpful responses to earlier versions.

NOTES

1. Ironically, Bonner's advertisement of Fern's salary served not only to advertise his newspaper but also to make that information public knowledge and grounds for public conjecture concerning Fern and her earnings.

2. Similar literary appropriations of popular American women writers were not uncommon across genres in the burgeoning capitalist culture of the nineteenth century. Mary Kelley notes that E.D.E.N. Southworth's heroine Capitola from *The Hidden Hand* inspired "Capitola hats, suits, and boots," while the popularity of Augusta Evans Wilson's *St. Elmo* resulted in the title's use for "female academies, a cigar, a Southern punch, steamboats, and thirteen towns stretching from New York to California" (27).

REFERENCES

Barr, Roseanne. *Roseanne: My Life As a Woman*. New York: Harper & Row, 1989.

Benstock, Shari. "Authorizing the Autobiographical" in *The Private Self: Theory and Practice of Women's Autobiographical Writings*, ed. Shari Benstock (Chapel Hill: U of North Carolina P, 1988), 10–33.

Berlant, Lauren. "The Female Woman: Fanny Fern and the Form of Sentiment." *American Literary History*. Fall (1991): 429–454.

Brodhead, Richard H. "Veiled Ladies: Toward a History of Antebellum Entertainment." *American Literary History* Summer (1989): 273–294.

Cooke, Rose Terry. "The Memorial of A.B., or Matilda Muffin." *Atlantic Monthly* Feb. 1860: 186–191.

Dobson, Joanne. "The Hidden Hand: Subversion of Cultural Ideology in Three Mid-Nineteenth-Century American Women's Novels." *American Quarterly* 38 (1986): 223–242.

Editorial. *New York Ledger*. 9 Nov. 1872.

Fern, Fanny. *Fern Leaves from Fanny's Portfolio*. n.p.:Auburn, 1853.

———. *Fresh Leaves*. New York: n.p., 1857.

———. *Ginger Snaps*. New York: n.p., 1870.

———. "A Rainy Day." *Olive Branch*. 14 Feb. 1852.

Foucault, Michel. *The History of Sexuality*. New York: Vintage, 1980.

Harris, Susan K. "'But is it any *good*?': Evaluating Nineteenth-Century American Women's Fiction." *American Literature* 63 (1991): 43–61.

Heilbrun, Carolyn G. *Writing a Woman's Life*. New York: Norton, 1988.

Jehlen, Myra. "Archimedes and the Paradox of Feminist Criticism," *Signs* 6:4 (1981): 575–601.

Kelley, Mary. *Private Woman, Public Stage*. New York: Oxford UP, 1984.

Mason, Mary G. "The Other Voice: Autobiographies of Women Writers." In *Autobiography:Essay Toward Theoretical and Critical*, ed. James Olney. Princeton: Princeton UP, 1980. 207–235.

McGinnis, Patricia I. "Fanny Fern, American Novelist." *Biblion: The University Library Journal: State University of New York at Albany* (1969): 2–37.

Miller, Nancy K. "Women's Autobiography in France: For a Dialectics of Identification." *Women and Language in Literature and Society*. Ed. Sally McConnell-Ginet, Ruth Borker, and Nelly Furman. New York: Praeger, 1980. 262.

Smith, Sidonie. *A Poetics of Women's Autobiography: Marginality and the Fictions of Self-Representation*. Bloomington: Indiana UP, 1987.

Spacks, Patricia Meyer. *Imagining a Self*. Cambridge: Harvard UP, 1976.

———. "Selves in Hiding." In *Women's Autobiography,* ed. Estelle C. Jelinek. Bloomington: Indiana UP, 1980. 112–32.

Warren, Joyce W. *Fanny Fern: An Independent Woman*. New Brunswick: Rutgers UP, 1992.

———., ed. *Ruth Hall and Other Writings*. New Brunswick: Rutgers UP, 1986.

Wood, Ann D. "The 'Scribbling Women' and Fanny Fern: Why Women Wrote." *American Quarterly* XXIII (1971): 4–24.

Excising the Text, Exorcising the Author:

Margaret Fuller's *Summer on the Lakes, in 1843*

Dorothy Z. Baker

Margaret Fuller's *Summer on the Lakes, in 1843* has presented a challenge to the reader and critic since the moment of its publication, such that it is now virtually impossible to introduce a study of the text without acknowledging the objectionable contemporary reviews and the conflicted stances of its many modern critics. The root of the difficulty in approaching *Summer on the Lakes* is primarily generic. As Susan Belasco Smith graciously puts it, "The book has always defied easy classification" (*Summer* vii). Described variously as a Transcendental travelogue, a sketchbook, and a social and political tract, the text has only recently been examined on its own terms.[1] Moreover, serious consideration of *Summer on the Lakes* has been compromised by its unusual publication history, the study of which reveals the remarkably diverse texts that are titled *Summer on the Lakes*.

When Fuller returned from her 1843 voyage to Niagara Falls and the Midwest, she set to work on a book-length manuscript, based in part on her travel journal.[2] The project was completed in the new year, and *Summer on the Lakes* appeared with Little and Brown in May 1844. After three printings in Fuller's lifetime, Arthur Buckminster Fuller, her brother, severely abridged the book for inclusion in a posthumous collection of her works, titled *At Home and Abroad; or, Things and Thoughts in America and Europe*, which he published in 1856. Consequently, when Arthur Fuller edited the six-volume *Collected Works*, appearing first in 1860 and reprinted in 1869, 1874, and 1909, he included his blue-pencilled version. After these publications, Arthur Fuller's truncated edition, rather than the original, became the received text of *Summer on the Lakes*. Mason Wade's 1941 edition of *The Writings of Margaret Fuller* drew from the *Collected Works*, as Wade believed that Arthur Fuller did a "good job of editing in this case" (4).[3] Wade's evaluation is seconded by Joel Myerson, who concludes that "the artistic success of *Summer on the Lakes* was hampered, though, by an unconscionable padding" (5). In short, critical opinion was unanimous: Arthur Fuller rescued the book from failure. The brother's edition supplanted the sister's authorial vision.

Among the early Fuller scholars, only Madeleine Stern takes exception to the abridged edition of *Summer on the Lakes*. In 1972, she published a facsimile edition of the 1844 text—the first reprinting of the original book in more than one hundred years—and commented that "Arthur Fuller's version of *Summer on the Lakes* deleted much of the so-called extraneous material and while it retained the narrative of the journey it stripped from it much of the spirit of the narrator" (xxxiv, v). Recent essays by William W. Stowe and Stephen Adams have drawn attention to the 1844 edition and its narrative strategy and coherence that can be seen only in the full version.[4] Moreover, Susan Belasco Smith's 1992 publication of the 1844 edition has prompted critics to revisit the unabridged text.

While new studies of the original text are needed for a full evaluation of Margaret Fuller's work, it is fruitful to reconsider the abbreviated version to determine not only what was altered but why. This essay will examine the editorial hand of Arthur B. Fuller, his deletions and emendations, and will argue that a careful examination of his editorial decisions will reveal not only an aesthetic but a personal agenda.

In the social climate of the mid-nineteenth century, devoted to notions of the "true woman" and the "angel in the home," Arthur Fuller surely understood that his sister, an exceptional woman in many respects, was unconventional. Edgar Allan Poe once remarked that there were three kinds of human beings—men, women, and Margaret Fuller.[5] In addition, contemporary reviews of her writing often included personal attacks. In the press, she is termed a "heathen priestess" (Brownson 546) and a "he-woman" ("Memoirs of Margaret Fuller" 168). We can infer from this commentary that Margaret Fuller was viewed as somehow aberrant as a woman. Although Arthur Fuller could not ensure that his sister would be remembered as exemplifying the cultural ideal or even the social norm, he could, however, refashion the most autobiographical of her works to represent the author as other than completely deviant, relative to the standards of the nineteenth century. Arthur Fuller modulated his sister's voice, erased the outré, and reshaped the argument of *Summer on the Lakes*. By doing so, he sought to mitigate her questionable reputation; by excising the text, Arthur Fuller might exorcise the author in the eyes of her readership.

By all accounts, Margaret and Arthur Fuller enjoyed the best of family relationships. The sixth of the Fuller children, Arthur was Margaret's much-loved baby brother. In a letter to her father, she refers to Arthur as "my pet."[6] When she was away from home, Margaret wrote frequently to her brother, and in many letters, she assumes a warm, maternal, and professorial tone, exhorting him to proper behavior and study habits. She tempers this tone as Arthur matures, and in late 1840, in recognition of their changing relationship, she closes a letter by writing, "But I will not play Mentor much, lest I make you adverse to write to your very affte (sic) sister Margaret" (II: 196). Brother and sister remained close as adults, and Margaret—during her 1843 trip to the Midwest—helped to secure a teaching position for Arthur in Illinois. His dedication to her manuscripts and publishing projects is ample evidence that he admired her greatly. One can assume that Arthur Fuller simply wished the world to think well of his sister.

However, Orestes Brownson—one of Margaret Fuller's earliest and harshest critics—did not. He railed against *Summer on the Lakes* on many counts, especially in that she fell short of his expectations of a woman author. His criticism of her literary style falls along these lines: "Miss Fuller seems to us to be wholly deficient in a pure, correct taste, and especially in that tidiness we always look for in women" (546). Where Margaret Fuller lacks feminine authorial qualities of purity, correctness, and consistency, in the eyes of Brownson, Arthur Fuller's work exhibits the tidiness we expect from editors. He modernizes spelling and diction: "burthen" is changed to "burden," "shewed" to "showed," and "phizzes" to "faces." He also standardizes the spelling of place names: "Chamouny" becomes "Chamonix," "Boon county" becomes "Boone County," and "Ottowa" becomes "Ottawa." At times, Arthur Fuller strives for assertive, more obviously literary phrasing in the text, rewriting "Do you climb the snowy peaks . . . ?" to read "Climb you the snow peaks . . . ?" (*Summer*, 81; *At Home*, 74), although one could rightly claim that this high-toned phrasing is inconsistent with the tone of the narrative.[7]

The contemporary critical reviews did not focus exclusively on such minutiae, and the subsequent editorial hand of Arthur Fuller was not limited to copyediting. The critics charged that *Summer on the Lakes* was an *omnium gatherum*, and, as such, an incoherent text. Caleb Stetson, for example, objected to the inclusion of

> things connected by no apparent link of association with the objects which seem to fill her eye and mind. . . . Tales also unexpectedly appear which have no connexion with the scenes she visited, except the accidental fact that they occurred in the course of her reading or were called up from the depths of her memory by some mysterious association. (275)

Arthur Fuller would later directly address the issue of coherence in his introduction to and revisions of the text.

Of particular significance to Arthur Fuller was the critics' virulent attack on Margaret Fuller's character. Brownson's review depicts the author as "a heathen priestess, though of what god or goddess we will not pretend to say." Brownson issues an equally harsh evaluation of her personal philosophy and religious convictions: "We detest her doctrines. We know nothing more abominable. . . . We believe no person has appeared among us whose conversation and writings have done more to corrupt the minds and hearts of our Boston community" (546–47). Ralph Waldo Emerson echoed Brownson's statement when he later wrote that "there was something a little pagan about her; . . . that her fancy, or her pride, had played with her religion" (*Memoirs* I: 219). In his role as editor, Arthur Fuller was compelled by and responded to these attacks on both the text and its author.

Arthur Fuller partially concedes to Margaret Fuller's critics in the introduction to the 1856 edition of *At Home and Abroad*, where he discusses his editorial strategy and speaks to the issue of abbreviating the manuscript of *Summer on the Lakes*. Arthur Fuller complains that the 1844 edition contained

> extracts from books which [Margaret Fuller] read in relation to the Indians; an account of and translation from the Seeress of Prevorst, a German work which had not then, but has since, been translated into English, and republished in this country; a few extracts from letters and poems sent her by friends while she was in the West, . . . and the story of Marianna (sic) . . . and also lines to Edith, a short poem. . . . The episodical nature of [*Summer on the Lakes*] enabled the editor to make these omissions without in any way marring its unity. . . . The reader will notice that nothing affecting the unity of the narrative is here wanting, the volume even gaining in that respect by the omission of extracts from other writers, and of a story and short poem not connected in any regard with Western life. (ix-x)

Arthur Fuller's major obstacle as editor of *Summer on the Lakes* is his tacit assumption that the text is centrally and exclusively concerned with "Western life." Consequently, his role centers on maintaining strict unity of theme within the framework of the western travel account. He appears to be unaware of the larger interests of the text, that concerns for nature and the development of wilderness are related to the role of women in society, the treatment of Native Americans, and the general leadership of the nation. And, if aware of these major thematic elements, he wished to censor these issues as either wrongheaded notions or inappropriate public concerns for a female author.

Although anecdotes and observations of Native Americans would normally be considered germane to a western travelogue, many are omitted in the revision. Most obvious is a twenty-page lacuna in the abridged version that accounts for much of Margaret Fuller's commentary on the Native American.[8] This section offers the reader a compendium of information about Indian culture, including its myths, religious rites, rituals of fasting, purification, and prayer. Margaret Fuller includes details about Indian languages and numerous stories that give insight into their hospitality, social etiquette, and business ethics. Throughout these twenty pages are accounts of exemplary men and women, tales of courage and heroism, and information about prominent chiefs. The author adds credence to her narrative with statements from white men who had been adopted by the Indians or had lengthy, felicitous sojourns with them and recognized "the tie of brotherhood" with them (124). Yet, this material is deleted in Arthur Fuller's edition. Likewise, the editor omits stories of unscrupulous traders and cruel white men who view their barbarity "as a joke" (131). He also blue-pencils many of the author's passages that implicate the American settlers in the Native Americans' pervasive and chronic alcohol abuse. Nonetheless, in other sections of *Summer on the Lakes*, Arthur Fuller chooses to retain descriptions of Indian squalor, poor hygiene, and drunkenness, as well as commentary about their begging and their dependence on governmental assistance, including one missionary's assertion that "even those Indians who had been converted, and who had adopted the habits of civilizations . . . were as selfish, as deceitful, and as indolent, as those who were still heathens . . . and are, in fact, but little superior to brutes" (120). In short, Arthur Fuller deleted most accounts of Native American morality and civility and settlers' immorality and hostility, while he retained many accounts of Native Americans as savages and European Americans as victims and frustrated citizens.

In her extensive treatment of Native Americans in *Summer on the Lakes*, Margaret Fuller works toward a balanced account of relations between the whites and the Indians, neither canonizing nor villainizing. She is sympathetic to both and sees flaws in both. Yet, balanced presentation was not her brother's priority. One can only conclude from Arthur Fuller's editorial decisions that "to give the ages a glimpse of what was great in Indian life and Indian character" would detract from the reader's evaluation of the text and its author (142). He perhaps worried that the settlers' violence toward Native Americans is inappropriate or unseemly subject matter for a genteel female author. And he was undoubtedly concerned that recognizing Indian spirituality would somehow demean Christian religiosity in the eyes of nineteenth-century Americans.

Because of his single-minded view of *Summer on the Lakes* as a monologic travel narrative, Arthur Fuller misunderstood many passages as superfluous to the central goals of the book. In a sketch written in Milwaukee, for example, Margaret Fuller comments on the wild roses in the oak thickets. They are red and lush, evocative of the first red roses, white blooms stained with the blood of Venus. This allusion brings Margaret Fuller to a description and explication of Titian's "Venus and Adonis," an apparent digression for which the author apologizes: "I will insert here, though with no excuse, except that it came to memory at the time, this description of Titian's Venus and Adonis" (69). Margaret Fuller's apology would appear to offer Arthur Fuller an invitation to delete this brief passage, were her words of apology meant to be understood literally. If Margaret Fuller were truly of the opinion that this piece were a mere digression, she would have omitted it herself. Instead, she includes the passage with disarming, prefatory remarks that invite the reader to ask why it "came to memory at the time." This answer is not in the art itself but in the author's personal reaction to the painting, that of indignation. The portrait of Venus clinging to Adonis leads the author to puzzle why "women always try to detain and restrain what they love" (70). Arguing that women's posture of obsessive, controlling love is enfeebling for both men and women, she offers the following advice for women in the nineteenth century: "Be less lovely— less feminine" (70). Arthur Fuller chose to omit the entire passage, perhaps owing to concerns that this counsel was, to his mind, overstated or contrary to the interests of men in the nineteenth century. However, he ignores evidence that this passage continues her discussion of women settlers and of the tale of Mariana, which immediately precedes this meditation; it also anticipates the Seeress of Prevorst and the folk tale of Muckwa. The contemplation of Venus and Adonis furthers the central argument of the text, which Stephen Adams has identified as an "expression of disappointment in the relationships be-tween men and women" (261). However, as Arthur Fuller deletes three of these four segments of *Summer on the Lakes* (the tales of Mariana, the Seherin von Prevorst, and Muckwa and the She-Bear), consistency might compel the editor to delete the commentary on Venus and Adonis as well.

One might also argue that Arthur Fuller had exceptional reservations about Margaret Fuller's description of Titian's painting in that she finds that "Adonis is not beautiful," yet "Venus herself is very beautiful; especially the body is lovely as can be" (69). Her celebration of the physical beauty of the woman while dismissing that of the man might, in Arthur Fuller's view, mark his sister as sexually aberrant and lend credence to Emerson's portrait of Mar-garet Fuller as a "burly masculine" sort who "put[s] upon" other women (*Mem-oirs* I:280).[9] Emerson further documents his suspicions about Margaret Fuller's sexuality with personal information about her female relationships. In *Mem-oirs*, he recalls that "her friendships, as a girl with girls, as a woman with women, were not unmingled with passion, and had passages of romantic sacri-fice and of ecstatic fusion, which I have heard with the ear, but could not trust my profane pen to report" (I: 281–82). After this characterization of Margaret Fuller in an 1852 publication, Arthur Fuller might have viewed his role in the 1856 text, *At Home and Abroad,* as an opportunity to counter the public por-trayal of his sister. Therefore, to delete this passage of *Summer on the Lakes* would not only tighten the text, in his view, but would also suppress a presen-tation of the author as independent, irreligious, and homosexual, which, in the eyes of nineteenth-century America, constitute a triad of sins against "true womanhood."

Recent studies of *Summer on the Lakes* lament the omission of the lengthy tales of Mariana and Die Seherin von Prevorst in the 1856 text and expose the importance of these narratives in the 1844 publication. Indeed, Stephen Adams demonstrates convincingly that the wider themes of "disjunction and disappointment," of squandered natural resources and wasted human potential are the central argument of the text but only in a full presentation that includes the tales of these gifted and ill-used women (252). Yet, these tales also offer an exposé of marriages that are destructive to women and suggest female superiority in the case of Die Seherin and homosociality in the case of Mariana. As such, Arthur Fuller would have understood these narratives, like the discussion of Venus and Adonis, as damaging to the feminine ethos of his sister.

By citing contemporary reviews of *Summer on the Lakes,* we can partially account for Arthur Fuller's desire to omit the tale of Mariana and other narrative and meditative passages from his 1854 edition. Arthur Fuller was undoubtedly responding to charges that the text was not fully coherent. Given the uniform evaluation of contemporary critics, it would be understandable that Fuller would focus on streamlining the text. However, were this his sole motivation, how do we then account for his retaining certain passages that—under this very criterion—might have also been deleted?

In the second chapter of *Summer on the Lakes*, Margaret Fuller narrates a tale that only immediately relates to the "plot" of the text in that the tale is set in Detroit and is currently being retold in a boat coming from Detroit.[10] The anecdote itself is thrice removed from the teller. A fellow passenger, identified only as "Mrs. L.," tells Margaret a story that was told to her by her parents, this tale containing yet another story told by another unnamed woman. The tale of Captain P. and his wife, Fanny, is not a commentary on boat travel in Michigan but a statement on marriage. The main character, Captain P., is presented as a man of "distinction and popular esteem which his wide knowledge, talents, and noble temper commanded" (13). A tale within the tale, which Margaret receives fourth-hand, reveals that a youthful indiscretion forced Captain P. into marriage with a woman "whose coarse and imperious expression showed as low habits of mind as her exaggerated dress and gesture did of education" (13–14). Married life with Fanny was a source of misery and embarrassment for the captain, but it also gave witness to his masculine virtue. As a young man, he accepted full responsibilities for his actions, and, as a husband, he would not abandon the marriage vow.

Interesting as the story may be, it is curious that Arthur Fuller did not consider this anecdote expendable. Similar to the others he deleted, it appears on first reading to be a digression from the travelogue. However, Arthur Fuller might have seen some value in the moral of this story, illustrated by the depiction of the disparate female characters. In the example offered by this tale, the poor, uneducated young woman who forsakes virtue to ensnare a rich man will never find happiness in her marriage. Instead, the young wife becomes a coarse, vituperous drunkard. In contrast, "soft and retiring" women, such as Mrs. L.'s mother, are shocked insensible when confronting Fanny, a perverse image of femininity: "Confounded, feeling scenes and ideas presented to her mind equally new and painful, [she] sat trembling; she knew not what to do, tears rushed into her eyes." Mrs. L.'s mother is rescued by her husband, who "led his wife to her own room" (14). The reader is asked to sympathize with the mother and to dismiss Fanny. Thus, this moralistic tale derides one woman's aberrant behavior while it celebrates another woman's innocence and gentility, serving as a testimony to "true womanhood." Furthermore, whereas Mrs. L.'s story speculates on the motivations and frame of mind of Captain P., the reader is never invited to consider why Fanny "fell into the habit of drinking" after "a few years" of marriage (17). The psychology of the gentleman being complex and worthy of investigation, Fanny's emotional life is banal, self-evident, and abhorrent.

In the context of the mid-nineteenth-century's passion for reform, the story of Captain P. also reverses the classic character roles of the temperance tale. Women, too, can be compromised by demon rum, forcing men to be their innocent victims. Moreover, in the context of the full text of *Summer on the Lakes*, the story of Fanny P. finds a parallel in the tales of the Native Americans, whom Fuller repeatedly describes as "now accustomed to drunkenness and every way degraded" (113). Margaret Fuller, like many nineteenth-century women authors—Child, Sedgwick, and Stowe among them—links issues of race and gender within *Summer on the Lakes* to assert that any people whose value and significance are unrecognized often react in kind, by devaluing themselves with self-abuse and self-destruction. However, because Arthur Fuller omitted many of the author's tales of systematic, social degradation of the Native Americans, this argument is blurred in later editions.

It appears likely, then, that although Arthur Fuller was interested in creating a tighter volume, he was also compelled by the critics' personal criticism of his sister as "pagan." To delete the tale of Captain P. would be to sacrifice evidence to the contrary. In remarks prefatory to the tale, Margaret Fuller avers that she "dwell[ed]" on the story and that its "moral beauty touched me profoundly" (13). The anecdote of Captain P., although no more germane to a travelogue than the story of Mariana, remained essential to the text in the eyes of Arthur Fuller because it represents his sister as a champion of conventional social values.

The same argument can be made for Arthur Fuller's retaining the dialogue of Free Hope, Old Church, Good Sense, and Self-Poise. In the 1844 version, this passage serves as an introduction to Margaret Fuller's precis of Justinus Kerner's *Die Seherin von Prevorst*. Because Kerner's book addresses women's physical, emotional, and spiritual health, Fuller's prefatory remarks offer her "own mental position on these subjects" (78). Arthur Fuller chose to omit the account of *Die Seherin* from his version, so one might question why he would retain the prefatory remarks. Yet, Margaret Fuller, who asks the voice of Free Hope to represent her views, emerges as the voice of reason in the dialogue. She acknowledges the wisdom of all parties, rejects their parochial perspectives, but honors each contribution. As such, the person of Margaret Fuller appears sensible, sensitive, and, perhaps most importantly, pious throughout. If Arthur Fuller sought a religious ethos to amend public opinion of his sister as "heathen priestess," this spiritual dialogue would serve that end.

In general, Arthur Fuller chose not to trim his sister's text of passages that extol virtue when virtue is attributed to men. As editor, he retained a lengthy portrayal of Morris Birkbeck, identified as an Illinois settler, visionary, author, philanthropist, businessman, and public servant. Margaret Fuller laments that Birkbeck's reputation was sullied for unsubstantial reasons but is convinced that a newer, wiser generation will appreciate his greatness. Likewise, Arthur Fuller does not delete a lengthy description of the Flemish dramatic hero Philip Van Artevelde, whom Margaret Fuller depicts as "a man religious, virtuous and sagacious" (64). Omitted, however, is the original opening paragraph explaining that the author's motivation for including this material is its importance for the story of Mariana. Margaret Fuller sees Van Artevelde as that man who would be "of sufficiently great soul" to recognize the gifts of an uncommon woman (64). Thus, her primary interest in this figure is as a helpmate to women. A second, subordinate paragraph extols his public virtue, but this second paragraph is the sole presentation of Arthur Fuller's Van Artevelde. This issue aside, in the 1844 edition, the brief sketches of Birkbeck and Van Artevelde are parallel to the jettisoned tale of Mariana, a woman with the potential for greatness, who, as the men, is limited by public misunderstanding. Likewise, the tale of Birkbeck's honorable death is similar to a deleted account of an Indian woman who also allows herself to die in place of her son (141). In the abridged edition, the symmetry is lost. The reader sees only the laudable countrymen. The great countrywomen have been excised.[11]

Margaret Fuller's goals for *Summer on the Lakes* and Arthur Fuller's expectations of his edited text are radically different. The original version of the collection situates itself squarely in the public domain; the text's political statement is direct and challenging. As Chevigny puts it, "although Fuller never used the word, ideology was a recurrent preoccupation in her travels" ("To the Edges" 185). Margaret Fuller's work on this collection was bracketed by her writing "The Great Lawsuit: Man *versus* Men; Woman *versus* Women" in 1843 and *Woman in the Nineteenth Century* in 1844, both public, political texts. *Summer on the Lakes* is likewise motivated. The chronology of Arthur Fuller's posthumous editions is equally significant. Arthur Fuller's work on *Summer on the Lakes* immediately followed the 1852 publication of *Memoirs* that challenged his sister's piety, sexuality, and social demeanor. The reminiscences of her friends—especially those of Emerson—were, in the eyes of nineteenth-century America, public attacks on her character. Such remarks were consonant with earlier attacks on *Summer on the Lakes* made by her most critical reviewers, Brownson among them. One could then view Arthur Fuller's commitment to editing and republishing his sister's writings as his response to the challenges addressed to her both during and after her life.

Arthur Fuller's republication of *Summer on the Lakes* was not his first attempt to alter the legacy of Margaret Fuller. His earliest editorial project was the 1855 publication of *Woman in the Nineteenth Century*, his lengthy preface to this edition forthrightly announcing his effort to recast the authorial persona of his sister. The introduction distances the author from any feminist or suffrage "clique or sect" (6) then hammers out his vision of Margaret Fuller as nothing short of a "true woman." Arthur Fuller admits that

> it is often supposed that literary women, and those who are active and earnest in promoting great intellectual, philanthropic, or religious movements, must of necessity neglect the domestic concerns of life. It may be that this is sometimes so, nor can such neglect be too severely reprehended; yet this is by no means a necessary result. (6)

Fuller portrays his sister as a counterexample to the stereotypical bluestocking and, in subsequent pages of the introduction, rehearses "a tribute to her domestic virtues and fidelity to all home duties" (7). Testifying at great length to her religious devotion, he offers the evidence of her Bible, "which she so diligently and thoughtfully read, and which bears, in her own handwriting, so many proofs of discriminating and prayerful perusal" (9). Arthur Fuller argues that his authority on the author issues from his knowledge of Margaret Fuller "at *home*, where best the *heart* and *soul* can be known,—in the unrestrained hours of domestic life" (8). This introduction, written in May 1855, announces his plans to publish in the near future a volume containing *Letters from Europe* and *Summer on the Lakes*. This proposed project would become *At Home and Abroad*, published the following year.

The brother's campaign on behalf of the sister did not end with the publication of *At Home and Abroad*. Arthur Fuller edited yet another collection of his sister's writings in 1860, this time a collection of essays, reviews, and poems, which he titled *Life Without and Life Within*. His introduction to this book again reveals his desire to mitigate his sister's reputation as an outspoken public figure and to establish Margaret Fuller as a private, religious, and domestic woman. He insists that the world has long recognized his sister's intellectual and literary gifts, the life without. Yet, he wishes the world to appreciate "the richness and the beauty of her inner life" (6).

The ironies of Arthur Fuller's editorial role in *Summer on the Lakes* appear to be threefold. First, of course, is his desire to edit radically a previously published book. Although he was not a man of letters, Arthur Fuller undoubtedly acted on patriarchal conviction that Margaret Fuller's writings needed to be "fixed" and that he knew better than she how to present her ideas and herself to her public. Second, when Arthur Fuller abbreviated *Summer on the Lakes* to adhere to the conventions of travel literature in the nineteenth century, he was responding to standards of unity that did not exist for this popular genre. Any generic lines drawn between the travelogue, the essay, and fiction had been previously blurred by Irving's 1820 *Sketchbook*, which is replete with seemingly ancillary tales. So, too, are Catharine Sedgwick's *Letters from Abroad to Kindred at Home* (1841) and Lydia Sigourney's *Scenes in My Native Land* (1844), among many others.[12] On the contrary, Margaret Fuller's work became the model for the literary travelogue, most notably Henry David Thoreau's *A Week on the Concord and Merrimack Rivers* (1849). Finally, in editing *Summer on the Lakes*, Arthur Fuller worked at cross-purposes. His revisions and his prefatory remarks indicate that he strived to eliminate the wandering and seemingly capricious tenor of the text. The abbreviated edition is more direct and spare, as a classical, male-authored text might be. Margaret Fuller describes her method of composition as stringing "all these beads that take my fancy" (148), and she closes her work with a self-reflexive poem depicting the art of writing as analogous to preserving the flavor and sweetness of fruit in jam (156). The edited text, however, defies Margaret Fuller's distinctly feminine metaphors for her narrative construction as stringing beads or making preserves and destroys the conversational tone of the text. The editor leached the narrative of these feminine traits and installed masculine unity and order in their place. At the same time, in a contrary impulse, Arthur Fuller sought to present the author as a "true woman"—or at least as a "truer" woman than her reputation would have her. Thus, while he reworked her narrative form as masculine, that is, direct and lean, not fleshy, rounded, and circular, his competing and contradictory editorial goal was to present the author as "truly feminine," soft and pious, gentle and genteel.

Arthur Fuller's republication of *Summer on the Lakes, in 1843* was not the only instance of well-meaning, albeit biased, editors attempting to alter the persona of Margaret Fuller by altering her manuscripts. Chevigny discovered that the two-volume *Memoirs of Margaret Fuller Ossoli* was posthumously revised before first publication:

> In what they construed as Fuller's interest, the editors, Emerson, James Freeman Clarke, and William Henry Channing, freely suppressed and altered her papers, literally cutting them, blue-penciling "private" passages, splicing together disconnected materials, and substituting their language for hers. ("To the Edges" 194)[13]

Yet the editors nowhere acknowledge their significant and substantial emendation of Fuller's work.[14]

The aggressive stance of Margaret Fuller's editors is not an anomaly in the literary history of nineteenth-century women authors. Women writers of fiction and nonfiction alike often found that their editors demanded radical revision of their work in advance of any publication agreement. Moreover, writing and revising according to specific editorial guidelines that put forth the author's assent to the norms of "true womanhood" were regular requirements of publication for the nineteenth-century woman. One of the earliest female serialists, Judith Sargent Murray, broke her relationship with the *Massachusetts Magazine* in 1795 when the editors attempted to censor her Universalist views as unpopular with their Calvinist readers (Granger 171). As Constantia of *The Gleaner*, Murray admits in remarks prefatory to her work that she is more interested in writing comic sketches than didactic morality essays but will combine both because she is "solicitous to obtain an establishment in the bosom of virtue," that is, to develop a pleasing ethos that will result in commercial success (13-14).[15] Whereas Mary Abigail Dodge complained publicly in her 1870 publication, *A Battle of the Books*, of financial disputes with editor James T. Fields, she spoke privately of authorial woes, specifically her difficulty in preserving her works as she had written them. In a letter to James Redpath of the *North American Review*, she writes:

> I wonder if in the Heaven to which I hope my way leads, I shall have to argue and beg for leave to speak as I do in this world. I not only, you see, have to write my articles to suit myself but I have to reason and wrestle with the Editor to force him into the belief that it suits him![16]

Fiction writers, too, found their work shaped by their editors' vision of feminine authorship. They could not rely on the guise of fiction—as opposed to the more direct ethical appeal of the essayist—to ensure a more liberal reception of their literary work and their literary personae. Louisa May Alcott authored many anonymous and pseudonymous mystery stories and surely had several reasons for distancing herself from these works; one reason was undoubtedly to escape the disapprobation that a female author would incur for writing indelicate material. Madeleine B. Stern has chronicled Alcott's multiple revisions of *A Modern Mephistopheles*, which was originally rejected by her editor for being "too sensational." Her final version deletes several scenes: Rosamond is offered as stakes in a card game; the heroine is married in a sham wedding ceremony then acts as a married woman; Rosamond finds a corpse and is committed to a madhouse. Without determining whether Alcott's revisions resulted in a stronger novel, it is clear she was sensitive that what the editor understood as "sensational" is actually outré and unspeakable on the part of a conventional woman. *A Modern Mephistopheles* eventually appeared in the No Name Series of Boston publishing company Roberts Brothers. The publication was anonymous, lucrative, and would not taint the author's self-described reputation as purveyor of "moral pap for the young" (296). Because the original manuscript is extant, we are able to trace the author's work before it was "censored" by society and the constraints of its marketplace. Once again, this is not an isolated event in an author's career. Ruth K. MacDonald has detailed the revision process of Alcott's *Moods*, in which the author conforms to contemporary standards of realism and works toward a more conventional resolution of the plot.

Jean Fagan Yellin discovered that Rebecca Harding Davis's 1862 novel, *Margret Howth*, was radically edited according to explicit direction from Davis's editor. In 1861, the author submitted to the *Atlantic Monthly* a manuscript titled "The Deaf and the Dumb," which James T. Fields accepted with the proviso of specific and substantive revision of the piece he described as "gloomy." It appeared the following year in serialized form as *Margret Howth— A Story of Today* with a more socially acceptable and physically attractive heroine and a new ninety-page conclusion that was more optimistic. In Yellin's words, "*Margret Howth* presents an important instance in which the leading member of the white male literary establishment required that a nineteenth-century woman writer 'feminize' her text" (297).

The publication history of Fuller's *Summer on the Lakes*, Alcott's *A Modern Mephistopheles* and *Moods*, Davis's *Margret Howth*, as well as the testimony of Murray and Dodge issue a disturbing statement about the relationship between the nineteenth-century woman and her editor. One can assume that— with further bibliographic and textual research on women authors in this period—the list of authors and titles would be ever the longer. More than interesting bibliographic information, such case studies challenge the confidence with which the twentieth-century reader can approach a female-authored nineteenth-century text. Without a thorough study of a given text and its revisions— if they are indeed extant—how can the reader be secure that s/he is gaining an understanding of the author as she sought to present herself and her work? One must question further if the twentieth-century scholar has inherited a needlessly filtered vision of nineteenth-century women—"true" or otherwise—as well as the texts they authored.

NOTES

1. In addition to Smith's introduction to the 1991 edition of the text, see Stephen Adams, "'That Tidiness We Always Look For In Woman.'" William W. Stowe's essay, "Conventions and Voices in Margaret Fuller's Travel Writing" is an important addition to Fuller scholarship on *Summer on the Lakes*.

2. For a thorough discussion of the transformation of the travel diary into the published book, see Nicole Tonkovich, "Traveling in the West, Writing in the Library."

3. In his introduction, however, Wade complains that Emerson, Channing, and Clarke,

who edited the *Memoirs of Margaret Fuller*, "took unpardonable liberties with the material before them" in that they "bowdleriz[ed]" Margaret Fuller's manuscripts (vi). Wade also admits that Arthur Fuller "took similar liberties when transcribing his sister's works and letters . . . as the *Works of Sarah Margaret Fuller Ossoli*," but he apparently believed that Arthur Fuller's work on *Summer on the Lakes* was a singular exception to his otherwise poor editorial performance (vi).

4. Jeffrey Steele's astute preface to *The Essential Margaret Fuller* concentrates on this very point in its introduction of *Summer on the Lakes*. Annette Kolodny, too, has observed that material once seen as peripheral to the travelogue is in fact integral to the text (*The Land Before Her* 125). This view is reiterated by Susan Belasco Smith in "*Summer on the Lakes*: Margaret Fuller and the British," 194.

5. Cited by Perry Miller, 192.

6. Letter of 21 May 1842 (1: 138). See her letters in 1 (5 July 1837):289–90; 1 (31 Dec. 1837): 319–20; and 1 (19 Feb. 1838): 325–26.

7. Unless otherwise indicated, all references to the 1844 text of *Summer on the Lakes, in 1843* are from the 1992 Belasco Smith edition and will be cited parenthetically.

8. Beginning with the final two paragraphs on 123, Arthur Fuller deleted 124–43 with the following exceptions: paragraph 3 of 128, the final two paragraphs of 135 that continue on 136, and the first and final three paragraphs of 143.

9. Mary E. Wood outlines the biographical and textual information that is construed as homosocial or homosexual in nineteenth-century society in "'With Ready Eye': Margaret Fuller and Lesbianism in Nineteenth-Century American Literature." In this important essay, Wood focuses on Margaret Fuller's *Woman in the Nineteenth Century* as homoerotic narrative in a literary tradition that constructs the essay as masculine discourse.

10. Indeed this tale opens much like the story of Mariana, which begins with a cursory account of Fuller's unexpected meeting with a former schoolmate's aunt at dinner, after which she solicits news of yet another schoolmate, Mariana.

11. This argument may also explain why Arthur Fuller retained the poem, "Ganymede to His Eagle, Suggested by a Work of Thorwaldsen's," which speaks to a young boy's meditation on and preparation for "the highest ministry" to the gods.

12. In fairness, many popular nineteenth-century travel narratives written by prominent authors also relied on a more structured framework, that of the day-by-day, site-by-site account that, of course, produces a more obviously unified text. These include, for example, Nathaniel P. Willis's *Pencillings by the Way* (1853), Harriet Beecher Stowe's *Sunny Memories of Foreign Lands* (1854), and Julia Ward Howe's *From the Oak to the Olive* (1868). The contemporary readership accepted diverse narrative approaches to the travelogue. See William W. Stowe's investigation of this subgenre (242–50).

13. See also Chevigny's earlier study of *Memoirs*, "The Long Arm of Censorship: Mythmaking in Margaret Fuller's Time and Our Own." Marie Urbanski corroborates Chevigny's finding, claiming that Emerson, Clarke, and Channing "not only destroyed and defaced original manuscripts but also rewrote Fuller's work, changing her writing style" (5).

14. Among the heavily edited materials in *Memoirs* is the tale of Mariana, which the editors identify in a footnote as material original to *Summer on the Lakes* (I, 42). Most radically foreshortened is the following passage from the 1844 edition, in which the boldface material is deleted in *Memoirs*:

> It was at this time that I came to school, and first saw Mariana. Me she charmed at once, for I was a sentimental child, who, in my early ill health, has been indulged in reading novels, till I had no eyes for the common greens and browns of life. The heroine of one of these, "The Bandit's Bride," I immediately saw in Mariana. Surely the Bandit's Bride had just such hair, and such strange, lively

ways, and such a sudden flash of the eye. The Bandit's Bride, too, was born to be "misunderstood" by all but her lover. But Mariana, I was determined, should be more fortunate, for, until her lover appeared, I myself would be the wise and delicate being who could understand her.

It was not, however, easy to approach her for this purpose. (55)

Until the appearance of this passage, the editors of *Memoirs* leave Fuller's work intact. Yet the intensity of Fuller's attachment to Mariana and her frank desire to fill the place of a male lover gave them sufficient reason to blue-pencil much of this language. Furthermore, the editors conclude the narrative prematurely with Mariana's withdrawal from school, and the reader is left with a simple, moralistic story of a girl who learns not to make a display of herself in public. The original narrative has other goals. Omitted from *Memoirs* is the account of Mariana's unhappy marriage to a merchant who has neither the intellectual nor emotional power to complement her. Furthermore, the editors of *Memoirs* excise Fuller's commentary on Mariana and her larger views of exceptional women whose talents and needs cannot be limited to "the appointed lot of woman" (64). The editors sacrifice adult narrative and social commentary to offer the reader mere boarding school reminiscence.

15. In her introduction to the 1992 edition of *The Gleaner*, Nina Baym explains that Murray's use of a male pseudonym was to ensure that her work would be received "without the typical bias against women writers" (xi).

16. Qtd. in Coultrap-McQuin 132. In an 1877 letter to H. L. Ensign, managing editor of *Alliance*, she addresses this issue directly: "I always lay out my work by reducing my editors to subjection. It is impossible to accomplish anything so long as an editor is liable to pop up at the critical moment with a will of his own; when he is properly subjected the rest is easy!"

REFERENCES

Adams, Stephen. "'That Tidiness We Always Look For in Woman': Fuller's *Summer on the Lakes* and Romantic Aesthetics." *Studies in the American Renaissance*. Ed. Joel Myerson. Charlottesville: UP of Virginia, 1987. 247–64.

Alcott, Louisa May. *Louisa May Alcott: Her Life, Letters, and Journals*. Ed. Ednah D. Cheney. Boston: Roberts Brothers, 1889.

Brownson, Orestes. "Review of *Summer on the Lakes*. By Margaret Fuller." *Brownson's Quarterly Review* 6 (1844): 546–47.

Chevigny, Bell Gale. "The Long Arm of Censorship: Myth-making in Margaret Fuller's Time and Our Own." *Signs: Journal of Women in Culture and Society* 2.2 (1976): 450–60.

———. "To the Edges of Ideology: Margaret Fuller's Centrifugal Evolution." *American Quarterly* 38.2 (1986): 173–201.

Coultrap-McQuin, Susan. *Doing Literary Business: American Women Writers in the Nineteenth Century*. Chapel Hill: U of North Carolina P, 1990.

Fuller, Margaret. *At Home and Abroad; or, Things and Thoughts in America and Europe*. Ed. Arthur B. Fuller. Boston: Crosby, Nichols, 1856.

———. *The Collected Works*. Ed. Arthur B. Fuller. Boston: Taggard, 1860.

———. *The Essential Margaret Fuller*. Ed. Jeffrey Steele. New Brunswick: Rutgers UP, 1992.

———. *The Letters of Margaret Fuller*. Ed. Robert N. Hudspeth. 4 vols. Ithaca: Cornell UP, 1983.

———. *Life Without and Life Within; or, Reviews, Narratives, Essays, and Poems*. Ed. Arthur B. Fuller. Boston: Brown, 1860. Rpt. Upper Saddle River, NJ: Literature House, 1970.

———. *Margaret Fuller: American Romantic*. Ed. Perry Miller. Ithaca: Cornell UP, 1963.

——. *Memoirs of Margaret Fuller Ossoli*. 2 vols. Boston: Phillips, 1852.

——. *Summer on the Lakes in 1843*. 1844. Intro. Madeleine B. Stern. Nieuwkoop: De Graaf, 1972.

——. *Summer on the Lakes, in 1843*. 1844. Intro. Susan Belasco Smith. Urbana and Chicago: U of Illinois P, 1991.

——. *The Writings of Margaret Fuller*. Ed. Mason Wade. New York: Viking, 1941.

Granger, Bruce. *American Essay Serials From Franklin to Irving*. Knoxville: U of Tennessee P, 1978.

Kolodny, Annette. *The Land Before Her: Fantasy and Experience of the American Frontiers, 1630–1860*. Chapel Hill: U of North Carolina P, 1984.

MacDonald, Ruth K. "*Moods*, Gothic and Domestic." *Critical Essays on Louisa May Alcott*. Ed. Madeleine B. Stern. Boston: Hall, 1984. 74–78.

"Memoirs of Margaret Fuller." *New Quarterly Review* 1 (1952): 168–70.

Murray, Judith Sargent. *The Gleaner*. 1798. Intro. Nina Baym. Schenectady: Union College P, 1992.

Myerson, Joel. *Margaret Fuller: An Exhibition From the Collection of Joel Myerson*. Department of English, University of South Carolina Bibliographical Series No. 8. Columbia: U of South Carolina P, 1973.

Smith, Susan Belasco. "*Summer on the Lakes*: Margaret Fuller and the British." *Resources For American Literary Study* 17.2 (1991): 191–207.

Stern, Madeleine B. Introduction. *A Modern Mephistopheles and Taming a Tartar*. By Louisa May Alcott. New York: Praeger, 1987. vii–xxi.

——. *The Life of Margaret Fuller*. Contributions in Women's Studies, No. 123. 2nd ed. Westport, CT: Greenwood, 1991.

Stetson, Caleb. "Notice of Recent Publications." *Christian Examiner* 37 (December 1844): 275.

Stowe, William W. "Conventions and Voices in Margaret Fuller's Travel Writing." *American Literature* 63.2 (June 1991): 242–62.

Tonkovich, Nicole. "Traveling in the West, Writing in the Library: Margaret Fuller's *Summer on the Lakes*." *Legacy: A Journal of American Women Writers* 10.2 (1993): 79–102.

Urbanski, Marie. *Margaret Fuller's "Woman in the Nineteenth Century": A Literary Study of Form and Content, of Sources and Influence*. Westport, CT: Greenwood, 1980.

Wood, Mary E. "'With Ready Eye': Margaret Fuller and Lesbianism in Nineteenth-Century American Literature." *American Literature* 65.1 (March 1993): 1–18.

Yellin, Jean Fagan. Afterword. *Margret Howth*. By Rebecca Harding Davis. New York: Feminist, 1990.

Literary Cross-Dressing in Old New York:
Ann Sophia Stephens as Jonathan Slick
Beatrice Jacobson

There were five or six cages full of little yaller birds a hanging among the bushes and right back of the tree stuck over with oranges, stood a marble woman a holding up a bunch of grapes cut out of marble, with a lot of green leaves twisted round it as nateral as could be. It was awful harnsome, but I swan if it didn't make me feel streaked to look at her a standing there among the bushes, for she hadn't the least rag of kivering on, and it raly was enough to make a feller blush to see her a holding the grapes over head, as if she wanted to make people look at her.

Think sez I, is this the swarry that Cousin Beebe has bought to show his company: I reckon he'd better have bought a calico frock or something of that sort to kiver over it.

Jonathan Slick

Of course, Jonathan Slick's inclination "to kiver over" the nude statue that he discovers in the arboretum of his cousin's house could be interpreted as a reaction borne of rustic prudery. A newcomer to the city, he is repeatedly astonished by the liberties New Yorkers take with, among other virtues, modesty. In his cousin's artificial Garden of Eden, he wants to veil the marble depiction of female sexuality from the eyes of profane viewers, including his own. Yet elsewhere and often, responding to related but somewhat conflicting motives, Jonathan rejects disguises or distortions of the human form: "I raly didn't know which looked the worst, men running about among decent people with dirty brustles under their noses, or women a trying tu make themselves look humpbacked so as tu be in the fashion" (61). Jonathan's determination to see through the sham that surrounds him so infuses his descriptions of *High Life in New York* that it encourages a shift of attention to the book's author and the salt-and-pepper trousers Ann Sophia Stephens figuratively dons when she adopts a male persona. Much like the young heroine of E.D.E.N. Southworth's *The Hid-*

den Hand, Capitola Black, who dresses like a boy to make a living on the streets of New York, Stephens finds in authorial cross-dressing a way to explore the social and literary worlds of New York, a way to be humorous, and a way to survive.

It was difficult for women to be accepted as beings capable of humor in the nineteenth century. Not only was the humorous tradition of the period anti-feminine, as Zita Dresner observes, but society's alignment of women with gentility and domesticity made a humorous woman suspect (138). Not only did male-dominated humor contain a strong element of misogyny, but to be humorous went against what Alfred Habegger describes as the "longstanding tradition in the U.S. that women have, or ought to have, a basic incapacity for humor or wit" (115). Additionally, as Habegger points out, women were assigned to domesticity, which required earnestness and dedication; a woman who took time to laugh at herself or her world was judged to be "not quite consistent with respectability" (140).[1]

Yet women found ways to be humorous without resorting to misogyny or irresponsibility. Nancy Walker asserts that female humorists "waged a little-recognized but persistent war" against hypersentimental women such as Emmeline Grangerford or Betsey Bobbitt ("Wit" 6). Humor implied an assertiveness, Walker observes, that worked against the passivity of the sentimentalized woman, thus providing a means of expressing ideas and feelings that society suppressed.

Ann Sophia Stephens's position as a nineteenth-century woman humorist is complicated since, unlike Frances Whitcher or Marietta Holley, who created female characters (the Widow Bedott and Samantha Smith, respectively), Stephens adopts a male persona, the Down East rustic Jonathan Slick. Further, as Linda Morris argues, Stephens regards the world that Jonathan Slick explores with ambivalence: she—and he—are both repelled by and attracted to the high life of the city (52). Especially in view of their focus on sentimentalism, the episodic and interrupted series of letters she produces in Jonathan's voice is an uneven text revealing ambivalence but also a sorting out of motives, materials, and strategies useful in her later work. Such literary cross-dressing lets Stephens try out, assess, and reconsider ways of surviving in both the social and the literary worlds.

Born in Humphreysville, Connecticut, in 1810, Ann Sophia Winterbotham had been determined to be a writer since childhood.[2] After marrying Edward Stephens, she edited the *Portland Magazine*, a periodical her husband published in Maine, from 1834 to 1837; they then relocated to New York so she could pursue her literary career. There, Ann Sophia Stephens became her family's primary wage earner, writing for and editing several important magazines, including *Peterson's*. In the 1850s, her many serialized novels began appearing in book form. In 1860, her novella *Malaeska* became the first Beadle

Dime Novel. A prominent literary figure throughout her life, Stephens continued writing and editing until her death in 1886.

Her early years in New York, when she was establishing herself as a promising writer and editor, mark a crucial period of transition and growth. In *Doing Literary Business*, a study of women and publishing in mid-nineteenth-century America, Susan Coultrap-McQuin describes exactly Stephens's agenda. Her struggle with what Coultrap-McQuin characterizes as "the cultural prescriptions and social circumstances" that shaped her literary context (7) can be sensed in the eccentric Yankee persona of Jonathan Slick. Preceding the Slick letters, however, is "Women of Genius," an essay Stephens first published in *Ladies' Companion* and then republished in 1839 in *Hesperian*. In the essay, Stephens acknowledges the prejudice against women who excel in writing. While flowing with sentimentality ("Why do they write? Why does the bird sing . . . ") and praising the domestic talents of women of genius in the United States, the piece demonstrates the tensions between the woman writer who would participate in the public sphere and the pressures placed on her to conform to the doctrine of "true womanhood." Thus, *High Life in New York* might best be read as an attempt to test the waters, to explore what a woman writer might do through a male persona, exercising the male prerogative of humor and trying out, albeit in jest, a series of strategies that would find their ways into the strongest of her later works.

High Life in New York, a series of letters written by a Yankee hailing from the onion farms of Weathersfield, Connecticut, belongs to her first years in New York City and represents her only extensive venture into humor. Dates for the publication of the individual pieces in the *New York Express* are uncertain; however, persons and events described link them to the early 1840s. A collection of the letters first appeared in book form in 1843. In *Women Vernacular Humorists*, Linda Morris describes the letters as an epistolary novel (50), yet the collection reads more like a compilation of newspaper columns, albeit with repeating characters and occasionally continuing plots. The letters never achieve more than episodic cohesion: some plot threads are abruptly dropped, and characters appear and disappear without explanation. Readers are even denied a satisfactory conclusion: although we are told in the preface that Jonathan ultimately left Weathersfield, the final letters do not even hint at his departure. The problematic structure of the series perhaps reflects the bewilderment and fascination of Jonathan Slick, a newcomer to the city who bumbles his way through new and confusing social codes as he attempts to succeed as a columnist for the *Express*. Both as a newcomer to the city and an aspiring writer, Slick parallels Stephens's own position—fresh from Maine and determined to make a literary reputation for herself.

The primary purposes of the letters are to report Jonathan's observations of the city and to trace his development as he responds to urban life. Inescapably, however, his identity is linked to a series of literary forerunners. Slick's persona is derived from the Yankee Doodle figure and a tradition of Down East characters.[3] Although the Yankee fancies himself as shrewd, he is limited in experience. A lanky youth, he typically leaves his rustic home, establishes an identity for himself apart from his family, and eventually finds himself involved in the workings of the young democracy. In the late 1820s and early 1830s, a divergence of regional types occurred, forming one particular group of New England figures, the Down Easters. This type might be a farmer, a peddler, or a politician; he (and there are no women Yankees until several years after *High Life*) applies a dose of Yankee wit and common sense to the situations he encounters, reports of which he usually writes in amusing letters to his family or to his editor back home.

Homey wit and dialect, presented in the humorous letters of a rustic who is usually traveling and finding himself playing a role in the destiny of the nation, characterize the Yankee figure that Stephens chose to work with. In doing so, she had two immediate models, Seba Smith's Jack Downing and Thomas Chandler Haliburton's Sam Slick.[4] Stephens knew Seba Smith and was familiar with his work. The letters he wrote in the persona of Jack Downing were addressed to Jack's relations back in Downingsville and focused mainly on politics, revealing the state legislature's lack of common sense and his own political naiveté. Downing gradually becomes involved in politics, considers running for office, advises President Jackson, and receives a commission in the Army. Yet he always holds to his rural ways, depending on native wit—and not formal education—to solve his problems.

Whereas Seba Smith concentrates on the political scene, Thomas Chandler Haliburton devises a character who is the epitome of the Yankee peddler— shrewd, economical, and conservative. Sam Slick travels Nova Scotia, relating his observations, stories, and reflections to an acquaintance. To inspire Canadians with Yankee enterprise, Haliburton uses Slick as a voice detached from his native land, reciting formulated saws and Tory views that would be, according to Walter Blair, more conservative than the most reactionary New Englander's (55). Additionally, Sam Slick is particularly critical of women, often describing their "points" and their temperaments in elaborate equine analogies. Sam Slick feels arrogantly confident of his method for handling women, which in one case involves beating a friend's half-dressed wife—evidence of the misogyny that Habegger and Morris perceive in nineteenth-century humor (Habegger 119; Morris 19).

In *High Life in New York*, Stephens simultaneously acknowledges conventions established by Smith and Haliburton and distances her project from theirs. At several points in her series, Jack Downing is mentioned. Jonathan is familiar with Jack's letters, and his editor suggests that he write about politics as Jack has done, a request that leads to Jonathan's one disastrous venture into the political scene. Later, when readers of the *Express* ask if Jack Downing writes Jonathan's letters, Jonathan takes the opportunity to emphasize his authorship: "Neither the Portland Major Jack Downing, nor the New York Major Jack Downing, nor our Sam, nor nobody else, has a finger in my dish; but all the letters that has my name and picter to 'em are writ by me" (30). In another letter, despite the fact that he has claimed Sam Slick as his older brother, Jonathan is critical of the vulgar language of Sam's latest book, *The Letter Bag* (1839): "I wanted to stick up for Sam but I'll be darn'd if I could see how to du it, for the book's an allfired smutty thing, and that's the fact" (144-45).

In terms of the Down East character, therefore, Stephens identifies Jonathan with his literary brethren through his rural New England origins, his lack of sophistication, his use of dialect, and his ongoing commentary on events and experiences. Yet the contrasts that she establishes are important. Unlike Sam Slick, Jonathan is emotionally tied to his rural roots. Audience differs as well: whereas Sam Slick's comments are addressed to a chance acquaintance, Jonathan's are addressed to family members, who know him well and who care for him. As Jonathan moves about New York, he is constantly aware of his family's beliefs regarding drinking, theater, actresses, and gambling. In fact, this tension between rural and urban values provides the letters' central dynamic.

Unlike Sam Slick and Jack Downing, Jonathan maintains a refreshing vulnerability throughout his city experiences. He does not become a hardened city-dweller or a cynic outside the mainstream. Even after his literary and social successes and his meeting with President John Tyler, he is still vulnerable, especially to feminine beauty. In one of the last incidents, he is taken in by the glamorous Miss Sneers and her gambling associates.

Another departure from the Down East Yankee tradition is Stephens's focus on the manners of fashionable New York society. While Sam Slick and Jack Downing offer humorous critiques of gentility, Jonathan's fascination with the manners of the upper-middle class and the wealthy is striking. Fashions, entertainments, parties, and theater are the topics he most frequently writes about. Repeatedly, the subject of his letters is "parlor sentimentalism," Karen Halttunen's term for the period's regulations of genteel behavior (56), to which Jonathan's growing literary reputation exposes him. As Linda Morris suggests, the focus on fashion and society is one trait that distinguishes Stephens (and sister vernacular humorists Whitcher and Holley) from male vernacular humorists (21).

Like other Down East characters, Jonathan Slick writes in a recognizable Connecticut dialect, replete with misspellings and regionalisms, drawn from Stephens's neighbors in Humphreysville. Dominating American comic writing during the nineteenth century, dialect humor reflected an awareness of political and social differences among Yankees, Southerners, frontier settlers, and city dwellers. Morris notes that use of the vernacular implied a distancing of the speaker from the literate reader and even from the scenes that the speaker describes (4-5). Further, Blair links the popularity of dialect humor to an emphasis, in the wake of Andrew Jackson's election, on the common people and the important role played by every American, however well or ill educated, in the democratic process; thus the backwoodsman who had been a stock figure in low comedy comes to be seen as the embodiment of American values, as, for example, when Davy Crockett evolves from a "bar" killer to a legislator (39). Lastly, as Nancy Walker notes, dialect humor of this period reveals most Americans' distrust of "both big words and those who used them" (*Tradition* 3). This anti-intellectualism also suggests the dichotomy between what Habegger describes as the cultured and largely feminine values of civilization and the spontaneous and largely masculine values of the frontier (115-125).

In the hands of Stephens, however, dialect reinforces honest sentiment and critiques affectation. Moreover, Stephens manipulates dialect so that it becomes not just a curiosity or a source of humor but also a way of assessing parlor sentimentalism from the rustic outsider's point of view. Attending a "swarry" given by his cousin, Jonathan learns what refined dancing is like:

> Wal, the music begun, and one of the fellers that had the hair on his lip, begun tu slide about with his eyes half shet and his hands a hanging down, and looking as doleful as if he's jest come away from a funeral. Did you ever see a duck swim a mill-dam, or a hen turning up its eyes when it's a drinking? If you have you can get some idea how the lazy coot danced. . . . Think, sez I, when it comes my turn, I'll give you a little specimen of ginuine dancing. . . . A young lady, with her hair twisted all up with little white flowers, balanced up tu me, jest as you've seen a bird walk, and then it come my turn. I took two steps for'ard and then I cut a peeler of a pigeon-wing, and ended off with a little touch of the double shuffle, but my trousers was so plaguey tight that I couldn't make my legs rale limber . . . besides, the music warn't much more like a dancing tune than Greenbank or Old Hundred. (63)

Stephens's use of dialect is most effective when, through it, Jonathan transforms experience—usually by fitting an urban experience into the context of rural life. Imaginatively, he is never far from his Weathersfield onion farm. At one point, having become infatuated with city women, he reflects on love, starting with a cliché and moving toward a comparison derived from rural experience, not without inadvertent humor:

> Love, according to my notion on it, is a good anchor for us on this 'ere voyage of life!—it brings us up so all a standing when we put on too

much sail. It puts me in mind, now I think on it, of our cruise through Hell Gate in Captin Doolittle's sloop; for jest as the tide and the wind was a carrying us on the rocks, we dropt anchor and kept off. I look on the freshet that in the spring brings down the Connecticut the rale rich soil for the meadows in Weathersfield. They make a great deal of splutter and fuss in their spring-time, with their rustles and their ribbons, and their fooleries, I know; but when they light on a feller for good, they are the rale onion patches of his existence. (117)

The movement in this passage from a platitude to a personal sentiment suggests the most important difference between Jonathan Slick and other more cynical Down East characters. Rather than becoming a type, he remains an individual who constantly responds to the world around him, not only making judgments but more importantly exploring his heartfelt reactions to urban gentility. More than just observing and critiquing, Jonathan repeatedly tests the values of New York against the values of Weathersfield. Thus Jonathan offers Stephens a crucial vantage point: through his persona, Stephens is able to describe how the city appears to a newcomer without revealing her own newcomer status. As a sensitive man, his sentimentalism demands more notice than that of a woman's, whose emotional vulnerability would likely be dismissed as stereotypical.

Because of his emphasis on feeling, Jonathan's observations provide a commentary on the evolution of sentimentalism from a valuable configuration of social behavior to an artificial show of empty form. During the nineteenth century, as growing city populations became distanced from the religious and social values that originated in small hometown communities, expressing personal feelings caused embarrassment, or they might, at crucial junctures, put one at risk. The conflicts between rural and urban behavior codes become, at points, too strenuous for Jonathan, who periodically retreats to the countryside, claiming nostalgia, or ill parents, or his own poor health as an excuse.

In one encounter with his friend Captain Doolittle, Jonathan is particularly troubled. He has been leading a busy social life and has become disillusioned with the artificiality of city women and distressed by the plight of single working women in New York. Thus discouraged, ill, and missing "the prime fresh onions right out of the arth," Jonathan is weeping when Captain Doolittle enters. When Jonathan denies that he has been crying, Doolittle, detecting a lie, claims that Jonathan has "deginerated":

Jonathan . . . there was tears in your eyes jest as I come in, and you was ashamed on 'em. Now, sich tears as a smart, honest young man may feel in his eyes naturally, are nothing to be ashamed on; when he gets to thinking of hum or old friends . . . the drops that come up unawares to moisten his eyes are wholesome to his natur. . . . ginuine tears that come from tender thoughts, Jonathan, darn me if they ain't the rain that keeps the young shoots green. (177)

Jonathan's "degineration" lies in his shame at being homesick, an indication that city life and the artificiality it demands are affecting him. Later, he summarizes Weathersfield's most useful lesson for life in New York: "A good outside for the world and a good heart within" (201). The consistency between interior and exterior behavior that Jonathan seeks is precisely the kind of transparency that sentimentalism encouraged, behavior that revealed an individual's authentic feelings or beliefs. Thus hiding his tears from Doolittle is a violation of that code—a form of "degineration." Yet the alternative—the world of artificiality and pretense—is, with few exceptions, exactly the world of New York.

Depicting the falseness of city life, *High Life in New York* demonstrates many of the tensions examined by Karen Halttunen in *Confidence Men and Painted Women: A Study in a Middle-Class Culture in America, 1830-1850.* As rural-based honesty and transparency of feelings gave way to urban materialism and artificiality, society adopted an agenda of shows of emotion, signs of attitude or feeling that were enacted whether or not the attitude or feeling actually existed. Jonathan, for example, describes at length the changed appearance of his cousins, John and Mary Beebe, who have adopted city manners (17, 58-59). Both their dress and their behavior have been affected. Their parlor has become what Halttunen describes as the stage setting for *acting* honestly and sincerely, the hostess serving as a sort of stage manager (101). Certainly affected manners are the rule with the Beebes: when cousin Jonathan first arrives, Mary greets him not with a familial embrace but with a contrived curtsy:

Instid of coming up and giving me a good shake o' the hand or a buss— there wouldn't a been any harm in't as we were cousins—she put one foot for'ard a little and drew t'other back kind o' catercornering, and then she sort o' wriggled her shoulders, and bent for'ard and made a curchy, city fashion. (22)

Not to be outclassed, Jonathan decides to do her one better, performing an outlandish gesture that ends "jest as a feller shuts a jack knife when he's afeard of cutting his fingers" (22).

Cosmetics also confound Jonathan. When he visits the boudoir of a woman who has attracted him, he is astonished to see her without her "public face." By accident, he happens into her dressing room—another violation of the code, according to Halttunen, for back rooms were off limits (101)—and sees a slovenly pile of articles that include her hairpiece and a glass containing "three, nice, little, white teeth" (85).

This particular scene enlightens and saddens Jonathan, but other demonstrations of artifice enrage him. Repeatedly, Jonathan is confronted with the fact that New York is largely a world of false fronts. His wealthy cousin, Jason Slick, for example, has equipped himself with all of the accoutrements of the nouveau riche, including liveried servants and a sham coat of arms. When Jason expresses embarrassment over his family's plebeian bloodlines, Jonathan explodes with a speech recalling with pride Jason's lowly beginnings and claiming that their grandfather, a shoemaker who fought in the Revolution, was as noble as any British lord. He concludes that American nobility will not have titles but will be traced back to the rosters of those who fought in the war.

Perhaps the most revealing symptom of Jonathan's incompatibility with urban social mores is his inability to understand the imaginary world of the theater. Time and again, he fails to distinguish between the actors and the roles they play. He is confused, for example, when an actor later appears onstage as a different character. He interprets a gesture made by an actor to the audience as a real—not a theatrical—signal. When Jonathan goes back stage at the Park Theater, he is surprised to see how homely the sets really are. An actor comments, "it's bad enuf, but then we put the best side out" (218). Over and over, Jonathan expects authenticity and sincerity, failing to realize the function of artifice in urban gentility. As Halttunen observes, "the sentimental demand for sincerity that had given rise to the complex code of genteel conduct had fallen away, leaving behind the social forms themselves" (196). These forms become the theatrics, both on the stage and in the grand parlors that bewilder and often mislead Jonathan.

Jonathan's confusion over the theater and fancy dress balls is ironic in view of Stephens's authorial disguise as a male Yankee. Both his insistence that only he writes his letters and his description of his cousin's urban dress— "he looked more like a woman in men's clothes than anything else" (17)— underscore Stephens's authorial deception. Yet on occasion and in significant ways, the mask slips and a less masculine personality is detected in Jonathan's writings. For example, his focus on dress, gesture, and social behavior is more typical of women humorists; as Nancy Walker demonstrates, while both men and women humorists focused on the incongruity between ideals and realities, women have preferred the "more private areas of home and human relationships" to the public areas of politics and business (*Tradition* 8)—a fair description of the letters of Jonathan Slick who, after one chaotic experience at a political assembly, selects domestic and social settings as his focus and who often *confuses* public and private arenas with, of course, humorous effect. More importantly, while Stephens treats parlor manners, decoration, fashion, and courtship humorously, she does not abandon sentiment in her critique of vulgar and hollow forms of gentility. Rather than rejecting the value of sentimental behavior, Stephens supports genuine sentiment and appropriate social forms and urges reform: a realignment of those social forms with inner feelings, the elimination of artificiality, and a restoration of sincerity.

Rather than ridiculing New York gentility outright, most of the humor of *High Life in New York* stems from Jonathan's inability to comprehend the urban world around him. He does not understand a number of words, never making the link between "swarry" (which he mistakenly identifies with the nude statue in his cousin's arboretum) and "soirée" and being forever intrigued by the delights of "sham pain." Further, he misreads gestures and situations. Continually the outsider, Jonathan longs to fit in, to conduct himself in an informed way. Indeed, the verbal abuse that Jonathan occasionally doles out to African-Americans stems from his own sense of social inferiority; among urbanites whose ways puzzle Jonathan and whose codes he cannot interpret, the sophistication of black servants who do understand and who are indeed well versed in urban decorum makes Jonathan feel all the more inadequate. Indeed, Stephens's attitude toward blacks in the early 1840s seems at best ambivalent, yet her positive inclusion of a young African-American at a celebration for President Tyler suggests that Jonathan's irritation stems more from class insecurity than from racism.

Another slip of the mask and a marked departure from Down East humor and from the general tone of *High Life in New York* is a lengthy section dealing with the plight of the underpaid female worker. When he meets Susan Reed, another migrant from Weathersfield, Jonathan sees that her job has run her down physically and psychologically. The sequence of letters describing Susan's plight lacks humor; Susan is a cause of concern—and hence her case probably derived from Stephens's observation of working conditions for single women. Similar problems are treated realistically in her later fiction,[5] but in *High Life*, Susan awakens Jonathan's social consciousness:

> I never see one of them harnsome young criters going along hum, arter working hard all day, to arn something to live on, and mebby to feed their pars and mars with, but I git to thinkin how much a ginuine chap ought to prize them for keeping honest, and industrious, and vartuous, when they haint much to encourage them to du right, and generally have a good deal to tempt them to du wrong . . . it's my opinion that there ain't a place on arth, where the people try to stomp each other down to the dirt more than they du here in York. (146)

The seriousness of the passage violates the mood of the rest of the work, but Stephens must have sensed that otherwise her portrait of New York would be incomplete.

Another slip of the mask is Stephens's handling of Jonathan's meeting with President Tyler. A stock convention in the adventures of many Yankee figures, this political apotheosis of the rustic underscores the democratic principle that all are created equal and therefore all are worthy to associate with the president and perhaps to become president as well. When Jonathan meets Tyler, however, the humor stems in part from Jonathan's feeling that this meeting is just as much of a treat for the President as it is for him. He describes the crowds as being as enthusiastic about his own presence as they are about Tyler's. Further, Stephens domesticates this conventionally public encounter: sensing that Tyler is exhausted from the day's hectic events, Jonathan sneaks him off to Captain Doolittle's sloop for some rest and relaxation. He offers Tyler some of his mother's doughnuts and a mixture of vinegar and molasses: "He didn't need much urgin, for the switcher was ginuine stuff, sweety and yet sort of tart, and cool as a cowcumber, and the doughnuts beat all natur" (266). Jonathan's perception of the President's needs and the care he takes of him in private are a radical departure from Jack Downing's political affiliation with Andrew Jackson or Sam Slick's appointment to the Court of St. James. Sensitive to the private person and not just the political official, Jonathan, true to his instincts, does not hesitate to nurture.

Detailing the ways in which *High Life in New York* develops a more feminine Yankee figure only partially reveals the significance of Stephens's authorial cross-dressing. There is particular irony in her assumption of male garb in order to charge New York society with artificiality and deception. When he observes that Cousin John Beebe's clothes make him look more like a woman, Jonathan comes daringly close to naming his own truth, that his letters are written by a woman who created him and who is responsible for his more "feminine" attributes as well as his focus on parlor sentimentalism. Occasionally, as in his observations of conditions for working women, the mask slips, the humor falls away, and the exploitation that makes the capricious social life of New York possible is revealed.

To conclude that Stephens dons Jonathan's salt-and-pepper trousers simply in order to be humorous without blame—that is, to be humorous as a man is allowed to be humorous—misses the more complicated function of *High Life* as a stage both in Stephens's acculturation to New York's social and literary worlds and in the development of women's humor. A newcomer to New York, taken aback by the duplicity of urban gentility, yet wanting to succeed as a woman writer, Stephens uses *High Life* as a way to sort out her reactions to city life and to experiment both with sentimentalism, the most popular and accepted form of women's narrative, and with humor, a terrain labeled for men only. By mocking the artificial sentimentality of genteel social life through the persona of an authentically sentimental yet humorously uninformed Yankee, Stephens expresses her serious hesitations about the value of parlor melodrama—as well as the role ascribed to women writers as narrators of parlor life—without the risk of alienating herself from the literary culture.

Thus *High Life in New York* may be viewed as transitional in two important ways. First, for Stephens herself, writing as Jonathan Slick allows her to straddle urban and rural values, humor and sentimentalism, realism and melodrama. By doing so, she learns how to position herself vis-à-vis the world of literary publication—a world intolerant of women's humor and ambivalent toward any woman writer critical of parlor etiquette or concerned about the economic survival of working girls. Through the persona of Jonathan Slick, Stephens develops techniques that she would employ in her later fiction, the best of which (*The Homestead, Fashion and Famine*, and *Malaeska*) cut the sentimentalism with healthy doses of realism—a mixture somewhat analogous to Jonathan's favorite combination of molasses and vinegar. Second, through its alternately sympathetic and humorous treatment of women's experience, *High Life* opens the door for Widow Bedott and Samantha Smith, Down East female Yankees whose creators, Frances Whitcher and Marietta Holley, were able to address women's roles and, in the case of Holley, women's rights, without needing to resort to cross-dressing.

NOTES

1. For a review of U.S. women's humor and an analysis of its suppression, see N. Walker and Z. Dresner's introduction to their anthology of women's humor, *Redressing the Balance: American Women's Literary Humor from Colonial Times to the 1980s* (Jackson: UP of Mississippi, 1988). For wider ranging and more extensive discussions of women's humor, see Walker's *A Very Serious Thing: Women's Humor and American Culture* (Minneapolis: U of Minnesota P, 1988) and *Women's Comic Visions*, ed. June Sochen (Detroit: Wayne State UP, 1991).

2. In *Women's Fiction: A Guide to Novels by and about Women in America, 1820-1870*, Nina Baym groups Stephens with two other women writers, Mary Jane Holmes and Marion Harland, all of whom chose to write because they wanted to, all of whom were motivated by their intellectual energies and the desire to shape their own lives; they were not primarily motivated by financial need (177).

3. A description of the Yankee Doodle character in verse, drama, and sketch is provided by Walter Blair in *Native American Humor* (39).

4. Another more remote model is Washington Irving's Jonathan Oldstyle. Although he does not conform to the character of the Down East rustic, Oldstyle is significant because his humor was directed at the very subject Stephens chose, fashionable New York society. In addition, interest in theater is echoed in Jonathan's fascination with dramatic productions at, for example, the Park Theater.

5. For example, in *Fashion and Famine*, Stephens graphically describes the conditions of women imprisoned in the Tombs; despite the dominant tone of melodrama, she also presents models of independent women living successfully in the city.

REFERENCES

Baym, Nina. *Women's Fiction: A Guide to Novels by and about Women in America, 1820-1870*. Ithaca, NY: Cornell UP, 1978.

Blair, Walter. *Native American Humor*. New York: Chandler, 1960.

Coultrap-McQuin, Susan. *Doing Literary Business: American Women Writers in the Nineteenth Century*. Chapel Hill: U of North Carolina P, 1990.

Dresner, Zita. "Women's Humor." *Humor in America: A Research Guide to Genres and Topics*. Ed. Lawrence E. Mintz. New York: Greenwood, 1988. 137-161.

Habegger, Alfred. *Gender, Fantasy, and Realism in American Literature*. New York: Columbia UP, 1982.

Haliburton, Thomas Chandler. *The Sam Slick Anthology*. Ed. Reginald Eyre Walters and Walter Avis. Toronto: Clarke, 1969.

Halttunen, Karen. *Confidence Men and Painted Women: A Study of Middle-Class Culture in America, 1830-1850*. New Haven: Yale UP, 1982.

Morris, Linda A. *Women Vernacular Humorists in Nineteenth-Century America: Ann Stephens, Frances Whitcher, and Marietta Holley*. New York: Garland, 1988.

Smith, Seba. *Life and Writings of Major Jack Downing*. Boston: Lilly, 1834.

Sochen, June, ed. *Women's Comic Visions*. Detroit: Wayne State UP, 1991.

Southworth, E.D.E.N. *The Hidden Hand* (1859). Ed. Joanne Dobson. New Brunswick: U of Rutgers P, 1987.

Stephens, Ann Sophia. "Woman of Genius." *Hesperian*. August 1839: 242-244.

———. *High Life in New York (1843)*. New York: Bunce & Brother, 1854.

———. *Fashion and Famine*. New York: Bunce & Brother, 1854.

———. *The Old Homestead*. New York: Bunce & Brother, 1855.

Walker, Nancy. "Wit, Sentimentality, and the Image of Women in the Nineteenth Century." *American Studies* 22.2 (Fall 1981): 5-22.

———. *The Tradition of Women's Humor in America*. Huntington Beach, CA: American Studies, 1984.

———. *A Very Serious Thing: Women's Humor and American Culture*. Minneapolis: U of Minnesota P, 1988.

——— and Zita Dresner, eds. *Redressing the Balance: American Women's Literary Humor from Colonial Times to the 1980s*. Jackson: UP of Mississippi, 1988.

Gender and the Jeremiad:
Gail Hamilton's Antisuffrage Prophecy
Sherry Lee Linkon

America was founded on the rights of man: why do we set our affections on silks and satins? . . . Never had any nation such opportunity as ours. Here is the race-course ready, the battle-ground prepared. It needs only that we be swift and strong. . . . It is ourselves alone that will fail if there be failure; not opportunity. It is for us to rise to the height of the great argument. . . . Give us full and free development. Tear away these gilded fetters, and let the children of God have free course to run and be glorified. Throw off allegiance to trifles, and with the heart believe, and with the mouth make confession, and the upright life attest: There is no God but God.

This can be done only when women and men will work together to the same end.

Gail Hamilton, *A New Atmosphere* (83–84)

Although the book quoted here is almost completely unknown today, its lamentation and call to virtuous action are features familiar to the American jeremiad. In this genre, the speaker first bemoans the failure of Americans to live up to the country's promise and then exhorts his listeners to return to the "true" path, thus ensuring the success of American culture. I say the speaker exhorts "his" listeners because critical work on the American jeremiad usually examines the speeches and writings of men.[1] This is not altogether surprising, since men, especially educated white men, have historically been more active in politics and public life than members of other demographic groups. They have had access to public platforms and the authority to deliver speeches and publish essays that exemplify the genre. Yet women writers and speakers have also employed the jeremiad to their advantage, often revising it slightly to fit their somewhat different version of public authority. However, women's use and revisions of the form have not received significant scholarly attention.

Nor have scholars considered how an author's awareness of a gendered audience might lead to revisions in the jeremiad, which, after all, performed the cultural work of creating consensus, or the illusion of consensus, in a diverse culture. Given the importance of this ideal of a common mission, it is not surprising that most nineteenth-century jeremiads ignore gender, which, along with race, marked a central cultural divide. Indeed, writers and speakers could only achieve the goal of consensus by either ignoring their female audiences or presenting their messages as appropriate for both women and men. Yet when we read the jeremiads of women writers, especially those written by conservative women, we see a clear acknowledgement of gender differences within a framework of shared values and goals, suggesting that women varied the form in significant ways that deserve critical attention.

Perhaps the most visible and memorable women "jeremiahs" have been those involved in the struggle for women's rights. Suffragists in the nineteenth century and feminists in the twentieth have argued that Americans have not lived up to their ideals of democracy and equal rights because they deny or limit the legal, political, and economic rights of women. But while some nineteenth-century women used the jeremiad to argue that women should have the same rights as men, others wrote jeremiads arguing against women's rights and suffrage. In essays and fiction, antisuffragists addressed male and female readers, describing how American culture had fallen away from its true path. Unlike other "jeremiahs," however, these antisuffragists gave men and women separate instructions on how to regain American virtue, and they imagined the ideal citizen as a good woman, not a male voter.

One of the least remembered but most active of these antisuffrage "jeremiahs" was Mary Abigail Dodge, who wrote under the pen name "Gail Hamilton." Her essays address a wide range of public issues, such as the "Woman Question," government spending on Civil War hospitals, and the actions of prominent members of Congress, and her literary reputation, limited though it may be, is based on her skills as an essayist. She wrote for many newspapers and magazines, including the *Atlantic Monthly*, the *Independent*, and the *New York Tribune*. During her lifetime, she published several collections of essays and three book-length commentaries on women's roles, marriage, and suffrage.

Her gendered jeremiad appears most strongly in the latter works. Like many suffragists, she describes the failures of American culture, especially the destructive effects of economic values and excessive individualism. Like most of her sister antisuffragists, however, she rejects the suffragists' argument that women should solve social problems by following the male model of legal and political rights and offers instead the feminine model of the home with its caring interpersonal relationships and Christian values as an alternative approach to social change. While affirming the power of good womanhood, she explicitly rejects the idea that winning the right to vote would benefit women or American society.

Instead, Hamilton calls for limitations on individualism, viewing self-interest and economic competition as central problems in nineteenth-century American culture. She argues that by respecting individual dignity and caring for others, women and men could repair the social problems that women face and thereby benefit the entire community. She calls upon her readers to act virtuously, set aside personal pride, and value human relationships over material goods. She also views women as the models of virtuous citizenship and the moral and emotional centers of the home and the community. Like most jeremiads, Hamilton's messages are usually conservative, but they also reveal her efforts to resist and revise her culture's dominant ideas about gender.

Hamilton's version of the jeremiad is strongly gendered in both form and content. Her sometimes awkward use of a traditionally male form highlights the limitations of feminine authority in nineteenth-century discourse, and her criticisms and prescriptions emphasize her struggle to balance the consensus that is central to the form with her own belief in the importance of gender difference. Her essays exemplify the "women's jeremiad," based upon but also challenging the male tradition. An examination of her long works on gender politics can help us understand the issues raised when writers attempt to insert gender into a form that resists difference. I want to focus on three aspects of Hamilton's jeremiads: her self-conscious appropriation of the jeremiad's public authority, her attention to distinct male and female audiences and roles, and the tension between this gendering of the jeremiad and the form's inherent conservatism.

A close look at Hamilton's efforts to claim and refuse authority in her jeremiads highlights the opportunities and problems involved when women adopt what George Landow terms the voice of the public "sage" (23). Hamilton presents her jeremiads to the public not in literal speeches, as many of her male contemporaries did, but in popular magazine and newspaper columns and in book-length essays published under her pseudonym. While Hamilton, like other women writers of the period, had little difficulty gaining access to public discourse through print media, her adoption of the role of the sage was not without complications related to her gender. By mid-century, women had many opportunities to enter into public discourse,[2] but they also knew that writing raised questions about their femininity; conservative women especially may have felt internal conflicts between their belief that women could best exercise their influence in the home and their professional interests in writing about the issues of the day. Like the "literary domestics" Mary Kelley has studied, Hamilton separated her public and private lives through her use of the pseudonym, keeping her identity secret even from her publishers early in her career. By publishing as "Gail Hamilton," she could protect her privacy and emphasize the difference between her public voice and her private self. Yet, as Malini Johar Schueller notes in *The Politics of Voice*, the power of Puritan political rhetoric, including later jeremiads that inherit many of the features of Puritan writing, derives from the "role of the speaker," a necessarily public role. Indeed, Schueller argues, "later American writers" continue the tradition by "emphasizing their speaking voices, and attempting to address the culture at large" (2). Thus, in writing a feminine jeremiad, Hamilton had to weigh her desire to divide her public voice from her private self against her goal of addressing her culture from a position of authority, which required the public presentation of the self.

Although some women spoke in public during the 1860s and their speeches were reported and even reprinted in newspapers, Hamilton's letters show that she clearly felt more comfortable expressing her ideas in private, in letters or in conversation, than in public.[3] She spent many years living in Washington, D.C., and interacted regularly with senators, Supreme Court justices, and first ladies. While she was apparently comfortable holding political conversations in private settings with such important public figures, she expressed dismay that readers might connect the public persona of the "Washington letters" in the *Congregationalist* with her private identity.[4] In a letter home about these political commentaries, she implores her family to *"lie like fury,* but don't say I wrote it" (*Life in Letters* 188). Like other women writers, Hamilton was clearly aware that some of her writing might be seen as improper, and she seems to have been especially worried about her political commentaries. As Susan Coultrap-McQuin has noted, Hamilton's fears were justified, for although she gained a reputation as a political essayist and a witty commentator, her writing was criticized by at least one of her contemporaries as "shrewish" and "didactic" (qtd. in Coultrap-McQuin, "Introduction," xi). Not only did Hamilton "speak" publicly through her writing, she frequently took on unfeminine topics, criticized individual men and men as a group, and displayed a wit and sharpness that could not have been read as a proper feminine voice. Her concerns about the propriety of her own writing may have led her to adopt the jeremiad, hoping that the form itself would lend authority to her ideas, but her writing also reveals her discomfort, at times, with that authority.

Hamilton's doubts about the propriety of her social criticism appear in *A New Atmosphere* (1865). She seems especially conscious of the politics of a woman writing critically to and about men. In parts of the book, she addresses men directly as "you," arguing, for example, that "You lower [marriage] to the level of the market" (20). But while the messages of the book are clearly aimed at male readers, Hamilton writes most of it about men rather than to them. For example, when she argues that men take advantage of women in the workplace simply because they can, she refers to "men" and "Man," not "you." Even her final and forceful call for reform uses third person rather than second: "Therefore opinion needs to be right, prejudice removed, and society renovated; and men must do it" (305). This indirect form of address illustrates Hamilton's clear understanding of mid-century gender politics. As Catherine Stimpson suggests, women writers often adopted strategies that both demonstrated and masked their self-assertion because they did not have the power to be "vastly nonconformist" (166–7). For a good woman, a direct challenge to men might have shown too much aggressiveness, and, as Kelley suggests, women writers needed to maintain feminine public personae to avoid being discredited.[5] If Hamilton could not always tell men what to do, she could and did offer her prescriptions for change in explicitly gendered terms. Her male readers would certainly have known when she was addressing them, even when she uses the third person.

The closing of *A New Atmosphere* further highlights both the usefulness and the limitations of the form for a woman writer. The book ends with a final prediction. While many women's idyllic dreams of a happy marriage have proven false, Hamilton insists, "there is a way whereby the wondrous edifice [of marriage] may be made as enduring as it is brilliant" (308). Someday, she promises in a closing description of clear skies and "ever-charmed hills," all women may find in marriage the ideal she envisions (309–310). She uses religious language, casting her ideas as the visions of a prophet rather than as the comments of an individual social critic. "O sweet my friend," she asks in the final section, "am I then a bird of evil omen?" No, she insists, she is not even responsible for writing the book: "It is but the voice of a thousand aching hearts. Ten thousand dreary lives are wrought into its pages" (307–308). This claim of prophecy lends authority to the jeremiad. For Hamilton, as for other "jeremiahs," this claim suggests a higher source for her own ideas. At the same time, however, it allows her to disclaim the criticisms she makes of men, attributing them to "the voice of a thousand aching hearts." Thus she gains the authority to speak while protecting herself from judgments about her audacity.

Hamilton uses the jeremiad to gain this authority and to de-emphasize her own agency in political writing, an ironic but necessary double-edged act that highlights the problem of cultural power for nineteenth-century women writers. Because it would have been familiar to Hamilton's readers and because it is cast as prophecy instead of mere opinion, the jeremiad form lends authority to Hamilton's voice, but her use of it, as a woman writer and as a woman writing to men, is inherently suspect. Although women's "moral superiority" was discussed widely in books and periodicals of the day, the idea of women "preaching" was still questionable. Women enacted their ministry most appropriately within the home, and a woman's congregation was to be her family and circle of friends, as many antisuffragists argued. Hamilton clearly steps outside those boundaries. Many women writers did, but Hamilton's sermon in *A New Atmosphere* is especially vehement. Moreover, she does not use the more typical feminine form of fiction or even the light-hearted bantering commentary of her own and other women's short essays.[6] Instead, she borrows what was arguably the most forceful and traditional form in American rhetoric. By criticizing men specifically, Hamilton violates the ideal of good womanhood, which envisioned women "influencing" men through the silent example of feminine virtue rather than preaching to them. In her use of a gendered jeremiad, then, Hamilton attempts to challenge male authority, but her challenge is limited by the form itself, as well as by the contradictions of her own ideology.

We can identify the limitations of the form and the contradictions of Hamilton's conservative ideology most clearly by examining the content of her jeremiads. Formally, she follows the pattern established by Old Testament prophets. As summarized by Thomas Scott, the form begins with the speaker identifying the listeners' problems and blaming those sufferings on their "falling away from—God's law." Further miseries are promised if behavior doesn't change, but the jeremiad closes with a prophetic description of the "bliss that their listeners would realize if they returned to the ways of God" (qtd. in Landow 26). The purpose of the pattern, according to Sacvan Bercovitch, is to evoke anxiety but also express optimism and offer a promise of progress and ultimate triumph (6–7). Specifically, Bercovitch writes, the jeremiad attempts to manage the "religious and economic dangers of unfettered individualism" and control "the excesses . . . of self-interest" (25). Most important, he argues, the form repeatedly posits a common mission for all Americans, replacing cultural homogeneity, which faded soon after the Puritans arrived, with "consensus by calling and enterprise" (26). Thus, the jeremiad fuses individual salvation with national success and erases cultural difference by suggesting that all Americans share a common goal and destiny. In addressing the individual as part of the community, the speaker usually ignores gender in order to emphasize the common mission of men and women in forging a better society. By discussing gender differences and by addressing men and women separately, Hamilton seems to split that consensus.

Not all jeremiads have ignored gender difference, however, and there is precedent for Hamilton's configuration of the ideal citizen as a wife and mother. In his study of the jeremiad, Douglas Anderson recognizes that Puritans and their descendants were conscious of gender difference and that gender roles played a part in early jeremiads, but he sees this difference fading over time. Anderson notes that in "A Model of Christian Charity," John Winthrop placed the image of Eve at the center of his ideal vision of the American community and that he envisioned the community functioning as a family or household with each citizen as a wife and mother in that imagined home. By the late eighteenth and early nineteenth centuries, however, American writers no longer envisioned the citizen as mother. In the work of male writers, including Thomas Jefferson and Benjamin Franklin, Anderson sees a shift to a vision of the citizen as father. This shift coincides with the rise of gender consciousness that

Nancy Cott has described, suggesting that the gendered definition of the good citizen in both the masculine jeremiads Anderson studies and Hamilton's feminine version should be read as part of the nineteenth-century debate about gender roles and cultural power.

In the middle of the nineteenth century, readers may not have understood gender difference as a threat to American consensus. Carroll Smith-Rosenberg argues that Americans believed in gender complementarity, the "natural" division of gender roles, a social model in which difference and consensus could co-exist. Yet this model rarely appears in jeremiads, which usually ignore gender differences, perhaps because they usually focused on public life, thus excluding women from the citizenry addressed. When Hamilton and other antisuffragists exhort their male and female readers to play distinct roles, they challenge the jeremiad's traditional erasure of difference, but their vision reflects their culture's ideal of gender complementarity. This attention to difference also reveals cracks in this version of consensus and highlights places where men's and women's goals conflict and complementarity fails. In reading Hamilton's jeremiads, then, we must examine both the assumptions she seems to make about gender complementarity and her implied challenge to American consensus.

Hamilton "genders" her jeremiad, in part, by addressing men and women distinctly and differently in many of her essays. This difference appears clearly in two of her early pieces, published during the 1860s. "Men and Women" appeared in Hamilton's first collection of essays, *Country Living and Country Thinking* (1861). The first part of this extended essay is addressed to men, but Hamilton admits that she does not "flatter [her]self that what [she] may say will have the slightest tendency to modify the views or the practice of any one of [her] masculine readers" (101), and she soon dismisses them and turns directly to her female audience. "You, O maidens and matrons beloved," she scolds her readers, have failed to live up to the promise of true womanhood. The remainder of the essay discusses women's failures and predicts the triumph of women's "moral rectitude" (202). While the pattern of her essay follows the usual declension-and-promise model of the jeremiad, by writing distinctly and separately to men and women within this long essay, Hamilton also revises the jeremiad tradition. She continues this process a few years later in *A New Atmosphere*, her book-length essay directed primarily at men. While *A New Atmosphere* offers some advice for women and closes with a section addressed specifically to them, most of Hamilton's complaints and instructions relate to men's attitudes and behavior.

A closer look at "Men and Women" and *A New Atmosphere* shows that Hamilton's distinctions go far beyond the gender of her audience. She not only addresses men and women separately, she offers specific advice for each sex. At the same time, she assumes that her readers, male and female, share the common goal of creating a good society. She calls for a social order that will nurture strength and pride in women and develop moral goodness and selflessness in men. To achieve such social virtue, Hamilton suggests, American women must renew their commitment to their true work as God's representatives on earth, and American men must learn to value true womanhood, voluntarily limit their own power over women, and accept their own moral power within the "feminine sphere" of the home. Hamilton's division of her audience suggests that men's and women's failures are different, and she suggests different roles for men and women, yet she calls on both to embrace a caring, selfless, morally virtuous role in society—a vision drawn from her ideal of good womanhood. In short, both women and men must become more "womanly." Hamilton offers men and women different instructions, though the advice she offers each sex suggests that both men and women must become more androgynous. Thus she simultaneously breaks and mends the traditional jeremiad. She splits the assumed consensus of the nongendered jeremiad by offering different advice to different audiences, but she fuses the two halves into one by suggesting a shared goal. How are we to read the prophecy of Hamilton's jeremiad? What does her emphasis tell us about women's use of the jeremiad?

In "Men and Women," Hamilton focuses on women's failure to accept their position in society, arguing that the suffragists' attempts to change women's place violate God's intentions. "You are where God has placed you" (141), she tells her female readers; if they would only embrace that position, their "soul[s] shall calmly sit in the evening-tide of a serene life, waiting the voice of the Lord" (161). This position offers women great power, Hamilton claims, but they have abdicated that power. By accepting the false idea, "propagated" by "aesthetic young lady-writers and sentimental penny-a-liners . . . that feebleness and fragility are womanly and fascinating" (120), women have made themselves weak and foolish. Women can gain both personal satisfaction and social influence, Hamilton argues, only when they return to true womanliness, based on strength and bravery (123–125). "The stronger [a woman] is," she writes, "the truer she is to her womanly instincts" (124). Woman's problem is not that her role is so limited, but that women "are far too apt to be content with small attainments and ignoble ends" (111) or to be "absorbed in dress, visiting, pleasure-seeking" (140). Women's rights activism is merely the "natural reaction" to such useless occupations, "a move too far in the right direction, or rather an injudicious means to compass worthy ends" (111). Women's work may not be great, she admits, but "the world . . . needs your moral heroism" (144). Throughout the text, Hamilton decries women's selfishness, vanity, and weakness, but she repeatedly points out that women are responsible for these traits and that their duty requires them to choose selflessness, virtue, and moral strength in order to create a better society. By placing blame directly on women and by emphasizing her vision of women's "true work," Hamilton prepares her women readers for the feminine prescription she will eventually offer to solve women's and society's problems. Women's failures, in her lament, harm everyone, but women alone are responsible for them. Men, in Hamilton's vision, have their own failures.

Even as Hamilton's gendered jeremiad suggests that women's role is central to American society, her prescription for women raises questions about the importance of their role. After all, as many twentieth-century feminist critics have pointed out, "moral rectitude" does not always produce direct results. Hamilton's readers, especially the suffragists, may well have doubted the efficacy of her prescription. Hamilton anticipates and attempts to respond to this doubt. After many pages of complaining about women's failure to live up to the possibilities of their sex, Hamilton follows the traditional jeremiad pattern and ends with a grand call for women to uplift themselves:

> O, if this latent power could be aroused! If woman would shake off this slumber, and put on her strength, her beautiful garments, how would she go forth conquering and to conquer, —how would the mountains break forth into singing, and the trees of the field clap their hands,— how would our sin-stained earth arise and shine, her light being come, and the glory of the Lord being risen upon her! (201)

Hamilton envisions women as the light of the world, its conquering saviors. While her use of religious language suggests great moral power, her vision of woman is inspirational but not substantive. With this airy ideal, Hamilton sweeps aside any real problems facing women. She describes her model woman as "a slight, pale girl, orphaned, homeless, neglected," who "seems to have drawn to herself, by some magnetic power, all the good of all persons by whom she has been surrounded, and to have fed her own soul thereon" (196). This juxtaposition of real economic problems and an idealistic vision of the redemptive power of feminine virtue highlights the weakness of Hamilton's plan.

Like most jeremiads, her prophecy does not call for anything truly new. Rather, it views the ideals of the past as valuable and useful models for the future. As Landow suggests, the sage does not necessarily criticize conventional wisdom; rather, s/he often argues that people have "abandoned orthodox wisdom or reduced it to an empty husk. . . . When a people ignores the wisdom that lies at the heart of its society and institutions, then the sage recalls that people to it" (23). Hamilton does not ultimately challenge orthodox ideas about gender; instead, she argues that her readers must rededicate themselves to traditional gender roles. Indeed, in the next paragraph, Hamilton explicitly returns women to the role of supporters of men. Women may not "be directly and actively engaged in fighting the battle," she admits, but they can treat men's wounds, offer "a cup of cold water to the thirsty and fainting,—give help to the conquered and smiles to the victor" (201–202). Thus, after exhorting women to moral heights and extolling the glory of women's strength, she returns them to their original position, at home, caring for and inspiring men. She does not suggest a change in women's roles, only a more satisfied and zealous acceptance of them. In offering a conservative closing, Hamilton drops her insistence on the good woman as a model for citizenship and allies herself more closely with the accepted notion of gender complementarity.

Her jeremiad for men seems to argue for somewhat more real change, as she calls on men to respect women's power and embrace a more feminine role, though in the end she returns men, too, to their original roles as the more active members of society. The majority of *A New Atmosphere* argues for a change in men's attitudes toward marriage and the home. Hamilton begins by criticizing American culture for teaching young women that their sole purpose in life is to get married; girls learn to measure their own value in terms of their success in the marriage market, based largely on their attractiveness to men (7). Using economic terms in her critique, she accuses men of "depreciating" marriage: "you degrade it to a question of political and domestic economy" (20). She extends her argument about men's economic power to the workplace, criticizing men because they pay women low wages and deprecate women who work as less than truly feminine. Rather than using their economic power to subordinate women, Hamilton argues, men should accept their economic responsibility for women. Women, she explains, are "reduced to want, to shame, to ignominy, to starvation, and degradation and death, through the meanness, the misconduct, or the inability of their natural protectors" (51). Men, she maintains, are "at the bottom of every evil under the sun" (263). They claim to value the home and family, but their actions show that they value money more:

> What men really believe in is making money, not making true men and women. They believe that the greatness of a nation consists in its much land and gold and machinery and ability to browbeat another nation, not in the incorruptibility of its citizens. Wealth and fame, purple and fine linen and sumptuous fare, brute force of intellect, position, and power, one or another or all forms of self-indulgence,—these, not purity, love, content, aspiration, and hearty good-will, they take to constitute blessedness. (290–291)

Where "Men and Women" blames women for their own problems, *A New Atmosphere* shifts the blame explicitly to men for falling away from true Christian values and letting their individual material interests outweigh their responsibilities to the community.

The "promise" of Hamilton's male jeremiad emphasizes a vision of men softened by love, becoming more aware of their wives' and daughters' feelings and rejecting economic values. She calls for men to consider the sacrifice a woman makes when she marries and to "constrain her to forget, in the fervor and efficacy of his love, the fruit which once her soul longed for. If he cannot prevent the sacrifice, he can cause that it shall not have been made in vain" (107). If a man will treat his wife properly, with love and respect, Hamilton says, he will discover "in the commonplace, insipid domestic weakling he scorns an angel unawares" (169). Indeed, after charging women with the responsibility for uplifting their own souls and supporting the souls of men in "Men and Women," Hamilton calls for men to take responsibility for themselves and their families. Men cannot count on women to reform them, she warns:

> If a husband be intemperate, or given over to money-getting, or money-saving, or money-spending,—if he be ill-tempered, indelicate, ignorant, obstinate, arrogant,—no wife, be she ever so prudent, wise, affectionate, can make the home what it ought to be. . . .
> Let us know the pretext upon which a full-grown man charges a delicate woman, who has had little if anything to do with him until he became a full-grown man, with the cure of his soul? (138–139)

Rather, she argues, men must take responsibility for their share of moral influence, on their wives as well as their children. If men are indeed stronger than women, she suggests, then they should be responsible for improving women, not vice versa.

Yet Hamilton cannot or will not completely overturn her own and her society's steadfast belief in women's influence over men. In the last thirty pages of *A New Atmosphere*, she moves back and forth between assigning men the primary role and giving women moral precedence. She claims that "men make women, and men and women together make society" (304), but she also charges men to accept "God's help proffered in woman" (292). After arguing for men to become more motherly, she finally insists that men and women have separate and distinct roles in society: "Men are the rocky stratum, women the soil which covers it. Men determine the outline, the level, the general character; women give the curves, the bloom, the grace" (305). As in "Men and Women," Hamilton's jeremiad ends not by calling for significant change but in repeating orthodox ideals. She predicts a better life when "man and woman . . . go together, he bringing his sturdy strength to shorten, she lending her manifold grace to lighten, the path that leads up thither" (306). This vision resolves the tensions Hamilton creates between men and women, and her jeremiad again seems to offer less of a challenge to existing social values and power relations and more of an affirmation of the idea of gender complementarity.

Hamilton's jeremiads clearly take gender difference into much greater account than other, more familiar jeremiads. Yet, like some others, Hamilton's essays offer only limited visions of social change, repeating instead conservative social ideas. Part of this seems to be a limitation of the form, which always ends with a vision of the glories of reclaiming past traditions. While Hamilton encourages men to become more like women, she cannot finally present womanhood as a complete model. She moves toward establishing a more radical version of Winthrop's model of the mother as the ideal citizen, but she will not, or cannot, set aside her culture's belief that the differences between men and women are ordained by God and that they are complementary. She cannot make a convincing argument either that women's influence is sufficient to create social change or that men should fully embrace a feminine model. Both texts end with images that reinforce clear divisions between men's and women's roles. Hamilton's message to women that they should be content to inspire and care for men reinscribes women's submissive, secondary position in the culture. She tells men, on the other hand, that "opinion needs to be right, prejudice removed, and society renovated; and men must do it" (304), repositioning men as the dominant force. In both texts, Hamilton seems torn between her belief in gender complementarity and her faith in the virtuous power of good womanhood. In both, she ends by re-establishing consensus but not offering significant social change.

Hamilton's gendered jeremiad is typical of those written by women who opposed suffrage.[7] Antisuffrage rhetoric combined criticisms of male greed and selfishness with claims that women had failed to live up to the promise of true womanhood. "Antis" also saw hope for the future in women's return to feminine virtue and men's conversion to the Christian values of home and community. Unlike suffragists and other "jeremiahs," who established consensus by attempting to make women more like men (by giving women the same rights men enjoyed), "Antis" attempted to maintain a consensus based on gender complementarity. Like Hamilton, however, most "Antis" wanted both women and men to become more womanly. Their vision failed because it could not transcend the conservative ideal of feminine submissiveness and influence partnered by masculine dominance and power. Antisuffrage women could revise the jeremiad by inserting gender difference into the common form, but they could not plausibly offer a woman-centered society as an alternative because the existing consensus and their own conservative ideas limited women's claims to social power. "Antis" simply could not reconcile the contradiction between gender difference and the female model citizen.

In addition, as Hamilton's texts reveal, women writers who embraced this contradictory vision of gender difference faced particular difficulties in attempting to use the authoritative form offered by the jeremiad. Hamilton's discomfort in using the jeremiad suggests that public authority did not quite fit an antisuffrage vision of feminine power. The endings of "Men and Women" and *A New Atmosphere* assign men the more active role of creating social change and instruct women to wait on the sidelines. For a woman to claim an active role in public discourse, especially by using a rhetorical weapon most often used by men, required her to reject such a sideline position. She could not embrace the roles of muse and caretaker while lecturing on social problems. For Hamilton, at least, the jeremiad seems to have offered authority but also, perhaps, to have challenged her ideas about the nature of feminine power. This irreconcilable tension in her essays reveals both Hamilton's resistance and the limitations of that resistance. She resists by insisting that the dominant form of American discourse recognize gender difference and thus explicitly include women, as well as by claiming a previously masculine form for her own, but she cannot envision a truly new paradigm from within the confines of her own conservative ideas about gender.

NOTES

1. To his credit, Sacvan Bercovitch identifies and briefly analyzes the use of the jeremiad by both conservative and radical women during the nineteenth century, including Catharine Beecher, Antoinette Brown Blackwell, Elizabeth Oakes Smith, and Elizabeth Cady Stanton (157–159).

2. For discussions of women's participation in public discourse during this period, see Baym, Kelley, and Moyle.

3. Hamilton's letters to John Greenleaf Whittier, George Wood, Henry James, Sr., and James G. Blaine—all prominent men—were frequently provocative, both ideologically and personally. While the writing style in these letters matches her witty public writings, the subjects and her directness with her friends suggest that she was more comfortable challenging individual men than she was challenging men as a class. See H. Augusta Dodge, ed., *Gail Hamilton's Life in Letters.*

4. Hamilton's letters describe many evenings spent in conversation with visitors to the houses where Hamilton lived, first with Gamaliel Bailey's family and later in the home of James G. Blaine, Speaker of the House. Although her early letters express some shyness, she later became quite comfortable with such interaction. See Hamilton's *Letters.*

5. Kelley cites the case of Fanny Fern, whose autobiographical novel *Ruth Hall* received harsh criticism for its unfeminine anger and implications of revenge against the writer's family as an example of the consequences of unfeminine writing.

6. See, for example, the works of Fanny Fern, as well as Hamilton's own writings, like "My Garden," in Coultrap-McQuin's *Gail Hamilton: Selected Writings.* Elements of Hamilton's usual witty style appear in all of her works, but in these jeremiads, that style regularly segues into a more serious, prophetic voice.

7. For examples of fictional versions of this, see Rose Terry Cooke, *Happy Dodd; or, She Hath Done What She Could,* and Rebecca Harding Davis, *John Andross.* For closer analysis of antisuffrage rhetoric, see my article on Cooke's writing about woman suffrage.

REFERENCES

Anderson, Douglas. *A House Undivided: Domesticity and Community in American Literature.* Cambridge: Cambridge UP, 1990.

Bercovitch, Sacvan. *The American Jeremiad.* Madison: U of Wisconsin P, 1978.

Cooke, Rose Terry. *Happy Dodd; or, She Hath Done What She Could.* Boston: Ticknor, 1887.

Cott, Nancy F. *The Bonds of Womanhood: "Woman's Sphere" in New England, 1780–1835.* New Haven: Yale UP, 1977.

Coultrap-McQuin, Susan. *Doing Literary Business: American Women Writers in the Nineteenth Century.* Chapel Hill: U of North Carolina P, 1990.

———. "Introduction." *Gail Hamilton: Selected Writings*. New Brunswick: Rutgers UP, 1992. xi– xxxvii.

Davis, Rebecca Harding. *John Andross*. New York: Orange, 1874.

Dodge, H. Augusta, ed. *Gail Hamilton's Life in Letters*. 2 Vols. Boston: Lee, 1901.

Dodge, Mary Abigail. *A New Atmosphere*. Boston: Ticknor, 1865.

———. "Men and Women." *Country Living and Country Thinking*. Boston: Ticknor, 1861.

Kelley, Mary. *Private Woman, Public Stage: Literary Domesticity in Nineteenth-century America*. New York: Oxford UP, 1984.

Landow, George P. *Elegant Jeremiahs: The Sage from Carlyle to Mailer*. Ithaca: Cornell UP, 1986.

Linkon, Sherry Lee. "Saints, Sufferers, and Strong-Minded Sisters: Rose Terry Cooke's Anti-suffrage Rhetoric." *Legacy* 10 (1994): 31–46.

Moyle, Geraldine. "The Tenth Muse Lately Sprung up in the Marketplace: Women and Professional Authorship in Nineteenth-century America." Diss. UCLA, 1985.

Parton, Sara. *Ruth Hall and Other Writings by Fanny Fern*. Joyce Warren, ed. New Brunswick: Rutgers UP, 1986.

Schueller, Malini Johar. *The Politics of Voice: Liberalism and Social Criticism from Franklin to Kingston*. Albany: SUNY P, 1992.

Smith-Rosenberg, Carroll. *Disorderly Conduct: Vision of Gender in Victorian America*. New York: Knopf, 1985.

Stimpson, Catherine R. "Female Insubordination and the Text." *Women in Culture and Politics: A Century of Change*. Ed. Judith Friedlander, Blanche Wiesen Cook, Alice Kessler-Harris, and Carroll Smith-Rosenberg. Bloomington: Indiana UP, 1986. 164–176.

The American Indian Story of Zitkala-Sa

Margaret A. Lukens

Zitkala-Sa is the pen name of Gertrude Simmons Bonnin, the first Native American woman writer to publish her own life story without the mediation of a non-Indian editor or ghost writer. Her autobiographical essays appeared at the turn of the twentieth century in the highly visible and influential *Atlantic Monthly*, and their publication won her instant recognition among the literati of the Northeast. However, despite her acceptance by people in the first circle of white society, what she wrote reflected her discomfort at occupying the liminal status of a white-educated Indian, placed, as she expressed it, "in the heart of chaos, beyond the touch or voice of human aid" (69).[1] In telling the story of her own growth to adulthood, Zitkala-Sa declared her love for Native culture as well as her ongoing and energetic concern for the necessity of Indian self-determination. She wrote to revise the dominant culture's assumptions about her people and the value of tribal culture, using a rhetorical strategy of contrast and inversion; she set the religious faith of the Sioux, the strength of family relationships, and the commitment to educating children in the context of the tribal community against the cruelty, ignorance, and superstition of the whites and their missionary system of education whose first principle was the removal of children from their homes. Zitkala-Sa thereby held up a mirror to her white readers and demonstrated that many cultural and racial prejudices they had long held about Indians actually reflected the worst inclinations of white America.

Born at the Yankton Sioux Agency in South Dakota, the third child of Tate I Yohin Win (Reaches for the Wind), a full-blood Dakota woman, and a white man who left the family before her birth, Gertrude Simmons learned the ways of her tribe for her first eight years of life. In 1884 missionaries arrived to recruit students for White's Manual Institute, a Quaker boarding school for Indians in Wabash, Indiana; their stories of the East featuring orchards full of apples may have persuaded eight-year-old Gertrude to leave for the distant school despite her mother's fears. Six years of missionary education, completed in 1895, led to studies at Earlham College from 1895 to 1897, and then to a teaching post at Carlisle Indian Industrial School in Pennsylvania during 1899 and 1900.

While employed at Carlisle, Gertrude began her quest to gain the attention of the powerful literary and political circles in the East as an Indian spokesperson. She initially published her autobiographical stories under the *nom de plume* Zitkala-Sa ("Red Bird" in Lakota) in the *Atlantic Monthly*'s first three issues of 1900 and rapidly developed a literary reputation among readers of that reputable journal. She was in good company in the pages of the *Atlantic*; among others whose work appeared there in 1900 were Edith Wharton, former President Grover Cleveland, Henry James, Jack London, and John Muir. At the turn of the century, the *Atlantic Monthly*, which through the mid-1890s had been a culturally conservative institution, was shedding its calm façade and beginning to publish politically and socially controversial material (Mott, *A History* vol. 4, 44). It had begun to "approach . . . that wide interest in the problems of the modern world which characterized the magazine under later management" (Mott, *A History* vol. 2, 513). The inclusion of articles by Zitkala-Sa showed the influence of the popular movement to reform U.S. policy toward Native Americans, begun in the 1880s with the publication of Helen Hunt Jackson's *A Century of Dishonor* and continuing into the first decades of the twentieth century.[2] When the U.S. military campaign to subdue Indian hostilities was succeeded by the reservation system and its management of all the surviving tribes in the United States, the Euro-American public found itself faced with the continuing presence of a subdued enemy and the guilt produced by reports on the wretched conditions endured by so many Native people. White Americans began to work out their guilt in a variety of ways. These ranged from assisting in the educational and political "improvement of the Indian" to popularizing the Indian in mainstream culture—in books, films, camp and scouting activities, and pictorial art, to name just a few.

This popular movement was also manifest in political developments among Native people around the country. Gertrude Bonnin became a member of the pan-Indian Society for the American Indian (SAI) in 1911. The SAI required that its members be of Indian blood; its aims were toward Indian self-determination but were essentially assimilationist. Bonnin and her husband, Raymond Talesfase Bonnin, moved to Washington, D.C., when she was elected secretary of the SAI in 1916; she served as editor of its periodical, the *American Indian Magazine*, during 1918 and 1919. Suffering the effects of strenuous internal disagreement, the SAI disbanded in 1920. Bonnin then turned her energies to working with the General Federation of Women's Clubs to found an Indian Welfare Committee.

In 1921, after the demise of the SAI, Gertrude Bonnin again assumed the role and name of Zitkala-Sa and collected her autobiographical stories and other previously uncollected short fiction and essays into one volume titled *American Indian Stories*. As Dexter Fisher states in her foreword to the 1979 reprint of *American Indian Stories*, Zitkala-Sa's autobiographical articles exemplified "one of the first attempts by a Native American woman to write her own story without the aid of an editor, an interpreter, or an ethnographer" (vi). In her freedom from the mediating judgment of an amanuensis, she was able to give voice to harsh criticisms of the dominant culture's methods of educating Native youth, the culturally genocidal intentions behind inducing Native students to learn European ways, and the government bureaucracy's inhumane mismanagement of the welfare of Native people as wards of the nation. These critical attacks are embedded in and intrinsically part of her own personal stories, and the sympathy the stories create in the reader leads the reader to adopt a critical position similar to the author's. In moving her mainstream audience to a new critical perspective, Zitkala-Sa hoped to make grassroots changes in national attitudes, which would improve the way her people were treated.

In "The School Days of an Indian Girl," Zitkala-Sa describes how the missionary school experience attempted to strip Native children of their tribal cultures and replace them with knowledge of Christianity, literacy, and the English language. It seemed at first to Indians like Gertrude's mother that the missionaries' offer of education "[began] to pay a tardy justice" (44) for the theft of Indian lands and was necessary for the advancement of their children in the white-controlled world; however, in fact, Gertrude discovered that her loss of Sioux culture and habits was not compensated by anything she gained from the white culture. Rather, she was left angry and isolated, alienated from her mentors in the white educational system and also from her own family, to the point of desiring to name herself anew as Zitkala-Sa. In the foreword to *Old Indian Legends*, Agnes Picotte notes that, although the author grew up speaking the Nakota (Dakota) dialect of the Sioux language, the name she chooses was from the Lakota dialect (xi). This act of self-naming was, in Dexter Fisher's estimation, an assertion of both her independence and her ties to Sioux culture (*AIS* x). However, that she chose a name from Lakota instead of one from her home dialect might indicate a more profound dislocation from her origins as well as a more conscious act of choice.

She wrote of these origins in the first of her *American Indian Stories*, "Impressions of an Indian Childhood," published in the *Atlantic Monthly* in 1900. The story reveals the humane childrearing practices among the Sioux and provides the context for early suspicions of whites that she imbibed from her mother. Sioux educational practices make a striking contrast with her later experiences at a school run by white missionaries; her mother takes pride in Gertrude's "wild freedom and overflowing spirits" (8), quite unlike the severe Quaker men and women who take over her training later. In fact, in the girl's early childhood, there were two modes of learning available to her, which she lost upon entering the white school system: learning experientially from her great degree of freedom and learning by imitating her mother and other older women of the tribe.

Gertrude learns her own physical limits by testing them:

> I tore away at my highest possible speed, with my long, black hair blowing in the breeze. . . . Having gone many paces ahead I stopped, panting for breath, and laughing with glee as my mother watched my every movement. . . . It was as if I were the activity, and my hands and feet were only experiments for my spirit to work upon. (8)

The act of running is not random play but rather an experiment for the spirit, and her mother gives full attention to Gertrude as she engages in the experiment. Similarly, she and her friends discover the natural world in their free playtime, practicing their recognition of the edible plants they have been taught to find:

> We each carried a light sharpened rod about four feet long, with which we pried up certain sweet roots. When we had eaten all the choice roots . . . we shouldered our rods and strayed off into patches of a stalky plant under whose yellow blossoms we found little crystal drops of gum. Drop by drop we gathered this nature's rock candy, until each of us could boast of a lump the size of a small bird's egg. Soon satiated with its woody flavor, we tossed away our gum, to return again to the sweet roots. (21)

Such essentially scientific skills of plant taxonomy are necessary for life on the land, as is a certain knowledge of the behavior of light and shadows. Knowledge of light and shadow was the way Gertrude learned to tell time, to understand where to position a dwelling or to plant vegetables, how to navigate on the trackless prairie. Zitkala-Sa narrates young Gertrude's attempts to catch her own shadow, noting, "Before this peculiar experience I have no distinct memory of having recognized any vital bond between myself and my own shadow" (24), illustrating the introduction of an important scientific concept into the mind of the youngster through playful interaction with the natural world.

Early expectations of Gertrude were that she would do her best to live up to the standards of her mother and the community. Skills and manners were inculcated by Gertrude's mother, both by strict admonition and by example. Although Zitkala-Sa writes "She taught me no fear save that of intruding myself upon others" (8), it is evident that her mother was strict about that and other rules of conduct. When she had something to teach, she was serious and firm:

The quietness of her oversight made me feel strongly responsible and dependent upon my own judgment. She treated me as a dignified little individual as long as I was on my good behavior; and how humiliated I was when some boldness of mine drew forth a rebuke from her! (20)

In tribal culture where community and communal values are so important, discipline is enforced by shame at one's exposure to community disapproval; in the white missionary system Gertrude falls into later, discipline is based upon guilt, which is the punishment of a society that centers on the individual. Zitkala-Sa's narrative of traditional Sioux childrearing emphasizes the humaneness and effectiveness of such community discipline, against which she intended to show the inhumaneness and sometimes the incomprehensibility to an Indian child of the way white missionaries maintained order.

The structure of learning and the curriculum of Gertrude's early training were deeply embedded in her Sioux culture. Whether attempting to create childish imitations of traditional styles of beadwork, which her mother insists be "sufficiently characteristic," or playing with her girlfriends at imitating their mothers, she is learning to perpetuate the culture of her tribe. She is taught to respect her elders, to be a generous host to guests in her home, and to be actively concerned for the welfare of all members of her tribe, particularly the ill or unfortunate.

One aspect of life that her mother teaches her in no uncertain terms is that in relationships between Indians and whites, the whites are villainous. In the first section of "Impressions of an Indian Childhood," young Gertrude tells her mother that she will draw water from the river when she grows big enough. Her mother replies, "If the paleface does not take away from us the river we drink." The girl asks who the "bad paleface" is, and her mother states unequivocally, "My little daughter, he is a sham,—a sickly sham! The bronzed Dakota is the only real man" (9). She goes on to tell the sad story of the deaths of Gertrude's sister and uncle, and even her father, blaming them all on the fraudulence and violence of the "paleface." At this point in the narrative, Zitkala-Sa turns away from strict narration of her own life, since records show that her own father was a white man named Felker (Fisher, AIS, ix). The truth and intensity of her mother's negative feelings are probably accurately represented, however, since he deserted the family before Gertrude's birth.

Despite the realities of friction between Gertrude and her mother, the mother is represented as a nearly prophetic voice of truth. When she submits to her daughter's wish to leave for school, it is partly because she believes their education of her daughter may begin to repay the "palefaces['] . . . large debt for stolen lands"; she lets the little girl go despite her knowledge that "[her] daughter must suffer keenly in this experiment" (44).

Zitkala-Sa tells a story designed to characterize the white missionaries which takes place before Gertrude is old enough to be tempted to leave home with them. Significantly, the incident is set in the winter, a time of confinement and probably some deprivation; it is, she says, her only winter memory. The missionaries have given her a bag of glass marbles. When Gertrude and her mother go walking by the river one day, she chances to observe the same colors in blocks of river ice as those in her marbles from the missionaries. She says,

> With my bare fingers I tried to pick out some of the colors, for they seemed so near to the surface. But my fingers began to sting with the intense cold, and I had to bite them hard to keep from crying.
> From that day on, for many a moon, I believed that glass marbles had river ice inside of them. (37–38)

The image of ice at the heart of the marbles, the only emblem she has for the missionaries, prefigures the cold heartlessness she will later experience at their hands. The image is echoed in later descriptions of the "palefaces": in the "glassy blue eyes" of white men who stare at the Indian children on their journey to Indiana (47), in her arrival at the missionaries' boarding school when "the snow still covered the ground, and the trees were bare" (52), and in her characterization of Earlham College students as "a cold race whose hearts were frozen hard with prejudice" (76).

The way Gertrude was raised by her mother contrasts starkly and deliberately in Zitkala-Sa's text with the practices at the missionary boarding school for Indians in chapter two of *American Indian Stories*, "The School Days of an Indian Girl." On the first leg of her journey to Indiana in the company of the "palefaces," she is "as frightened and bewildered as the captured young of a wild creature" (45); after only one day at White's Manual Institute, she will have become "only one of the little animals driven by a herder" (56). Every aspect of life, including eating meals, is now regimented in a new, strange way.

Food immediately becomes a problem for Gertrude. On the train trip, she tells us, one of the missionaries has made a game of tossing candies to the children, who have competed to grab the greatest quantity. Interestingly, her narration of the incident in *American Indian Stories* leaves out the last two sentences of the paragraph as it had appeared originally in the *Atlantic Monthly*. The omitted sentences said that:

> The missionary's generous distribution of candies was impressed upon my memory by a disastrous result which followed. I had caught more than my share of candies and gums, and soon after our arrival at the school I had a chance to disgrace myself, which, I am ashamed to say, I did. (*Atlantic Monthly* 185)

The reader assumes Gertrude's disgrace is that too much candy made her sick to her stomach, which is hard on one's reputation if it happens in public. The mystery is why, twenty-one years after the initial publication, Zitkala-Sa would choose to delete those sentences. They illustrate so vividly her early experience of "paleface" food, demonstrating its capacity to sicken rather than to nourish. The later version puts less emphasis on Gertrude's greedy participation, which helped bring down the consequences; in it the candy-toss is only a brief glimpse in a bewildering panorama of new experience.

Zitkala-Sa describes the "palefaces" as outstandingly rude, according to the manners she has been taught as a Sioux. Children and adults alike stare unabashedly at the Indian children, dressed in best dresses with newly beaded moccasins and belts for the journey. White mothers do not chastise their children for gawking, as Indian mothers would do, but instead point out the curiosity of each Indian child's blanket. Upon arrival at the school in Indiana, Gertrude experiences an affront to her dignity:

> two warm hands grasped me firmly, and in the same moment I was tossed high in midair. A rosy-cheeked paleface woman caught me in her arms. I was both frightened and insulted by such trifling. . . . My mother had never made a plaything of her wee daughter. (50)

This gesture, no doubt intended to loosen the child up and make her feel more at ease in her new surroundings, is an analogue for the attitude of whites who would, in the late nineteenth century, make playthings of Indians or attempt to assuage their own guilty consciences by bringing them into a situation of wardship. It also vividly illustrates the vast cultural chasm between Gertrude and her new teachers.

Zitkala-Sa repeatedly observes that the good intentions of the missionaries were wrong-headed and that, in many cases, the forms of white culture came as an affront to well-brought-up Indians. The fashion of women's clothing enforced at the school, dresses with tight-fitting bodices, strikes Gertrude as terribly immodest since she is used to concealing her own form in loose-fitting buckskin and a blanket over all. The manner of cutting hair is worse, since for the Sioux, "short hair was worn by mourners, and shingled hair by cowards [i.e. captured warriors whose hair was cut by the enemy]" (54). Zitkala-Sa narrates this conflict in the terms of a warrior's struggle, since she recognizes the system of white education to be a part of the violent destruction of her people and her culture. Gertrude runs and hides the day they are cutting hair, but to no avail; she is captured and suffers the consequences: "I felt the cold blades of the scissors against my neck, and heard them gnaw off one of my thick braids. Then I lost my spirit" (56). Clearly her cultural understanding of shorn hair takes precedence as she succumbs to mourning the death of her Sioux ethnicity.

Gertrude's resistance does not end there, however. The third section of "School Days" effectively juxtaposes two incidents of rebellion: the first instance is verbal, inadvertent, and disastrous; the second is nonverbal, intentional, and effective. In the first incident, Gertrude and three friends are caught playing in the snow against the rules, and they hastily rehearse the word "no" in hopes that it will exonerate them. By contrast to methods of discipline in which the community presence is vital, the missionary teachers create an atmosphere of paranoia in which punishment occurs by isolating the children from one another. The first of the three girls is asked questions like "Are you going to obey my word the next time?" (58) and suffers a hard spanking. The girls are caught between two cultures, and it is not their disobedience but their lack of access to the English language and their unfamiliarity with methods of interrogation that draw them the punishment.

The second incident is similar, but it is Gertrude alone who is called in for breaking a playground rule. Her punishment is to mash turnips for the noon-time meal. By this time, she has developed decided preferences concerning "paleface" food:

> I hated turnips, and their odor which came from the brown jar was offensive to me. With fire in my heart, I took the wooden tool . . ., grasping the handle with both hands, I bent in hot rage over the turnips. I worked my vengeance upon them. . . . as I sent the masher into the bottom of the jar, I felt a satisfying sensation that the weight of my body had gone into it. (60)

Gertrude's revenge is that the bottom of the jar breaks under her weight; the turnips end up on the kitchen floor rather than the dining room table: "As I sat eating my dinner, and saw that no turnips were served, I whooped in my heart for having once asserted the rebellion within me" (61). Once again, Zitkala-Sa depicts Gertrude as a young warrior in her resistance to white authority.

Zitkala-Sa turns the rhetorical tables on the religion and medical practices of white people, two areas in which "civilization" pretends superiority to tribal "superstitions"; in fact, she shows that from a Sioux point of view, the beliefs of the whites appear to be no more than superstitions. A section of "School Days" is devoted to Gertrude's experience of learning about the devil of Christianity and seeing a picture of the white man's conception of "the king of evil spirits." She is surprised to hear the immediacy of the white teacher's stories about the devil, since the elders of the Sioux "taught [her] to fear [evil spirits] no more than those who stalked about in material guise" (62). The white woman's story is "that this terrible creature roamed loose in the world, and that little girls who disobeyed school regulations were to be tortured by him" (63); the story is clearly designed to frighten the children into obedience, but it also assumes a degree of superstition and credulity that does not do justice to the students' spiritual training or to the sophistication of their native religion. Even as a child, Gertrude is capable of a judgment against this ignorant sort of belief: "I blamed the hard-working, well-meaning, ignorant woman who was inculcating in our hearts her superstitious ideas" (67). This woman is the antitype of Gertrude's mother, who has been her source of religious truth until her departure for school.

When Gertrude has a bad dream about the devil coming to get her, she takes her revenge on the ugly image that has polluted her consciousness. In a gesture that foreshadows her future as a writer who will write to reshape the contents of people's imaginations, she uses "a broken slate pencil" to scratch the picture from the book of Bible stories: "I began by scratching out his eyes. A few moments later, when I was ready to leave the room, there was a ragged hole in the page where the picture of the devil had once been" (64). She has met the devil as bogeyman and taken her complete revenge.

The most damning charge against the white missionaries is their inattention to the Indian children's physical ailments; Zitkala-Sa asserts that the whites are not just coldhearted, but that they are unaware of effective methods of treatment. All that seems to matter in the school is the student's presence at roll call: "No matter if a dull headache or the painful cough of slow consumption had delayed the absentee, there was only time enough to mark the tardiness" (66). When a classmate dies of a chronic illness, Gertrude observes no more effective remedy being applied than "the open pages of the white man's Bible." In her anger, she says,

I grew bitter, and censured the woman for cruel neglect of our physical ills. I despised the pencils that moved automatically, and the one teaspoon which dealt out, from a large bottle, healing to a row of variously ailing Indian children. (67)

The supposedly advanced medical science of the whites appears to be no more than a patent remedy, misapplied to a wide variety of ailments. And again, the white female teacher is the antitype of Gertrude's mother, having failed to nurture and protect the children placed in her care. The voice and vision of the "other," so degraded and misunderstood by the majority white society, is thus recuperated by Zitkala-Sa's subtle chronicle.

However, despite these failures, the system succeeds in holding Gertrude's interest in continuing her education. Her own very personal reaction to liminality aids in the decision as well. When she is home on the reservation for four years after her first three years of school, she gets little comfort from her older brother or from her mother, who cannot understand the intellectual split that literacy has produced in her daughter. The reservation itself has changed; there are "no more young braves in blankets and eagle plumes, nor Indian maids with prettily painted cheeks" (72). Gertrude might fit into the social activities where all the young people who have been to school and have "become civilized," wear suits and dresses, and speak English, except that she has discarded the fashions of the white school: "I had no hat, no ribbons, and no close-fitting gown. Since my return from school I had thrown away my shoes, and wore again the soft moccasins" (73). She does not value the outward trappings of white culture, but her rebellion against her mother prevents her from feeling at home on the reservation. In fact, the worst of the conflict sounds like a classic adolescent discontent with self and surroundings:

> Even nature seemed to have no place for me. I was neither a wee girl nor a tall one; neither a wild Indian nor a tame one. This deplorable situation was the effect of my brief course in the East, and the unsatisfactory "teenth" in a girl's years. (69)

Having been exposed to an alternative place, Gertrude attempts to find a solution to her alienation by going east to school once more in her quest for an education and a place where she feels right.

A high school diploma enables her to enter Earlham College, but these successes do not assuage Gertrude's feelings of belonging nowhere. The mostly white students at Earlham are "scornful and yet curious"(76); they are slow to seek her out and only do so after she succeeds publicly, winning an intramural oratorical contest. She narrates that she "hid" herself in her dormitory room, "pined for sympathey," and "wept in secret" (76). Gertrude Simmons later encountered overt racism at the Indiana State Oratorical Contest of 1896, at which she was the sole representative of Earlham College. Zitkala-Sa tells generally of "strong prejudice against my people" and "the slurs against the Indian that stained the lips of our opponents"; she also paints a vivid picture of "a large white flag, with a drawing of a most forlorn Indian girl on it. Under this they had printed in bold black letters words that ridiculed the college which was represented by a 'squaw'" (79). Zitkala-Sa characterizes the racist slur as "worse than barbarian rudeness" (79), putting the "savage" shoe on the white foot she believes it truly fits.

Zitkala-Sa depicts Gertrude's progress east in "An Indian Teacher Among Indians," the third chapter of *American Indian Stories* and her third story to appear in the *Atlantic Monthly*. Her progress opposes the westward movement of conquest pursued by the whites and takes her beyond the system of education into her life's work and eventual residence in Washington, D.C., as an advocate for Indian rights. She says,

> Since the winter when I had my first dreams about red apples I had been traveling slowly toward the morning horizon. There had been no

doubt about the direction in which I wished to go to spend my energies in a work for the Indian race. (81)

Her next step after Indiana is Carlisle Indian School in western Pennsylvania. Although the chapter title says she is "Among Indians," the only Indian she interacts with in the narrative is her mother while on a brief visit to Yankton. There she discovers that her brother has been replaced in his Indian agency job on the reservation; as her mother tells her, "the Great Father at Washington sent a white son to take your brother's pen from him. Since then Dawee has not been able to make use of the education the Eastern school has given him" (90–91). Evidently, the white world does not want to grant space, power, or autonomy to Native Americans despite its efforts to "civilize" and "Americanize" them. Dawee has taken the risk of being an advocate for his people, and, as his mother says, "The Indian cannot complain to the Great Father in Washington without suffering outrage for it here [i.e., on the reservation]" (91). Dawee's trouble helps propel Gertrude toward her eventual life's work and location in Washington, D.C.

Gertrude's observations of the corruptions and intentions of the system of educating Indians lead her to reflect bitterly upon her own role as a teacher and on the "civilized" visitors who come through her classrooms as if to a zoo. Her decision to leave her teaching post is predicated on the question the "palefaces" have failed to ask themselves: "whether real life or long-lasting death lies beneath this semblance of civilization" (99), which is the white system of educating Indians. Having "forgotten the healing in trees and brooks," she describes herself metaphorically as "a slender tree . . . uprooted from my mother, nature, and . . . shorn of my branches. . . . The natural coat of bark . . . scraped off to the very quick" (97). This image recalls the moaning telegraph pole of her childhood, of which she says, "I used to wonder what the paleface had done to hurt it" (48) The "cold bare pole" she has become expresses her desire for the chance to be a powerful communicator in a new medium on behalf of her people. The electric metaphor becomes a storm of unharnessed natural energy:

Still, I seemed to hope a day would come when my mute aching head, reared upward to the sky, would flash a zigzag lightning across the heavens. With this dream of vent for a long-pent consciousness, I walked again amid the crowds. (97)

Her own story is an exemplum of the long story of Native American survival despite all the powerful attempts of white people to accomplish the genocide of Native people and cultures; her literary resistance is a vital aspect of that survival, since she has taken control of the story and told it from an insider's point of view.

Zitkala-Sa depicts Gertrude's mother as the bearer of tribal religion in much the same way dominant cultural discourse created the white woman as the Christian "angel of the house." However, her mother is not limited and enfeebled by her association with her religion as white women were by theirs. In the face of the hard-heartedness, corruption, and disappointment she has encountered in mainstream America, Gertrude has temporarily lost her faith in the Great Spirit: "The Great Spirit does not care if we live or die! Let us not look for good or justice: then we shall not be disappointed!" Her mother replies, "Sh! my child, do not talk so madly. There is Taku Iyotan Wasaka, to which I pray" (92). The author's note on the deity's name reads "an absolute power"; she comments no further, but the straightforwardness of her note implies deep respect of the faith she thought she had lost. Her essay "The Great Spirit" provides further evidence of this.

"The Great Spirit," originally published in the *Atlantic Monthly* in 1902 under the title "Why I Am a Pagan," justifies her rejection of Christianity in favor of her Native religion. Describing herself as more religious than the converted Indian whom she characterizes as a "distorted shadow," she is attuned to "the loving Mystery" and treats "the solemn 'native preacher'" "with a compassion for all echoes in human disguise," listening "with respect for God's creature, though he mouth most strangely the jangling phrases of a bigoted creed" (101–105). As Royal Hassrick notes, Sioux religion was based on reconciliation with nature:

> Knowledge and interpretation of natural forces became the science of living essential to the very existence of the individual. The more comprehensive and in tune the understanding, the more forthright was the person's direction, the more assured his adjustment. . . .
>
> The forces of nature were so real, so close, and so great that disregard of their omnipotence was inconceivable. Rather, reverence and gratitude that man was permitted to exist in the midst of such an awesome world were the logical and realistic foundations of Sioux belief. (Hassrick 205–206, 213)

In her knowledge of "natural forces," Zitkala-Sa has achieved the forthrightness of direction and assurance necessary to discard Christianity, despite all the work of her missionary schooling. The essay contains a conversation between Zitkala-Sa and a "native preacher" whose message is preoccupied with "the after-doom of hell fire," echoing the lesson on the devil from the woman at White's Manual Institute. In spite of his narrow view, Zitkala-Sa says she "would not forget that the pale-faced missionary and the hoodooed aborigine are both God's creatures, though small indeed their own conceptions of Infinite Love" (107), demonstrating that she is capable of forgiveness while at the same time rejecting "the bigoted creed." Since Christianity justified so much of the cultural genocide against Native Americans, her rejection of the religion implies a more total rejection of the whole imperialist project.

Although her literary efforts and public recitations were received with overwhelming public acclaim, Zitkala-Sa's forthright criticism of the Indian boarding school experience caused an unhealable rift with her employer at Carlisle. According to Deborah Welch, Richard Henry Pratt, who had founded the school in 1879 with the purpose of acculturating Native children, characterized her stories as "trash." Pratt's displeasure with Zitkala-Sa's publications in the *Atlantic* led first to her reassignment as a recruiter—effectively a banishment to the West, away from the support of her literary coterie—and eventually to the end of her tenure at Carlisle. However, Zitkala-Sa parlayed this time in the West to her advantage, because this was where she collected the material for *Old Indian Legends*, her next major publication.

Dexter Fisher has argued that in publishing *Old Indian Legends* in 1901, Zitkala-Sa sought "to become the literary counterpart of the oral storytellers of her tribe" (1977, 229). The title page of the book bears out this intention: the stories are "retold by Zitkala-Sa"; the artistic decision to include illustrations by Angel De Cora, a Winnebago artist, gives a visual aspect to this published performance of traditional orature. The legends, including a number of stories of Iktomi, the Dakota Trickster, are stories traditionally told for entertainment as opposed to sacred tales. Zitkala-Sa retold and filtered these tales with the intention of reaching a culturally diverse audience of young people. Her work was popularly acclaimed, as illustrated by a testimonial letter from Helen Keller appended to *American Indian Stories* as an advertisement for *Old Indian Legends*. On August 25, 1919, Keller wrote:

Dear Zitkala-Sa:

I thank you for your book on Indian Legends. I have read them with exquisite pleasure. Like all folk tales they mirror the child life of the world. . .

Your tales of birds, beast, tree and spirit can not but hold captive the hearts of all children. They will kindle in their young minds that eternal wonder which creates poetry and keeps life fresh and eager. I wish you and your little book of Indian tales all success. (*AIS* 196)

Keller's letter praised the book for its "wild, strange music," and its inclusion in the volume lent Zitkala-Sa some of Keller's popular cachet.

According to Dorothea Susag, the image of the trickster Iktomi informs not only *Old Indian Legends* but also Zitkala-Sa's autobiographical essays and short fiction. As a representation of the trickery of white people, Iktomi stories instruct Native people to beware and not be fooled by smooth talk. Conversely, Susag sees Iktomi as a positive embodiment of creative and powerful ways for Native people to engage in cultural trickery in defense against cultural genocide, as Zitkala-Sa herself did by excelling in and seeming to accept the white world while holding with fierce pride onto Dakota traditions. As the years passed, Gertrude Simmons Bonnin became an increasingly devoted and influential advocate for Indian rights, and it was in 1924, during the height of her political activism, that citizenship was finally granted to Native Americans. That same year, the Indian Rights Association assigned her to investigate abuses in the government's treatment of some Oklahoma tribes; with two fellow investigators, she co-authored "Oklahoma's Poor Rich Indians," an exposé that resulted in the appointment of the Meriam Commission and its 1928 report to the U.S. Congress. In 1926 she founded the National Council of American Indians, serving as president from then until her death in 1938. Despite numerous discouragements, her energy was unflagging, and although she did not return to writing fiction after her work as editor of the *American Indian Magazine*, hundreds of pages of letters and articles written by and about Gertrude Simmons Bonnin and her work on Indian rights are contained in various archives around the country. When she died at age sixty-one of cardiac dilatation and kidney disease, she was buried in Arlington National Cemetery under a headstone proclaiming her to be "Gertrude Simmons Bonnin—'Zitkala-Sa' of the Sioux Indians—1876–1938."

Gertrude Simmons Bonnin strove to reach the public conscience of America through her work as Zitkala-Sa; she wrote with the clear purpose of re-creating in the imagination of her mostly white audience the idea of the people and the culture she had left behind her. Her stories, besides showing the Sioux from the inside, reveal the cruelties of white schooling of Indian children and dwell on her own feelings of liminality that resulted from that education. The life and letters of Zitkala-Sa exemplify the condition of a Native American writer in transition between two cultures. However, her success and achievement in the realm of published literature never overshadowed the truth that her inspiration had its source in the traditional oral culture of the Sioux.

NOTES

1. All references by page alone are to Zitkala-Sa, *American Indian Stories.* 1921. Fwd. Dexter Fisher. Lincoln: U of Nebraska P, 1979.
2. See Valerie S. Mathes's *Helen Hunt Jackson and Her Indian Reform Legacy.*

REFERENCES

Cutter, Martha J. "Zitkala-Sa's Autobiographical Writings: The Problems of a Canonical Search for Language and Identity." *Melus* 19:1 (1994): 31–44.
Dockstader, Frederick J. "Gertrude Simmons Bonnin." *Great North American Indians.* New York: Van Nostrand Reinhold, 1977. 40–41.

Fisher, Dexter. "The Transformation of Tradition: A Study of Zitkala-Sa and Mourning Dove, Two Transitional American Indian Writers." Diss. City U of New York, 1979.

———. "The Transformation of Tradition: A Study of Zitkala-Sa and Mourning Dove, Two Transitional American Indian Writers." *Critical Essays on American Indian Literature.* Ed. Andrew Wiget. Boston: Hall, 1985. 202–11.

———. "Zitkala-Sa: The Evolution of a Writer." Foreword. *American Indian Stories.* By Zitkala-Sa. Lincoln: U of Nebraska P, 1979. v–xx.

———. "Zitkala-Sa: The Evolution of a Writer." *American Indian Quarterly* 5 (1977): 229–38.

"Gertrude Bonnin (Zitkala-Sa)." *Native North American Literature.* Ed. Janet Witalec. New York: Gale Research, 1994. 169–176.

Hassrick, Royal B. *The Sioux: Life and Customs of a Warrior Society.* Norman: U of Oklahoma P, 1964.

Lukens, Margaret A. "Creating Cultural Spaces: The Pluralist Project of American Women Writers, 1843–1902 (Margaret Fuller, Harriet Jacobs, Sarah Winnemucca, and Zitkala-Sa)." Diss. U of Colorado, 1991.

Lukens, Margo. "Zitkala-Sa (Gertrude Simmons Bonnin)." *Native American Writers of the United States.* Ed. Kenneth M. Roemer. New York: Bruccoli, 1997. (forthcoming)

Mathes, Valerie S. *Helen Hunt Jackson and Her Indian Reform Legacy.* Austin: U of Texas P, 1990.

Mott, Frank Luther. *A History of American Magazines, 1850–1865.* Vol. 2. Cambridge: Harvard UP, 1938.

———. *A History of American Magazines, 1885–1905.* Vol. 4. Cambridge: Harvard UP, 1957.

Picotte, Agnes. Foreword. *Old Indian Legends.* By Zitkala-Sa. 1901. Rpt. 1985.

Stout, Mary. "Zitkala Sa." *Dictionary of Native American Literature.* Ed. Andrew Wiget. New York: Garland, 1994. 299–303.

———. "Zitkala-Sa: The Literature of Politics." *Coyote Was Here: Essays on Contemporary American Literary and Political Mobilization.* Ed. Bo Scholer, *The Dolphin 9.* Aarhus, Denmark: Seklos, 1984: 70–78.

Susag, Dorothea M. "Zitkala-Sa (Gertrude Simmons Bonnin): A Power(full) Literary Voice." *Studies in American Indian Literatures* 5 (1993): 3–24.

Welch, Deborah. "American Indian Leader: The Story of Gertrude Bonnin." Diss. U of Wyoming, 1985.

Willard, William. "Zitkala-Sa, A Woman Who Would Be Heard." *Wicazo Sa Review* 1 (1985): 11–16.

Young, Mary E. "Gertrude Simmons Bonnin." *Notable American Women, 1607–1950.* Ed. Edward T. James. Cambridge: Belknap, 1971. 198–200.

Zitkala-Sa. *American Indian Stories.* 1921. Fwd. Dexter Fisher. Lincoln: U of Nebraska P, 1979.

———. "Impressions of an Indian Childhood." *Atlantic Monthly* 85 (1900): 37–47.

———. "An Indian Teacher Among Indians." *Atlantic Monthly* 85 (1900): 381–86.

———. "The School Days of an Indian Girl." *Atlantic Monthly* 85 (1900): 185–194.

———. "Why I Am a Pagan." *Atlantic Monthly* 90 (1902): 801–803.

Contributors' Notes

Elizabeth Alexander teaches in the English Department at the University of Chicago. She is the author of two books of poems, *The Venus Hottentot* (University Press of Virginia, 1990) and *Body of Life* (Tia Chucha Press, 1996), as well as a play, *Diva Studies*, and many essays on African-American literature and culture.

Dorothy Z. Baker teaches American literature at the University of Houston. She is the author of *Mystic Masks in Self-Reflexive Poetry* and editor of *Poetics in the Poem: Critical Essays in American Self-Reflexive Poetry*. She has published many essays, primarily on nineteenth-century women's literature.

Judith Mattson Bean is an assistant professor of English at Texas Woman's University. She has published articles on Margaret Fuller and discourse analysis in *Studies in the American Renaissance* and *Southwestern American Literature*.

Beatrice Jacobson teaches English and Women's Studies at St. Ambrose University, Davenport, Iowa. Her doctoral studies at the University of Iowa focused on nineteenth-century American literature, and especially women poets, notably Emily Dickinson. Jacobson is also an associate of Centro de Estudios Interamericanos in Cuenca, Ecuador, where she works and teaches part of each year.

Laura Laffrado is an associate professor at Western Washington University. The author of *Hawthorne's Literature for Children* (1992), she is currently completing a book on gender and genre in American literature and culture.

Sherry Lee Linkon is an associate professor of English and coordinator of American Studies at Youngstown State University. She is co-editor of *Radical Revisions: Rereading 1930s Culture* (Illinois UP, 1996), and she has published numerous articles on American women's literature, pedagogy, and popular culture.

Margaret A. Lukens has been working in the field of Native American women's writing since graduate school at the University of Colorado, Boulder. She completed her disseration, which includes chapters on Zitkala-Sa and Sarah Winnemucca, in 1991. She teaches English at the University of Maine.

Shirley Marchalonis is a professor of English and Women's Studies at Pennsylvania State University and teaches at the Berks Campus. She is the author and editor of several books, including *College Girls: A Century in Fiction* (Rutgers UP, 1995) and *The Worlds of Lucy Larcom, 1824–1893* (Georgia, 1989).

Stephanie A. Tingley is an associate professor of English at Youngstown State University, where she teaches American literature, film, and composition. She is currently completing a critical study of Emily Dickinson's letters entitled *A Fairer House Than Prose.*

Index